Tom Stoppard

Tom Stoppard

Bucking the Postmodern

Daniel Keith Jernigan

McFarland & Company, Inc., Publishers
Jefferson, North Carolina, and London

LIBRARY OF CONGRESS CATALOGUING-IN-PUBLICATION DATA

Jernigan, Daniel K.
    Tom Stoppard : bucking the postmodern / Daniel Keith Jernigan.
        p.   cm.
    Includes bibliographical references and index.

    ISBN 978-0-7864-6532-3
    softcover : acid free paper ∞

    1. Stoppard, Tom — Criticism and interpretation.   I. Title.
PR6069.T6Z715 2012
822'.914 — dc23   2012037140

BRITISH LIBRARY CATALOGUING DATA ARE AVAILABLE

© 2012 Daniel Keith Jernigan. All rights reserved

No part of this book may be reproduced or transmitted in any form or by any means, electronic or mechanical, including photocopying or recording, or by any information storage and retrieval system, without permission in writing from the publisher.

Front cover painting: *Tom Stoppard* by Wendy Walworth Schrijver

Manufactured in the United States of America

McFarland & Company, Inc., Publishers
  Box 611, Jefferson, North Carolina 28640
    www.mcfarlandpub.com

For Joy

Table of Contents

Preface   1

1. Introduction   5
2. Normalizing *Magritte* and Tumbling Philosophers   35
3. Modernist Diversions   58
4. Intermission: *Night and Day*   84
5. Normalizing Postmodern Science   98
6. Metahistorical Detectives   127
7. The Narrative Turn: Re-innovating the Traditional in *The Coast of Utopia*   157

Encore: Rock 'n' Roll   186
Chapter Notes   197
Bibliography   206
Index   211

Preface

The central argument of this book is that Stoppard's career is dominated by a commitment to "Bucking the Postmodern," to critiquing and rejecting postmodern attitudes at every turn. In making this case, I also argue that Stoppard's career has followed a trajectory that runs counter to that of the 20th century generally, moving in turn from the postmodernism of *Rosencrantz and Guildenstern Are Dead* (1967) to the modernism of *The Real Thing* (1984) to the realism of *The Coast of Utopia* (2002) and *Rock 'n' Roll* (2002). It is not lost on me, however, that these two claims are partly at odds with each other. To be sure, nineteenth century dramatic realism is perhaps best understood as so fixated on ignoring its own artificiality that any overt attempt to critique (or otherwise engage) drama's self-referential qualities on the part of the playwright puts it at odds with realist conventions. Indeed, even the briefest reconsideration of Stoppard's most recent plays reminds us that while they do employ more dramatic realist techniques than the rest of his plays, they aren't really committed to dramatic realism proper; i.e., that while there is indeed a consistency to the way in which Stoppard appropriates realist conventions in order to defend positivist epistemology, the final result ultimately shares much more with contemporary neo-realism than it does with nineteenth century dramatic realism.

This realization quickly leads to a second one, which is that even while I spend considerable time arguing that Stoppard's rejection of the postmodern is suggestive of how Brian McHale describes the transition from the modern to the postmodern, albeit in reverse, it would be equally fair to say that just as Stoppard's late plays are never fully realist, so too his middle plays are never fully modernist. Yes, there is a minimalizing of the sorts of ontological playfulness that McHale would characterize as postmodern — and, consequently, a simultaneous re-assertion of epistemological doubt about how it is that we know what we think we know (Lieutenant Carr on his deathbed in *Travesties* being the most clear embodiment of this anti-epistemological attitude given that everything we witness has been channeled through his ailing consciousness). However, I am ultimately fairly skeptical of the idea that Stoppard ever gave himself completely over to the sort of epistemological doubt that is so central to the modern condition (e.g., placed side by side with the epistemological skepticism of Virginia Woolf, Stoppard comes across as downright positivist). In any case, I take it as correct all the same that as his career progressed Tom Stoppard committed himself more and more to belief in an objective material reality and, moreover, that he ultimately rejected both the postmodern and the modern in order to embrace this "real." However, I must emphasize that this transition could just as easily be described as progressive as regressive, and that any indication in the following discussion that I favor the latter perspective should be attributed to rhetorical and critical convenience.

Except for the inclusion of two of Stoppard's early short plays — *The Real Inspector Hound* and *After Magritte*— this book primarily focuses on the major stage plays, avoiding his many short plays of the seventies as well as his radio plays, screenplays, "translations," and his novel, *Lord Malquist and Mr. Moon*. It is the major plays, however, that are the one constant in his career, appearing every two to five years; as such, I would argue that they are the most important means to understanding the various aesthetic tendencies and developments of that career. It is with this understanding, however, that the six-year gap between *Rosencrantz and Guildenstern Are Dead* (*R & G*, 1966) and *Jumpers* (1972) presents something of a problem, especially considering that for most writers these years are quite formative. A look at the two short plays that fill this gap — *The Real Inspector Hound* (1968) and *After Magritte* (1970)— however, proves they were quite formative for Stoppard as well, which is why I use these two plays as a means of bridging that gap (indeed, the aesthetic and philosophical differences between *R & G* and *Jumpers* would come as quite a surprise without also considering these short transitional plays).

A final disclaimer: It might strike some as odd that at times I may well appear to conflate ontological issues with epistemological ones, especially since my thesis is so dependent on the way in which McHale relies on these two terms to differentiate modernist fiction (for how it raises epistemological questions) from postmodernist fiction (for how it raises ontological questions). This is perhaps most evident in my discussion of *Hapgood* in Chapter 5, although to one degree or another it crops up throughout. In Chapter 5 this is largely because I rely on Arkady Plotnitsky's conception of the way in which "anti-epistemology" is endemic in quantum mechanics; in fact, I distinctly remember Plotnisky suggesting to me when I was a student of his at Purdue University that McHale had it exactly backwards in his argument about the distinction between the modern and the postmodern. In any case, this conflation is at least partially resolved by the simple fact that even more important to my thesis than recognizing Stoppard's career transitions is that there is an even clearer and more general transition from bemused engagement with many different sorts of nontraditional (anti-epistemological and anti-ontological) modes of thinking and seeing the world to more traditional modes of thinking and seeing the world (or, to reference Lyotard, from evincing skepticism of grand narratives, to embracing them); as such, even when he is rejecting anti-epistemological attitudes, he is, in any case, tracking that same more general arc that defines my thesis.

I must begin my acknowledgments by thanking the various journals in which some of this work has previously been published. Chapter 5 is reprinted with minor revisions from *Comparative Drama* by permission of the editors. Chapter 4 is reprinted after substantial revision from *Text and Presentation*, and parts of the Introduction come from an essay in my own edited collection, *Drama and the Postmodern*. I would also like to thank the generosity of Nanyang Technological University for providing me with funding to visit the Harry Ransom Center at the University of Texas, where Stoppard's papers are archived.

While I am solely responsible for any of the weaknesses which might be found in this volume, there are quite a few people to whom I owe my thanks for any of its strengths. Tom Adler was a careful and conscientious reader of those sections which came from my dissertation. Joe Somoza and K. West nurtured a truly naïve — if enthusiastic — student of poetry. Reed Dasenbrock showed me that my intuitions about how to respond to literature were both reasonable and valuable, and, at least in part, instilled in me the sort of philosophical disposition which finds works such as Stoppard's valuable, while Tim Cleveland, Mark Moffett, and Jay Allman each played similar roles. Arkady Plotnitsky reignited my fascination with science just as it was waning after five years of doing a literature Ph.D. Zheng

Preface

Jie helped piece the hodgepodge together as deadlines loomed. Stacy Thompson, Chuck Tryon, Angela Frattarola, Bede Scott, Walter Wadiak and Brendan Quigley were valuable friends and colleagues when doing this sort of work. A special thanks to Neil Murphy, for both his friendship and for being just the sort of division head one needs to finally complete such work. And also to Joy Wheeler for, well, everything else.

1

Introduction

Stoppard expresses keen interest in certain intellectual, aesthetic, and ideological positions associated with postmodern art and drama, while he is at the same time antipathetic to, and even staunchly critical of, some of the more radical notions and claims of postmodern social theory and its image of the human subject. Stoppard does not, then, fully inhabit the postmodern terrain, but he often travels there and traverses it, speaking the language of the region faultlessly even as he stops occasionally to arraign it with deadpan irony or wit.
— Vanden Heuvel (213)

Of course I don't want to give any of them shallow arguments and then knock them down. No, you have to give the best possible argument for each of them. It's like playing chess with yourself— you have to try to win just as hard at black as you do with white.
— Stoppard interview with Ross Wetzsteon

Traversing the Postmodern

I find the above epigraph from Michael Vanden Heuvel's essay "'Is Postmodernism?' Stoppard Among/Against the Postmodern" to be the single most compelling statement that has been made by a literary critic attempting the difficult task of summing up the entirety of Tom Stoppard's career. To be any more precise about Stoppard's oeuvre is to risk making problematic and corrupt generalizations about a complex and nuanced career that defies such generalizations. Such a difficulty is, of course, at least partly a consequence of Stoppard's belief— as stated in the second epigram — that you must "try to win just as hard at black as you do with white." Such a commitment makes it extremely difficult to determine what side of an issue Stoppard finally falls down on, especially when these issues concern ontological or epistemological skepticism of one sort or another as he goes about critically engaging with the various features of the postmodern terrain.

In *Stoppard's Theatre: Finding Order Amid Chaos*, John Fleming takes what is perhaps a wiser path than I do by deciding "not to yoke [Stoppard's plays] to an overall thesis" because of the way in which "[a]n overarching thesis offers a certain clarity of focus, but often results in the manipulation and distortion of evidence to fit the preordained pattern" (7). And while I am sure that the occasional reader will conclude that I have done too much to "yoke the plays to an overall thesis," I'm not quite sure why we should be any less willing to forsake an attempt to "offer a certain clarity of focus" when it comes to Stoppard than when it comes to anyone else. For taking such risks is what critics do. Otherwise, it seems we may as well pack up and go home. To be sure, I take it more as a challenge than a warning that in plays such as *Indian Ink* and *Arcadia* Stoppard himself has ruthlessly parodied literary critics' tendencies to construct what they are looking for even while convincing themselves that theirs is an act of discovery. If in the final analysis what follows amounts to so much self parody, well, I hold out hope that at least it is a good one.

For much of what follows I take Vanden Heuvel's thesis as my own, albeit with the qualification that while Stoppard's career (at least until *The Coast of Utopia*) is consumed with addressing postmodern issues without ever committing to postmodern ideals, there is a gradual transition from a more generally favorable response to and aesthetic treatment of those ideas, to a less favorable one. John Bull provides a different means to making the same point:

> Tom Stoppard is as fascinated by systems of logic as was Jonathan Swift, and as suspicious of them. From Stoppard's very earliest work, audiences were drawn into worlds that declared themselves as rationally coherent, even as the events of the play set out to demolish the evidence [136].

In fact, I think that Bull has this exactly backwards. For while *Rosencrantz and Guildenstern Are Dead* (*R & G*) begins with the irrational flipping of heads some 99 times in a row, I would argue that this series of events becomes marginally more rational to the audience as it gradually comes to terms with the nature of the environment which allows for such a result — that is, the theater. A similar pattern plays out time and again in Stoppard's work, whether we are considering *After Magritte* (the very play which caused John Bull to make the disputed claim), *The Real Thing*, or *Arcadia*.

1. Introduction

As Stoppard traverses the postmodern terrain, more often than not contextualization serves to make the seemingly irrational, rational, and, moreover, does so with greater and more meaningful definition of purpose as his career progresses.

John Bull's confusion on this point is hardly surprising. Stoppard's metatheatrical playfulness — and how it addresses rational/irrational tensions — has tempted many a critic to unreflective hyperbole about the radical implications of his work. Indeed, Tom Stoppard's plays are so self-consciously experimental that it isn't at all surprising that a wide range of critics have referred to them as postmodern, especially considering that his career spans an era during which the term came to be used so widely (and loosely). Notable among those who have referred to Stoppard's work as postmodern are Rodney Simard, Katherine Kelly, Richard Corballis, Christopher Innes, and Marvin Carlson.[1] None of these critics, however, provides a sustained reading of Stoppard's plays from *Rosencrantz and Guildenstern Are Dead* (*R & G*) to the present; a significant oversight, as you get a much different impression of Stoppard when you are looking for trends that extend throughout his career than when he is considered piecemeal. Furthermore, there remains much clarifying work to be done when it comes to categorizing Stoppard's work as postmodern, if for no other reason than that so much of this criticism fails to apply the term "postmodern" in any kind of "strict" or "traditional" sense, completely avoiding reference to the major philosophical theorists of the postmodern such as Fredric Jameson and Jean-François Lyotard.

Michael Vanden Heuvel's essay is a notable exception. Vanden Heuvel's essay begins with the claim, "First, it is necessary to drive home the point early that Stoppard and his plays will frustrate any attempt to impose an either/or logic in terms of their relationship to postmodern ideas and aesthetics" (213). Vanden Heuvel sees Stoppard's commitment to investigating postmodern concepts as his central oeuvre, even while he ultimately refrains from deciding whether or not this sort of investigation marks Stoppard's work as postmodern. Jim Hunter makes a similar point in *About Stoppard*, although not within the context of "postmodernism" per se:

> Stoppard's lifelong response to the promulgators of uncertainty in the twentieth century is to take on their clothing, their materials, their apparatus, yet then, as it were from within their walls, to fight for the old faiths — not, admittedly

for Newtonian physics, but for the notions of "objective reality and absolute morality" and a moral order derived from Christian absolutes [34].

As descriptions of Stoppard's general attitude I find Vanden Heuvel and Hunter largely convincing, if imprecise.[2] I argue, by contrast, that despite Stoppard's tendency to "traverse" the postmodern without becoming postmodern himself, it is possible to note progressively changing attitudes towards the postmodern in Stoppard's work, as over the years he has become increasingly committed to "arraign[ing] it with deadpan irony or wit" even as he becomes ever more committed to "objective reality and absolute morality."

Versions of the Postmodern

Perhaps the dearth of theoretically informed criticism concerning Stoppard's postmodern characteristics derives from the very fact that drama itself hasn't been as fully theorized from this perspective as have other mediums, such as fiction and film. For while Jameson and Lyotard have each discussed fiction at length — as have numerous literary critics, including Brian McHale and Linda Hutcheon — critics devoted to describing the postmodern in drama have been both few and lacking in influence. Perhaps the most notable study of the postmodern in drama is Stephen Watt's *Postmodern/Drama: Reading the Contemporary Stage* (1998), which, upon recognizing the poor showing drama makes in various theorizations of the postmodern condition, suggests that the solution to this oversight is simply a matter of learning to read the postmodern in theater; for Watt, postmodernity is in the eye of the beholder. And were I not approaching Stoppard with an eye attuned to postmodern effects, I would certainly miss much of the way in which Stoppard engages postmodernity. However, Watt's very theory of postmodern drama is largely consistent with postmodern attitudes about how truths are constructed, itself an epistemological attitude that Stoppard becomes increasingly dissatisfied with. As such, at the end of the day I am too committed to trying to get at Stoppard's central oeuvre to give myself over to Watt's version of postmodernity in drama.

Equally important is Kerstin Schmidt's *Postmodernism in American Drama*, which ultimately argues that postmodernism in drama is explicitly concerned with disrupting traditional theatrical boundaries:

1. Introduction

Postmodern dramatists approach performance art as a valuable resource for their dramatic endeavors. Among others, the influence takes shape most vividly in the attempt to make the theatrical audience reconsider the traditional boundaries between performance and reality, art and life, fiction and autobiography [59].

Indeed, it is in Stoppard's explicit disruptions of traditional theatrical boundaries that I find him most thoroughly embracing a postmodern aesthetic (even as he stops ever shorter of embracing postmodern epistemologies and ontologies). All the same, I find that Jameson and Lyotard provide for a much more theoretically informed discussion of the postmodern in Stoppard, while Linda Hutcheon, Brian McHale and Ihab Hassan prove very useful for explaining his various formal techniques.

As such, Jean-François Lyotard's seminal theorization of the postmodern, *The Postmodern Condition*, provides a convenient starting point. For our current purposes, Lyotard's oft-repeated definition should prove sufficient: "Simplifying to the extreme, I define postmodern as incredulity towards metanarratives" (xxiv). Notably, what Lyotard recognizes when he looks out across Western society and culture is how, in so many ways, it has given up grand, universal metanarratives for what he calls "localized" narratives, "agreed on by its present players and subject to eventual cancellation" (66). Given that Stoppard has written about science himself (most notably in *Hapgood* and *Arcadia*) it ultimately proves quite useful to the current project that Lyotard sees this trend as rooted in the sciences; he speaks in turn of the indeterminacies of relativity theory, Gödel's incompleteness theorem, quantum mechanics, and chaos theory, which arrived in seeming quick succession after a long tradition of scientific determinism. It is implied — even if it is never overtly stated — that if even the so-called hard sciences are shot through with local truths (e.g., relative distances and quantum positions), so too go the rest of the natural sciences, to say nothing of the social sciences and (God forbid) the humanities (but much more on this specific treatment of "postmodern science" in Chapter 5's discussion of *Hapgood* and *Arcadia*).

Although much more invested in postmodern literary criticism, like Lyotard, Ihab Hassan also sees postmodernity as arising out of indeterminacy in the sciences, which makes his thinking on postmodern literature and culture an equally useful starting place for considering the postmodern in Stoppard. After discussing the impact of Einstein, Heisenberg/Bohr and

Gödel in turn, Hassan suggests that "mechanism, determinism, materialism recede before the flux of consciousness" and that "in such rarefied realms of reason a humanist, modern, or postmodern gasps for breath" (*The Postmodern Turn* 88–89). And while we will see, however, that Stoppard himself hardly stops to gasp — indeterminacy is for those who overthink reality — he has, perhaps, become increasingly prone to sputtering with contempt.

Even more important to the current project, however, is Hassan's recognition that there are two fundamental tendencies in the postmodern, indeterminacy and immanence. "Indeterminacy" in the postmodern will become increasingly familiar in this treatment of Stoppard for what it shares with Lyotard and McHale (and for how central it is in Stoppard's own flirtations with the postmodern). For as Hassan explains it, there is a growing tendency towards "openness, fragmentation, ambiguity, discontinuity, decenterment, heterodoxy, pluralism, deformation, all conducive to indeterminacy or under-determination," resulting in a literature where "our ideas of author, audience, reading, writing, book, genre, critical theory, and of literature itself, have all suddenly become questionable" ("From Postmodernism to Postmodernity" 4). By contrast, "immanence" in the postmodern is a more complicated and tenuous issue, and as Hassan explains it, looks to identify a feature of the postmodern most clearly identified by Fredric Jameson and Baudrillard (I quote at length in order to give due diligence to a feature of the postmodern given comparatively scant attention in the rest of this manuscript):

> These uncertainties or indeterminacies, however, are also dispersed or disseminated by the fluent imperium of technology. Thus I call the second major tendency of postmodernism immanences, a term that I employ without religious echo to designate the capacity of mind to generalize itself in symbols, intervene more and more into nature, act through its own abstractions, and project human consciousness to the edges of the cosmos. This mental tendency may be further described by words like diffusion, dissemination, projection, interplay, communication, which all derive from the emergence of human beings as language animals, homo pictor or homo significans, creatures constituting themselves, and also their universe, by symbols of their own making. Call it gnostic textualism, if you must. Meanwhile, the public world dissolves as fact and fiction blend, history becomes a media happening, science takes its own models as the only accessible reality, cybernetics confronts us with the enigma of artificial intelligence (Deep Blue contra Kasparov), and technologies project our perceptions to the edge of matter, within the atom or at the rim of the expanding universe ["From Postmodernism to Postmodernity" 5].

1. Introduction

One thing that intrigues me about this passage is how little it speaks to the postmodern issues I find in Stoppard. For Stoppard is all about indeterminacy. All about finding some new formal technique to address "openness, fragmentation, ambiguity, discontinuity, decenterment, heterodoxy, pluralism, deformation, all conducive to indeterminacy or under-determination" and doing so in a way which makes us reconsider our "ideas of author, audience, reading, writing, book, genre, critical theory, and of literature." And while much of Stoppard's work is ultimately devoted to favoring the determinate, that doesn't mean he isn't caught up in issues of determinacy and indeterminacy all the same (as Vanden Heuvel and Hunter remind us). As a consequence, a significant portion of what follows describes how Stoppard uses formal techniques to engage this very tension, and it is for just this reason, moreover, that I ultimately invoke Brian McHale's differentiation between the way in which modernist fiction raises epistemological questions while postmodern fiction raises ontological questions to describe Stoppard's transition from a postmodern aesthetic to a modern one.

It is much more rare, however, to find Stoppard even stopping to consider (let alone embracing) what Hassan refers to as immanence. In *Travesties* "fact and fiction" do blend. But it is a blending more committed to making us reconsider our "ideas of author, audience, reading, writing, book, genre, critical theory, and of literature" than it is about "the public world dissolv[ing] as ... history becomes a media happening." Immanence, as Hassan describes it, seems much closer to critiques of the way in which technology is part and parcel of what Fredric Jameson suggests has become "representational shorthand for grasping a network of power and control even more difficult for our minds and imaginations to grasp: the whole new decentered global network of the third stage of capital itself" (*Postmodernism* 38) and which, Baudrillard argues in *Simulacra and Simulation*, manifests itself in the form of a simulacrum: "We live in a world where there is more and more information, and less and less meaning" (79). Oddly enough, Baudrillard yet provides a sociological explanation for the appeal of Stoppard's metatheatrical tricks in postmodern society:

> The futility of everything that comes to us from the media is the inescapable consequence of the absolute inability of that particular stage to remain silent. Music, commercial breaks, news flashes, adverts, news broadcasts, movies, presenters — there is no alternative but to fill the screen; otherwise there would

be an irremediable void.... That's why the slightest technical hitch, the slightest slip on the part of the presenter becomes so exciting, for it reveals the depth of the emptiness squinting out at us through this little window [*Cool Memories* 139].

Time and again Stoppard draws our attention to such technical hitches. In any case, for Jameson and Baudrillard, there is something ideologically suspect about postmodern indeterminacy; it is both prefigured by, and results in, a defense of the status quo of multinational capitalistic enterprises.

In Stoppard, however, there is nothing (or at least very little) about the relationship between power and knowledge, or about the way in which power fosters indeterminacy concerning various privileged subjects. Perhaps just a bit in *The Real Inspector Hound* (*Hound*, 1968), as the two theater critics in the play draw attention to the power they have in making or breaking productions and careers (perhaps an unsurprising anxiety for a novice playwright, as Stoppard was at the time). And also, perhaps, a way of reading it into *Arcadia*'s (1993) representation of the girl genius Thomasina, alienated as she is by the status quo such that her discoveries in chaos theory are prefigured as having occurred centuries before their natural time. But then in *Night and Day* (1978), where we might expect such ideas to take full bloom given the text's commitment to uncovering the power struggle between labor and corporate power in the news media, the play is downright positivist in its attitude that the truth will out itself despite the concerns of the powerful and the privileged. So too in *Rock 'n' Roll* (2006), where the idea that there is any significant collusion between power and knowledge is once again rejected.

And while critics such as Linda Hutcheon have convincingly explored the relationship between a postmodern emptying out of traditional epistemological attitudes and how such emptying out has given new voice to the pursuit of various progressive agendas on the part of a wide range of novelists — usually in the form of alternate constructed realities which are intended to reject and/or take an ironically distancing attitude towards traditional realities — this observation on Hutcheon's part is only loosely relevant to the question at hand. In fact, there is every indication that Hutcheon would distance herself from the idea that there is a necessary causal connection between the way in which the postmodern opens the door to alternative voices (Lyotard's "small narratives") and the apparent

1. Introduction

resulting wave of authors whose postmodern bona fides reside in their progressive political opinions (a too often assumed reading of the importance of Hutcheon's work), and would agree that it is just as easy for conservative voices to step into the postmodern void as it is for liberal and/or progressive ones to do so.[3] And as further counterpoint to Hutcheon's focus on progressive voices in postmodernism, it is worth remembering how Jameson and Baudrillard suggest that the net effect of the postmodern proliferation of voices via a news media distributed by increasingly complicated and ever encroaching technologies is ultimately conservative in how it serves to divert attention away from any sort of meaningful engagement with reality. (The proliferating fictions of Sarah Palin — uncritically given voice by Fox News — come to mind as an obvious example.) In any case, I will take this ambiguity concerning the politics of postmodernism to mean that Stoppard's moderate conservatism is irrelevant as an indicator of his relationship with (and apparent rejection of) the postmodern (although I am tempted to argue that, if anything, it is in his self-proclaimed political moderateness that he makes his rejection of the postmodern most apparent, as it may well be symptomatic of a corresponding belief that nothing has been emptied out — and that, consequently, there is no room for radical voices of any stripe). In any case, while I will at times gesture towards ways in which my discussion of Stoppard's postmodernity is complicated by his occasional forays into political issues, in general I will allow myself to be comforted by the fact that his self-proclaimed moderate politics is beside the point when it comes to determining his thinking about postmodern epistemological and ontological issues.

Brian McHale's Ontological Postmodernism

The dearth of postmodern readings of drama and dramatic technique makes McHale very important to my attempt to better understand the importance of the metatheatrical techniques which are so prevalent in Stoppard's plays, especially because McHale is so focused on discovering ways in which novels transgress ontological boundaries (something which happens quite naturally in drama, and is prevalent throughout Stoppard's career). In turn, as sympathetic as I am to Vanden Heuvel's reading of Stoppard, a close reading of Stoppard through Brian McHale suggests that while Stoppard's early work (*R & G* and *Inspector Hound*, for instance) is postmodern, the remainder of his career essentially tracks backward from the way that McHale traces the literary chronological history of twentieth-century fiction, becoming "late modernist" through the mid-seventies (most notably in *Travesties*) and, finally, "modernist" in the 80s and 90s (in *The Real Thing* and *Arcadia*).

McHale begins his characterization of postmodernist fiction by contrasting it with modernist fiction proper, which, he explains, is best understood according to how it employs an epistemological dominant, asking questions concerning the state of knowledge:

> What is there to be known?; Who knows it?; How do they know it, and with what degree of certainty?; How is knowledge transferred from one knower to another, and with what degree of reliability?; How does the object of knowledge change as it passes from knower to knower?; What are the limits of the knowable?; etc. [*Postmodernist Fiction* 9].

According to this perspective, a short story such as Virginia Woolf's "The Mark on the Wall" isn't modernist so much because of the stream-of-consciousness style of its narration but, rather, because of how the narrator suggests that stream-of-consciousness reflection is every bit as legitimate a means of processing information and arriving at knowledge as are more conventional (even scientific) means of knowing.

In turn McHale describes postmodernist fiction in direct contrast to modernist fiction, suggesting that it should be understood by how it employs an ontological dominant, asking questions about existence rather than about knowledge:

> What is a world?; What kinds of worlds are there, how are they constituted, and how do they differ?; What happens when different kinds of worlds are placed in confrontation, or when boundaries between worlds are violated?; What is the mode of existence of a text, and what is the mode of existence of the world it projects?; How is a projected world structured? [10].

McHale sees fiction as postmodern not only when it raises questions about the existence of the world in which the reader resides, but also, and more importantly, when it raises questions about the existence of the world created within the pages of fictional texts themselves. It is hardly surprising, then, that much of McHale's critical attention focuses on novels wherein the boundaries between worlds break down, as happens, for instance, when an author explicitly enters into one of his or her own texts to comment

1. Introduction

upon that text. McHale explains that when such "metanarrative" commentary occurs explicitly, worlds collide; and, moreover, that these collisions raise ontological questions about the stability of the world described in the text. McHale calls the space where these collisions occur "the zone," a place where space is "less constructed than destructed by the text, or rather constructed and destructed at the same time" (45).

As we will see, "the zone" figures as the setting for many of the different types of narrative disparity examined by McHale, and, moreover, as the setting for much of Stoppard's early work as well. To this end, it is worth noting that in *Postmodernist Fiction* McHale argues that the theater provides an ideal environment for the morphological development of those metaleptic features which serve to distinguish a work as postmodern:

> This metaleptic function of character has especially been exploited in twentieth-century drama, paradigmatically in Pirandello's *Six Characters in Search of an Author* (1921), but also in plays by Brecht, Beckett, Jean Genet, Tom Stoppard, Peter Handke and others. Metalepsis appears so early in twentieth-century drama, and attains such precocious sophistication by comparison with prose fiction, for reasons which should be fairly obvious. The fundamental ontological boundary in theater is a literal, physical threshold, equally visible to the audience and (if they are permitted to recognize it) the characters: namely, the footlights, the edge of the stage [121].

And yet while McHale provides a promising list of playwrights given the scope of the current essay, he doesn't elaborate, and so it is unclear whether or not he considers such metadrama to be postmodern. The implication is, however, that if it were postmodern, it would be so as a consequence of having taken advantage of this "literal, physical threshold" which has such potential to be made prominent in the theater.

Pirandello's *Six Characters in Search of an Author* (1921) is an important case study for considering how McHale's ideas apply to drama, populated as it is by characters who are explicitly conscious of the fact that they are authorial constructs who have been left unfinished by their author. The audience is introduced to these characters only after they have already struck out on their own in an attempt to employ the help of a writer who can complete their existence. Instead, they find a director — and the play focuses on what ensues after they enlist that director's help. McHale's discussion of Vladimir Nabakov's *Look at the Harlequins* (1974) provides the appropriate point of comparison:

> I now confess that I was bothered ... by a dream feeling that my life was the non-identical twin, a parody, an inferior variant of another man's life, somewhere on this earth or another earth. A demon, I felt, was forcing me to impersonate that other man, that other writer who was and would always be incomparably greater, healthier, and crueler than your obedient servant [*Postmodernist Fiction* 208].

Here, Vadim correctly surmises that he is a fictional character in a novel, just as Pirandello's characters know that they are characters from an unfinished play. Thus, *Six Characters in Search of an Author* and *Look at the Harlequins* can be seen as similarly postmodern for how they share concerns about the ontological integrity of fictional worlds.

However, an even more poignant understanding of Pirandello's postmodern credentials can be found in McHale's discussion of what he refers to as "Chinese Box Worlds." For this analysis McHale turns to the Polish phenomenologist Roman Ingarden, whose theories help to identify how the worlds created by words are "partly indeterminate for the imprecise nature of language" (*Postmodernist Fiction* 31). For his part, McHale focuses on a scene from Gilbert Sorrentino's *Mulligan Stew* (1979) where "There is no kitchen, no porch, no bath. At this side of the living room, a staircase leads 'nowhere'" (quoted in McHale *Postmodernist Fiction* 32). McHale explains the connection to Ingarden as follows:

> All houses in fiction are like this, partly specified, partly left vague. Normally neither the reader nor the character who shares the same world with such a house notices this vagueness; Sorrentino's characters, however, are aware of being inside a fiction, and so find this house anomalous, with its permanent gaps where a real-world house would be ontologically determinate [32].

According to McHale this scene raises questions concerning the material stability of ill-defined fictional worlds. As a result, at least one ontological question is foregrounded: What is the mode of existence of a text?

In turn, Pirandello's *Six Characters* can also be seen as an early example of this same sort of investigation into ontological mystification, since it asks what might occur if an author were to create firmly defined characters and yet fail to create an appropriate setting for these characters to inhabit. It might be argued, for instance, that Pirandello's characters occupy a world that is even less well defined than the world of *Mulligan Stew*, since for Pirandello's characters there isn't even so much as a familiar staircase that might lead them to nowhere, but only nowhere itself—an alternate reality

1. Introduction

that is completely foreign to that of their expectations. All they have are familiar objects, such as sofas of a particular color and the various other objects which make up Madame Pace's brothel. When The Producer, for instance, has a green sofa brought in to help them stage one of their scenes, The Stepdaughter responds, "No, no, not a green one! It was yellow, yellow velvet with flowers on it." Self-consciousness about one's ontological vulnerability is, perhaps, a logical implication of this setting where existence itself has become so tenuous. And, consequently, the very same questions raised by *Mulligan Stew* are raised by Pirandello, with the notable difference that Pirandello wrote *Six Characters* some 60 years before Sorrentino wrote *Mulligan Stew*.

The fact that drama became so self-consciously theatrical even while fiction was engaged in various prototypically modernist experiments is suggestive, especially given Stoppard's own eventual transition away from postmodern drama even as the more radical experiments in postmodern fiction were coming into their own. For as we will see, Stoppard's own investment in the metatheatricalism of Pirandello is on full display in both *R & G* and *Hound*. And as this introduction continues, I will provide detailed explanations of how McHale's theorization of the postmodern provides a compelling means to understanding the philosophical implications of these two plays, both in order to convince the reader that Stoppard was fully invested in a metatheatrical tradition that extends back at least as far as Pirandello, but also to prepare the reader to recognize those subtle differences which serve to differentiate Stoppard's later modernist plays from his early postmodern ones. As such, after my treatments of *R & G* and *Hound*, I will conclude by introducing each of the later chapters in order to begin to direct the reader, at least briefly, towards those differences which I find so important.

Rosencrantz and Guildenstern Are Dead

Much has been made of the debt Stoppard's early work owes to Pirandello[4] and looking at *R & G* via McHale provides for a compelling case for such a connection. *R & G* is carefully constructed with Shakespeare's *Hamlet* as its template, except that rather than making *Hamlet* the focus of the play, Stoppard zeroes in on two of the minor characters, Rosencrantz

(ROS) and Guildenstern (GUIL). The play tracks their travels to Castle Elsinore, where they have been summoned to assist Claudius and Gertrude in diagnosing Hamlet's apparent illness. The fundamental morphological difference between *R & G* and *Hamlet* is that whenever the plot of *Hamlet* shifts away from ROS and GUIL, *R & G* keeps ROS and GUIL as its focus. Significantly, similar to an effect found in *Six Characters*, these are the very moments at which ROS and GUIL are most prone to floundering about and wandering aimlessly, apparently not knowing what to do in the absence of a script. It soon becomes evident that ROS and GUIL's reality is thoroughly circumscribed by the ontological limits of the theater itself, as well as by those few stage directions originally provided for by Shakespeare.

Moreover, as in *Six Characters* and *Mulligan Stew*, the very physical world that ROS and GUIL inhabit is ill-defined and ambiguous. Consider the following stage directions: "[Guildenstern] spins another coin over his shoulder without looking at it, his attention being directed at his environment or lack of it" (12). Notably, this "environment or lack of it" corresponds with the fact that these opening scenes from *R & G* were never fully described by Shakespeare (in fact, they weren't described by Shakespeare at all, as they do not appear in *Hamlet*), just as the setting of *Mulligan Stew* could never have been fully specified by Sorrentino (which was, of course, Sorrentino's point). Stoppard's work, then, might best be understood as providing a more generalized consideration of what McHale finds so fascinating in Sorrentino's work, as Stoppard asks that his audience question the indeterminacy that exists at the margins of all texts (including those of Shakespeare), not just at the margins of his own (and this some ten years before Sorrentino published *Mulligan Stew*).

Of course when ROS and GUIL arrive at Castle Elsinore their physical world, at least, becomes much more tangible, since it now contains points of correspondence with those scenes which are described in Shakespeare's text. It is at this point that Stoppard changes his target, replacing the indeterminate *setting* of the work with the indeterminate *character* of ROS and GUIL. Even in this case, however, the effect is similar to what is found in Sorrentino, for it is this very indeterminacy of character which explains why ROS and GUIL don't quite know where they are going, let alone why. When asked about the first thing he remembers, ROS can only say: "Ah. No, it's no good, it's gone. It was a long time ago." When pressed

1. Introduction

by ROS about the first thing that happened that day he can barely remember that very morning (notably, a scene that does not occur in *Hamlet*). After some prodding, he finally comes out with "That's it — pale sky before dawn, a man standing on his saddle to bang on the shutters — shouts — What's all the row about? Clear off — But then he called our names. You remember that — this man woke us up" (19). That this is pretty poor memory for so recent an event, even for characters as dimwitted as ROS and GUIL, is the point. It is almost as if their dimwittedness stems from the very fact that the events in question aren't specifically described in the text of *Hamlet*. Consequently, their memories of the event are as insubstantial as those which reside at the end of the staircase "described" in *Mulligan Stew*. For all intents and purposes, their memories are, quite simply, out of bounds. Or, as Jim Hunter explains it, "Though they are dressed as Elizabethans, Stoppard gives them twentieth century intellects. They attempt to make sense of their situation by rational means — we get scraps of traditional philosophical inquiry — yet they mistrust all perception (20)." While I am not sure I would be so kind as concerns their intellect,[5] in any case it is clear that Stoppard pushes ontological questions even further than Sorrentino does, and, moreover, that he does so by questioning the unique ontological ambiguities that accrue when putting dramatic scripts into performance.

This porous relationship between Shakespeare's text and Stoppard's own plays a substantial role in defining the very character (or lack of it) of ROS and GUIL. This resonance between what Stoppard pilfers from *Hamlet* and what are perhaps the defining characteristics of ROS and GUIL is featured most prominently in the scene in which Claudius confuses the two:

> CLAUDIUS: Welcome, dear Rosencrantz ... (*he raises a hand at GUIL while ROS bows— GUIL bows late and hurriedly*) ... and Guildenstern [35].

Claudius gets it right later, only to be "corrected" by Gertrude:

> GERTRUDE (*correcting*): Thanks, Guildenstern (*Turning to ROS, who bows as GUIL checks upward movements to bow too— both bent double, squinting at each other.*) ... and gentle Rosencrantz. (*Turning to GUIL, both straightening up —GUIL checks again and bows again*) [37].

The only textual difference between what we see in *R & G* and the original from *Hamlet* comes in the stage directions, which goes to show just

19

how clever Stoppard is at manipulating the text in order to highlight the fact that Claudius and Gertrude cannot distinguish between ROS and GUIL. And while it may simply be that Shakespeare is more subtle than Stoppard (and had intended this confusion all along), in any case, Stoppard takes the idea and runs with it such that the attitude of the scene is itself mirrored in the way that ROS and GUIL are prone to confusing their own names, as they do when they role-play what they might say when they try to "glean what afflicts" Hamlet:

> ROS: My honoured Lord!
> GUIL: My dear Rosencrantz!
> *Pause.*
> ROS: Am I pretending to be you?
> GUIL: Certainly not. If you like. Shall we continue? [48].

Notably, GUIL is embarrassed enough to try and cover for his mistake. But ultimately it is no use. Even as the play ends and first ROS and then GUIL himself finally and simply "disappear," he calls out for his friend: "Rosen—?/ Guil—?" (125). Clearly, Stoppard is transgressing well-defined literary boundaries, and he is doing so in such a way that forces his own characters to suffer the consequences of his manipulations.

Focusing on the way in which Stoppard puts the unique features of theater to metanarrative effect recalls another discussion in McHale's *Postmodernist Fiction*, where he explores how postmodernist authors manipulate the very physical characteristics of the book wherein their novel resides: "For one thing, there is the physical space of the material book, in particular the two-dimensional space of the page. It should be possible to integrate this physical space in the structure of the zone" (56). McHale's point is that a book can use the very words on a page in such nontraditional ways that they draw attention to their existence as signifiers (I am reminded of calligrams such as Gregory Corso's poem "Bomb," where the words on the page take on the very shape of an atomic explosion); on these occasions the book itself enters "the zone." It would seem, then, that Stoppard provides the precise theatrical complement to this metaliterary device in how he uses the unique three-dimensional aspect of the stage's various traditional characteristics to raise ontological questions about the world that the stage's characters inhabit. Conveniently, McHale himself provides a list of those physical characteristics of the theater that a postmodern playwright might take advantage of: "the footlights, the edge of the stage"

1. Introduction

(*Postmodernist Fiction* 121). According to this perspective, when theatrical objects are specifically referenced as footlight, as the edge of stage, or even as actor/actress, prop, or text, ontological questions proliferate about the boundary between stage and reality.

To be sure, there is much about *R & G* which leaves the audience with the distinct impression that it is being had. The audience is ever likely to find itself sympathizing with GUIL from the opening scene, in which we find GUIL considering whether the fact that he has called heads, spun, and lost more than 90 coins in succession means that "We are now within un-, sub-, or supernatural forces" (*R & G* 17). Ultimately we are left with the unmistakable impression that someone — or something — is making ROS the butt of a grand cosmic and/or literary joke (are we seeing the edge of the stage, perhaps?). That some trickster is, perhaps, making the coins fall in a way that does not comport with the laws of probability. GUIL considers the various possibilities:

> GUIL: [...] One: I'm willing it. Inside where nothing shows. I'm the essence of a man spinning double-headed coins, and betting against himself in private atonement for an unremembered past... Two: time has stopped dead, and a single experience of one coin being spun once has been repeated ninety times... (*He flips a coin, looks at it, tosses it to* ROS.) On the whole, doubtful. Three: divine intervention, that is to say, a good turn from above concerning him. [...] Four: a spectacular vindication of the principle that each individual coin spun individually (*he spins one*) is as likely to come down heads as tails and therefore should cause no surprise each individual time it does [16].

Determining just what this force is which allows the coin to fall heads so many times in a row is at the heart of the play's metatheatricality, as we must eventually come to the conclusion that the theater is just such a place where such a phenomenon is likely to occur. For the coins might all be two-headed props. Or, rather, each actor might simply pretend that heads has fallen, even when and if the coin onstage happens to fall tails up. This is the ontological environment Stoppard is working within and which he is so intent on drawing his audience's attention to. For as sure as a character can appear on the stage in front of a twentieth-century audience outfitted entirely in Elizabethan garb without the audience batting an eye given its collective understanding of the artificiality of the environment, so to can that same character spin heads 99 times in succession (or at least can claim to have done so) without the audience deciding, like the self-interested ROS, that it too must "have a good look at your coins" (14).

The fact that the artificiality of the environment explains the anomaly better than any of the theories put forward by ROS draws our attention to the fact that somewhere Stoppard is winking at us, goading us on to ever deeper understandings of the artificiality of the stage. ROS and GUIL catch only glimpses of the elusive hand of the creator behind the curtain — "as soon as we make our move they'll come pouring in from every side, shouting obscure instructions (85)" — as they begin to second-guess their autonomy in navigating their way through the play's narrative. Indeed, GUIL's use of the word "they" turns out to be one of the more astute observations that he has made about who controls his fate. For it is not Hamlet or Claudius or even The Player who does so, but, simply, "they," or, rather, all those people working behind the scenes in order to make sure productions such as *Hamlet* or *R & G* come off the way they are supposed to; it is the always and unseen production team, which, The Player reminds us, is particularly susceptible to the interfering hand of what "is written":

> PLAYER: There's a design at work in all art — surely you know that? [...] We aim at the point where everyone who is marked for death dies.
> GUIL: Marked? ... Who decides?
> PLAYER: (*Switching off his smile*) Decides? It is written [79].

Guildenstern comes even closer to understanding his fate as he describes what it is like to be on a boat in terms that are reminiscent of his situation in the play: "Our movement is contained within a larger one that carries us along as inexorably as the wind and current" (122).

Similarly, ROS's and GUIL's poor sense of direction is not just a manifestation of their indeterminate character but also an example of how the theater space itself can enter into "the zone." For even as ROS and GUIL attempt to get their bearings according to the position of the sun, GUIL gets so caught up in hypotheticals about where the sun might be that he fails to notice whether or not there even is one: "If it is [morning], and the sun is over there (his right as he faces the audience) for instance, that (front) would be northerly" (58). GUIL continues in this fashion until he has convinced himself that he has exhausted all of his options. The actual sun, however, remains elusive, so that sometime later GUIL seems to have given it up as a possibility entirely, explaining to ROS (who thinks that he has seen the sun rise) that he had not seen the sun rise at all, but, rather, "you opened your eyes very, very slowly. If you'd been facing back there you'd be swearing that was east" (85). ROS and GUIL's dilemma speaks

1. Introduction

to the fact that there is no sun within a theater, but only the misleading glare of the ever-present stage lights (thusly referenced, they too become part of "the zone").

It is also worth considering the ontological questions about theatrical space which arise as ROS and GUIL interact more directly with the audience:

> ROS *leaps up and bellows at the audience.*
> ROS: Fire!
> GUIL *jumps up.*
> GUIL: Where?
> ROS: It's all right — I'm demonstrating the misuse of free speech. To prove that it exists. (*He regards the audience, that is the direction, with contempt— and other directions, then front again.*) Not a move [60].

What Stoppard is alluding to here is a famous argument within political science which suggests that an individual's right to free speech should never be given such free rein as to allow for the shouting of "fire" in a crowded theater. And while the stage directions suggest that ROS doesn't explicitly acknowledge an audience, his surprise that no one moves is at least an indirect reference to one. Indeed, the ethical argument itself presupposes just such an audience, for this limit to universal free speech depends on the realization that, if someone yells "fire" in a crowded theater, the audience might panic, resulting in a dangerous stampede towards the exits. Who else but the audience does ROS refer to when he observes that there is "Not a move"? And that "They should burn to death in their shoes"? Thus, one of the unique characteristics of the theater that Stoppard takes advantage of is its live audience — an audience which is, in turn, also forced to inhabit "the zone" alongside ROS and GUIL.

As it turns out, The Player is especially well attuned to the possibilities of the theatrical environment, a feature which becomes most pronounced in how he practically revels in his foreknowledge of ROS and GUIL's fate:

> GUIL: You're evidently a man who knows his way around.
> PLAYER: I've been here before.
> GUIL: We're still finding our feet.
> PLAYER: I should concentrate on not losing your heads.
> GUIL: Do you speak from knowledge?
> PLAYER: Precedent [66].

The Player speaks from precedent because he has played the role before (apparently, during the play's previous performances). And as an actor himself, he is wiser to the ways of theater than are ROS and GUIL, whose fate is so thoroughly prescribed for them that even upon discovering Hamlet's trickery in swapping out the letter calling for Hamlet's death for a second letter calling for their own, they plod unwittingly towards their certain deaths all the same:

> Ros: All right then, I don't care. I've had enough. To tell you the truth, I'm relieved.
> (*And he disappears from view.*)
> GUIL: Our names shouted in a certain dawn ... a message ... a summons.... There must have been a moment, at the beginning, were we could have said — no. But somehow we missed it. (*He looks round and sees he is alone.*)
> Rosen—?
> GUIL—?
> (*He gathers himself.*)
> Well, we'll know better next time. Now you see me, now you —(*and disappears*) [125–126].

This passage alone has a lot to unpack. What precisely is GUIL referring to when he suggests that there must have been a moment at the beginning when they "could have said — no?" Or, that "we'll know better next time?" Clearly, GUIL is on the brink of discovering an essential truth about himself, or, at least, about those forces that have compelled him to his death against his will.

Consequently, as the play progresses and as ROS and GUIL become increasingly aware of their predicament as characters trapped in a narrative beyond their control, fated to die in the play's conclusion, the implication is, then, that "the zone" is a place where characters die not because of an inherent tragic flaw, or even because of a prophecy from an oracle, but, rather, because their fate has been prescribed to them by their author. This, then, is the zone where all texts reside; and, moreover, which Stoppard explicitly examines by showing how ROS and GUIL face up to their inevitable deaths. By implication, Oedipus' fated killing of his father and marriage to his mother is far more inescapable even than Oedipus finally realizes after having failed to escape his own fate; for he must, moreover, do so time and again, with each successive production of *Oedipus Rex*. According to this logic Sophocles is the oracle who has situated Oedipus in this predicament. This is the zone where all texts reside, and which Stoppard explicitly examines by showing ROS and GUIL face up to their inevitable deaths. And the fact that *R & G* resides within this zone makes

1. Introduction

it — Stoppard's first produced and published play — fully postmodernist according to McHale's criteria.

Finally, much of the critical discussion of the play has been directed towards asking, as John Fleming does, "To what degree can one apply that design to human life?" (60). Fleming cites Brassel — who argues, in essence, that the play suggests that we are meant to sympathize with "these two men groping in an existential void (54)" — and Delaney, who counters that rather than a void the play presents the idea that "there is a design at work in life as well as art (19)." Fleming is clearly quite concerned with this issue, ultimately deciding that "their 'characterness' (inability to define themselves sufficiently outside Shakespeare's world) is somewhat unsatisfying and prevents them from reaching 'Everyman' status" (65). While my own sympathies on this issue are with Delaney, it must be stressed that Brassel and Fleming are, quite simply, looking for the wrong thing given the play's postmodernity. For it is the very point of the play that Rosencrantz and Guildenstern cannot sufficiently define themselves "outside Shakespeare's world." This is a feature, not a bug.

The Real Inspector Hound

Equally important to understanding how fully invested Stoppard is in a postmodern aesthetics is his one-act play, *The Real Inspector Hound* (1968), which actually does *R & G* one better in how it explicitly transcends the boundary between the stage and the audience, as audience members appear to cross the theatrical threshold and join the action as it occurs on stage. As *Hound* begins, the audience's attention is focused on two theater critics, Moon and Birdboot, as if they were the subject of the play. However, soon enough "another" play begins which the audience — together with these two critics — becomes so intent on watching that they eventually identify with Moon and Birdboot as if they, too, are simply audience members. According to McHale, such boundary crossing is postmodern:

> What is striking about many postmodernist texts is the way they court confusion of levels.... Postmodernist texts [...] tend to encourage trompe-l'oeil, deliberately misleading the reader into regarding an embedded, secondary world as the primary, diegetic world. Typically, such deliberate "mystification" is followed by "demystification," in which the true ontological status of the supposed

"reality" is revealed and the entire ontological structure of the text consequently laid bare [*Postmodernist Fiction* 115].

Mystification in *Inspector Hound* happens at the very moment when the two critics suddenly appear as if they are part of the audience. Ontological "demystification" begins to occur when Moon and Birdboot find themselves caught up in the action of a new play within a play: "The phone starts to ring on the empty stage. Moon tries to ignore it." Finally losing patience, Moon ascends the stage and answers the phone. It is for Birdboot, and Moon calls him to the stage: "Birdboot gets up. He approaches cautiously. Moon gives him the phone and moves back to his seat. Birdboot watches him go. He looks round and smiles weakly, expiating himself" (32). At this point demystification is complete.

Upon demystification there are other intriguing developments, as the entire play begins to repeat itself with rather surprising results. For just as Simon had been secretly involved in a love triangle with both the mistress of the manor, Lady Cynthia Muldoon, and her houseguest, Felicity Cunningham (whom he wishes to dump for Cynthia), so too Birdboot is secretly involved with the actress who is playing Felicity and, in turn, immediately smitten with the actress playing Cynthia (causing him to want to dump the actress playing Felicity). Thus, when thrust onto the stage, Birdboot finds himself responding to the characters (or is it to their actor-counterparts?) in precisely the same way that the fictional Simon had. Moreover, just as Simon feels compelled to explain his mysterious appearance at Muldoon Manor in Act I, Birdboot feels similarly compelled to explain his own (perhaps, more mysterious) appearance within the play:

FELICITY: What are you doing here?!
BIRDBOOT: Well, I ...
FELICITY: Honestly, darling, you really are extraordinary—
BIRDBOOT: Yes, well here I am. (*He looks round sheepishly.*)
FELICITY: You must have been desperate to see me—I mean, I'm flattered, but couldn't it wait till I got back? [*Hound* 33].

Much of the dialogue is a word-for-word repetition of a similar scene in Act I. Yet this isn't just a case of a man stumbling onto a stage where he doesn't belong, since all of the other actors accept Birdboot into Simon's role without hesitation. Additionally, the scene works at many distinct ontological levels, since Felicity's words can also be seen as alluding to their "real world" affair—which makes his "strange" appearance on stage

1. Introduction

uniquely bizarre for her (i.e., couldn't he have waited until the play was over to see her?).

This is, however, more than an instance of trompe-l'oeil (with Moon and Birdboot switching ontological levels), but is, more specifically, what McHale refers to (after citing Douglas Hofstader) as a "Strange Loop": "The 'Strange Loop' phenomenon occurs whenever, by moving upwards (or downwards) through the levels of some hierarchical system, we unexpectedly find ourselves right back where we started" (Hofstader 10). The disruption of ontological levels that occurs in *Inspector Hound* employs just this sort of theatrical repetition, as the characters of the inner play unexpectedly find themselves "right back where they started," creating just the sort of "recursive structure" which "results when you perform the same operation over and over again, each time operating on the product of the previous operation." When the same scene plays itself out with Birdboot operating in the role of Simon, the resulting recursive structure causes interpretations to proliferate; so, too, do ontological questions concerning the boundary between stage and audience. When combined with the trompe-l'oeil, this recursive structure multiplies the layering of ontological levels in ways yet unexamined by McHale. In turn, with *Hound* we find the type of ontological questions which render a work postmodern proliferating, meaning that even while Stoppard's contemporaries in fiction are just beginning to adopt the morphological features described by McHale, Stoppard is already revolutionizing a tradition that extends back at least as far as Pirandello.

Something yet remains to be said about the play's genre, which is a satire of the murder mystery play popularized by Agatha Christie in the early 20th century. Significantly, Brian McHale suggests that "a modernist novel looks like a detective story" for how it raises epistemological questions even as it "revolve[s] around problems of the accessibility of knowledge, the individual mind's grappling with an elusive or occluded reality" (*Constructing Postmodernism* 147). However, as much as this play grapples with these issues, its metatheatricalism ultimately means that it grapples with ontological issues as well, such that it ultimately shares more with what McHale refers to as "anti-detective" stories for how it "foregrounds its own ontological status" and "reveals to us, behind the layers of patterns of events and misconstructions of patterns and retrospective constructions, the presence of the real author himself" (*Constructing Postmodernism* 151).

When every mystery is instead a trick played on us by the author, our attention is inevitably drawn to that author. Just as in *R & G*, the very reality of the stage is identified as a construct.

However, that *Hound* is also a parody means that the play's postmodernity is further complicated by what Fredric Jameson has said about how parody has been replaced by pastiche in the postmodern era:

> [Postmodernity] is the moment at which pastiche appears and parody has become impossible. Pastiche is, like parody, the imitation of a peculiar or unique style, the wearing of a stylistic mask, speech in a dead language: but it is a neutral practice of such mimicry, without parody's ulterior motive, without the satirical impulse, without laughter, without the still latent feeling that there exists something normal compared to which what is being imitated is rather comic [*Postmodernism* 17].

Whether or not what we are witnessing in *Hound* qualifies as parody or pastiche is difficult to determine. Most telling on this front is the dialogue of Mrs. Drudge, which sounds more like stage directions from a murder mystery play than it does like dialogue:

> Hello, the drawing room of Lady Muldoon's country residence one morning in early spring? ... Hello!— the draw — Who? Whom did you wish to speak to? I'm afraid there is no one of that name here, this is all mysterious and I'm sure it's leading up to something, I hope nothing is amiss for we, that is, Lady Muldoon and her houseguests, are here cut off from the world, including Magnus, the wheelchair-ridden half-brother of her ladyship's husband Lord Albert Muldoon who ten years ago went out for a walk on the cliffs and was never seen again [11].

Personally, I find this to be a fairly blank form of parody in its attitude towards the murder mystery play. Yes, Stoppard does identify various genre stereotypes which, having become predictable and stale, perhaps do need rethinking. However, it seems to me that Stoppard is having as much fun with the genre as he is critiquing it — a feature which, I would argue, does as much to honor the genre as it does to question it — meaning that even according to Jameson's definition the play leans postmodern. In any case, we will see that as his career develops Stoppard becomes increasingly overt in how he uses parody to critique various political and philosophical attitudes which he finds to be ontologically, epistemologically, and even aesthetically distasteful, pointing to one more way in which Stoppard becomes increasingly modern during the course of his career.

1. Introduction

At this point it is worth noting that *Hound* becomes so deeply metatheatrical that it begins to engage those larger social and political forces and institutions that give rise to the theater. For when Moon and Birdboot find themselves caught up in the action of the very play that they are watching, the audience not only sees through the realistic illusion distinguishing audience from actor but also begins to recognize the role that critics play in fashioning a successful production. That a death results from the interaction between the theater and its critics presents an apt metaphor, since critics have caused the death of many plays, actors, and actresses. (Of course, they have contributed to successful careers as well, and, at least on occasion, have done so via trading sexual favors, also intimated at in the play.) Consequently, the metadramatic window that opens up on those elements which make up the theater is extended so that the audience can see the larger social political forces which conspire in order to create a hit. Thus, while someone like Pirandello strives for nothing beyond an epistemological/ontological effect, there is at least a hint of ideological concern about the capitalistic forces that contribute to the successful production that Stoppard's *Hound* proved to be. It would seem, then, that in addition to engaging the textual sorts of indeterminacy described by Hassan, the play also flirts with what Hassan refers to as immanence. For even as the play goes out of its way to identify the way in which the so-called independent theater and independent press collude in the face of various market constraints, this would appear to become an investigation of the way in which "the public world dissolves as fact and fiction blend" and "history becomes a media happening" ("From Postmodernism to Postmodernity" 5).

It is also notable that after *Hound*—which as we have discussed would appear to employ postmodern technique to ideological effect in order to explore the complicity between cultural production and the power hierarchy—Stoppard begins his long transition away from the postmodern. (Along the way, he actively dismisses the relationship between ideology and representation in such plays as *Night and Day* and *Rock 'n' Roll*.) One way of reading this is that with *Hound* he recognized the potential ideological implications of postmodern formulations, such that he actively sought to reject such attitudes in his future work. (I will return to this point in this book's concluding chapter, "Encore.") Consider Hutcheon on the subversive potential of the postmodern:

As you will no doubt have noticed, since the prefatory note there is another fiction or construct operating here too: my own paradoxical postmodernism of complicity and critique, of reflexivity and historicity, that at once inscribes and subverts the conventions and ideologies of the dominant cultural and social forces of the twentieth-century western world [11–12].

According to this perspective, the postmodern is anything but moderate. It is either subversive of the status quo — or subversive in how it reinscribes that status quo. By contrast, we will find that Stoppard, the self-described moderate conservative, quoted by John Bull as saying "I'm a conservative with a small *c*. I am a conservative in politics, literature, education and theatre" ("Politics" 151) is not only ideologically moderate, but also epistemologically, ontologically and aesthetically moderate as well. It would seem these are poor credentials indeed for a postmodernist.

Reductive Postmodernity

While the treatment of Stoppard's remaining major plays (and one minor one, *After Magritte*) in the following chapters is chronological — as suits the needs of an argument making claims that Stoppard's career has evolved in a coherent and comprehensible way — as much as possible I have attempted to ensure that each chapter has its own thesis even as I seek to identify unique ways in which Stoppard resists the postmodern. That said, Brian McHale's work differentiating the modern from the postmodern in fiction is often — though not always — key to recognizing this "resistance." To this end it is significant that in addition to exploring the morphological differences between modern and postmodern texts, McHale goes on to explain that the difference between the two can be a fine one, wherein the raising of epistemological questions can easily tip over into the raising of ontological questions:

> Intractable epistemological uncertainty becomes at a certain point ontological plurality or instability: push epistemological questions far enough and they "tip over" into ontological questions. By the same token, push ontological questions far enough and they tip over into epistemological questions — the sequence is not linear and unidirectional, but bidirectional and reversible [*Postmodernist Fiction* 11].

My own position is that Stoppard actually succeeds in reversing this trend: "push[ing] ontological questions far enough [so that] they tip over into

1. Introduction

epistemological questions"; and, moreover, that to the extent that Stoppard accomplishes this, he transitions from a postmodernist author to a modernist one (albeit a modernist author who continues to actively engage postmodern concepts).

In explaining how epistemological questions merge into ontological ones, McHale references Beckett's trilogy (*Molloy*, *Malone Dies*, *The Unnamable*), arguing that *Molloy* is fully modernist for how it raises epistemological questions, while *Malone Dies* is "limit-modernist" because it hesitates on the border, simultaneously foregrounding both ontological and epistemological questions. McHale explains that in order for a text to remain essentially modernist even though it raises ontological questions, the ontological dominant must be recuperated as stemming from a more deeply relevant epistemological dominant. According to McHale, *Malone Dies*' ontological disparity can be recovered as merely raising epistemological questions once we realize that the ontological disparity[6] at work in the novel results from an unreliable narrator, making it yet "recuperable in epistemological terms, as a reflection or extension of Malone's consciousness" (12). Thus, *Malone Dies* becomes the prototypical limit-modernist text because "looked at one way [it] seems to focus on epistemological issues, while looked at another it seems to be focused on ontological issues" (13).

Conversely, according to this same criterion (and, of course, according to McHale's claim that the sequence is "bidirectional and reversible"), what at first looks like postmodernism would best be identified as modernist should all of its ontological mystification be "normalized" in one way or another, such as through the implementation of an unreliable narrator. As we will see, Stoppard's *Travesties* embodies the clearest reversal of the trend described by McHale, most especially in how its use of an unreliable narrator serves to normalize the ontological incongruities of the work as a whole. The fundamental argument of this volume, however, is that throughout the remainder of his career Stoppard continues to do much the same thing, albeit by finding new ways of normalizing what might otherwise be regarded as postmodern.

In Chapter 2 I begin to track this very transition from the postmodern to the modern in Stoppard's next two plays, *After Magritte* and *Jumpers*. While still employing theatrical techniques that are every bit as innovative as his first two plays — even to the point of exhibiting the same potential to subvert both epistemological and ontological norms—*After Magritte* and *Jumpers* are easily recognized as charting a very different theatrical path than what might have been expected after *R & G* and *Hound*, simultaneously reveling in—and normalizing—their overt theatricalism. *After Magritte*, for instance, begins by introducing such an odd collage of items to the audience that it can easily be interpreted as rejecting traditional ontological categories. On closer examination, however, we find that Stoppard's response to a Magrittean perspective of the world is to make sense of it, as each of the various visual anomalies is made sense of within the context of a larger narrative. Thus, in stark contrast to Magritte's paintings, Stoppard reinstates ("normalizes") a very traditional ontological picture of the universe. Moreover, it's also notable that in contrast with *Hound*, *After Magritte* doesn't just privilege coherence, but also privileges the idea that the empirical method helps to yield such coherence (and as we will see, the empirical method is privileged time and again during Stoppard's career). As with *After Magritte*, *Jumpers* also fills the stage with various odd creatures in need of further explanation, a troupe of acrobats who have day jobs as Cambridge philosophers. Apparently, the only way to *normalize* the excessive leaps of logic and pratfalls of common sense that philosophers are so prone to making is to put them in their place (i.e., by placing them in the shoes of actual gymnasts).

Chapter 3 argues that *Travesties* and *The Real Thing* do even more than their predecessors to reject postmodern attitudes. While very different from each other in form, they have a common concern for the way in which literary reputations are established (as do some of the later plays, including *Arcadia* and *Hapgood*). At the most superficial level, the suggestion is that the various figures in the two plays — most notably, James Joyce, Tristan Tzara and Vladimir Lenin in *Travesties*—have been artificially constructed by critics and historians, just as characters in a play are artificial constructs. However, unlike similar treatments of the way in which theatrical characters can be used to raise questions about the ontological status of real-world characters (Jean Genet, Luigi Pirandello), these plays ultimately suggest that there are real, identifiable characters beneath these artificial constructs (Carr's unreliability as a narrator in *Travesties* providing some assurance on this point). *The Real Thing* walks a difficult path in this regard, asking that its audience recognize that Stoppard himself is partly constructed by what he is willing to divulge about himself, even while

1. Introduction

problematizing any comfortable connections we feel like making between the central character, Henry (also a playwright), and Stoppard himself.

Night and Day, discussed in Chapter 4, is the oddball of the bunch. Focused as it is on defending uncompromisingly free-market attitudes towards freedom of expression, it is perhaps the only play (other than *Rock 'n' Roll*—which, because it comes so late, is less of an oddball) which does not traverse a postmodern terrain. Rather, I argue that it is best seen as an instance wherein Stoppard had every opportunity to invoke postmodern perspectives about truth and power in order to explore the power dynamic implicit in knowledge creation and distribution (a concept at least hinted at in *Hound*), but instead chose to reject such concepts in favor of an idealization of the press as "the last line of defense for all the other freedoms" (*Night and Day* 63).

Chapter 5 focuses on the science plays, *Hapgood* and *Arcadia*. In *Hapgood* Stoppard draws an analogy between the theory of quantum mechanics and international espionage, while in *Arcadia* he uses chaos theory to explain the difficulty that literary biographers confront when recovering the past. Although these works are not as theatrically experimental as Stoppard's earlier work (a compelling if not sufficient sign of having rejected the postmodern), they nonetheless engage the concerns of the postmodern era in their adoption of "postmodern science." In keeping with what is becoming a familiar pattern, much of Stoppard's investigation into these theories seeks to normalize their odder ontological and epistemological features according to various available classical interpretations of quantum mechanics and chaos theory rather than to revel in their anti-epistemological implications.

Chapter 6 begins by reconsidering the attitude Stoppard takes towards literary critics in *Arcadia* before moving on to also discuss his treatment of critics in *Indian Ink* and *The Invention of Love*. The plays share a common theme, as they each track the successes and failures of literary critics engaged in historiographic research. In *Arcadia* and *Indian Ink*, the work of these critics (each one, a fictional character) is largely derided as both prone to error and potentially "trivial." And while it is all too easy to read the plays as having something in common with contemporary (postmodern) theories of how readers construct meaning, I will argue that the plays ultimately favor historiography as an act of discovery rather than of invention. As such, *The Invention of Love* serves as something of a turning point, as Stoppard finally proves much more sympathetic to the famous classicist A. E. Housman than he is to the fictional critics he satirizes in *Arcadia* and *Indian Ink,* even though Housman has an even stronger commitment to the idea that an accurate picture of the past is recoverable through due historiographical diligence (i.e., through the proper use of the scientific method).

While Stoppard has occasionally been diverted from the overt theatricalism which stands as the defining feature in a distinguished career, Chapter 7 and "Encore" discuss his most recent plays, *The Coast of Utopia* and *Rock 'n' Roll,* which are much more straightforwardly sociorealist history plays and, as such, do not do nearly as much to add nuance to their thematic meaning through formalist experimentation with the morphological features of theater as do his other plays (notably, *The Coast of Utopia* has been linked with Chekhov for its overt socio-realism). Moreover, while Stoppard is well known for his playfulness, these works are deeply serious in their attitude as well as their theatrical style. This final chapter argues, however, that there is a significant link between these earlier works and Stoppard's larger canon — that is, that underneath his playfulness Stoppard has always engaged serious ideas, and, moreover, that despite the traditional theatricalism of these recent plays, there remains a resonance between these works' thematic vision and their form that is in keeping with the most metatheatrical of his plays. In *Rock 'n' Roll* in particular I conclude that only after working through a wide variety of theatrical techniques — each of which, in one way or another was directed towards self-consciously querying the postmodern uncertainty which surrounds him — Stoppard finally finds some comfort in the relative safety of dramatic realism in order to express his various politically positivist ideals.

2

Normalizing *Magritte* and Tumbling Philosophers

After Magritte and *Jumpers* are both much concerned with issues of appearance and reality. Notably, each play contains scenes wherein various characters are caught in odd and or compromising situations, only to have the strangeness of those situations clarified as the scene proceeds. In *Jumpers*, George references an aphorism concerning the philosopher Ludwig Wittgenstein which clarifies Stoppard's motivations for employing this technique:

> Meeting a friend in a corridor, Wittgenstein said: "Tell me, why do people always say it was natural for men to assume that the sun went round the earth rather than that the earth was rotating?" His friend said, "Well, obviously, because it just looks as if the sun is going round the earth." To which the philosopher replied, "Well, what would it have looked like if it had looked as if the earth was rotating?" [75].

This, in essence, is what we see so often in these two plays. Characters make assumptions regarding particular events "because it just looks as if" x interpretation of those events is correct. And then, at every turn, we find Stoppard stepping in to show x was really no more reasonable an interpretation of those events than y. This forces us to ask, "Well, what would it have looked like if it had looked like y had really been the case?" Stoppard asks a lot of his audience, just as Wittgenstein asked a lot of his fellow philosophers. Most notably, Wittgenstein famously wanted to cure philosophers of the desire to philosophize, which, as we will see, is an attitude shared by Stoppard.

After Magritte

When the curtain rises on *After Magritte* an image appears which presents such an odd collage of items to the audience that at first we are likely to assume that Stoppard is once again engaged in disrupting ontological truths in some of those same ways that have become so familiar in *Hound* and *R & G*. We find Mother lying on an ironing board, one foot propped up against an iron. She is wearing a black rubber bathing cap, and a black bowler hat sits on her stomach. Thelma Harris is on her hands and knees, expensively dressed in a full-length gown, while Reginald Harris is standing on a chair, bare to the waist, wearing fishing waders over his dress trousers. A lamp hangs from the ceiling, complexly counterbalanced by a basket of fruit. A police constable stares through the window stage rear. Notable for the fact that it might strike the policeman's interests, all of the furniture is seen to be blocking the front door as if forming a barricade. (One might ask: What would it have looked like if it did not look like it was forming a barricade?)

Anthony Jenkins explains that the play's title presents a double pun, referring both to the "chronological time of the play's action"—which takes place after the Harris family has attended a Magritte exhibit—and to the fact that it is "'after Magritte' *stylistically*, in the sense of 'in the manner of Magritte'" (208). Jenkins finds the closest stylistic resemblance in Magritte's *L'Assassin menacé*, which he describes as follows:

> Two large respectably dressed figures in overcoats and bowler hats stand on either side of what amounts to a proscenium.... The man on the left grasps a club whose knob resembles a human knee-cap; the one on the right holds a net at the ready ... a wooden table with a simple cloth supports a gramophone into the horn of which a man gazes as if listening to the record as he leans against the table ... a naked woman on a couch whose shape and unyielding surface suggests a coffin; a towel draped across her neck isolates her rather masculine-looking, bloodstained head. Beyond her ... the grille of a balcony above which rise the heads and shoulders of three impassive male observers [55].

The similarity of the play to the Magritte painting is that in each collage we recognize a combination of bizarre items grouped together in ways that are not commonly found in the real world. Stoppard also borrows other items from Magritte's artistic wardrobe, including a woman with a tuba.[1] Thus, for fairly obvious reasons many commentators on Stoppard's work have taken this play as an homage to Magritte.

In order to understand the epistemological and ontological attitudes under investigation in *After Magritte*, it proves fruitful to begin by examining *L'Assassin menacé* itself, which also appears specifically directed towards investigating ontological and epistemological issues. According to

2. Normalizing *Magritte* and *Tumbling Philosophers*

one reading, if we are to take *L'Assassin menacé* as a representative sample of the world's ontological artifacts, we might believe that the world quite naturally contained such odd collages as the ones contained there. As such, at the most cursory level it would appear that Magritte rejects coherence narratives about how the world typically arranges itself, instead suggesting that there is no quotably coherent pattern that might match that of the world's ontological wardrobe, and that the artist need not even attempt to represent the world accurately. According to this interpretation all conceivable patterns are constructed and not found, contingent and not necessary. Magritte, it seems, spoke his own private language to a small (but growing) group of admirers; the implication is that we all, similarly, speak our own private language. The artificially constructed is as coherent and meaningful as "the real" (whatever that is).

Michel Foucault's *This Is Not a Pipe*, which analyzes Magritte's painting of *The Treachery of Images*, among other works by Magritte, serves as a useful instruction manual for better grasping the epistemological and ontological issues commonly raised by the artist. According to Foucault, Magritte's work rejects the "traditional" idea that the artist's job is to create mimetic representations of reality. Indeed, Foucault emphatically rejects the idea that the painting—which depicts a pipe over the caption "Ceci n'est pas un pipe" ("This is not a pipe")—puts forward the "simpleminded" assertion that a painting of a pipe is not, after all, the same thing as a pipe: "But who would seriously contend that the collection of intersecting lines above the text is a pipe?" (19). For Foucault the issues raised by the painting concern, not just how symbols relate to their objects, but also—and more importantly—a rejection of the idea that we might better know the world by describing it and by establishing resemblances of it. The astute witness to the painting would generalize beyond the singular disclaimer of the drawing to a much more skeptical perspective on signified and signifier.

As his analysis continues, Foucault examines the entire range of Magritte's works, noting in particular how Magritte confronts modernist concepts about anti-representability in unique ways:

> Magritte allows the old space of representability to rule, but only at the surface, no more than a polished stone, bearing words and shapes; beneath, nothing. It is a gravestone: The incisions that drew the figures and those that marked letters communicate only by void, the non-place hidden beneath marble solidity [41].

Thus, a painting that is superficially realistic (for example, the realistic portrayal of the pipe in *The Treachery of Images*) is, ironically, recognized as more radically dismissive of the potentiality of representability than is a work which is explicitly and overtly anti-representative. In his introduction to Foucault's *This Is Not a Pipe*, James Harkness provides a useful summary of Foucault's argument:

> How to banish resemblance and its implicit burden of discourse? Magritte's strategy involves deploying largely familiar images, but images whose recognizability is immediately subverted and rendered moot by "impossible," "irrational," or "senseless," conjunctions. In *L'Explication* (1952), the most obvious thing about the carrot metamorphosis into the wine bottle is that it is not (does not reproduce, represent, or linguistically affirm) any actual carrot or bottle [8].

To assist with his explication of the radical epistemological attitude at work in Magritte, Harkness references Foucault's theorization of heterotopia in *The Order of Things*: "such things are 'laid,' 'placed,' 'arranged' in lists so very different from one another it is impossible to find a place of residence for them." Foucault continues: "Heterotopia are disturbing, probably because they secretly undermine language, because they make it impossible to name this *and* name that, because they shatter or tangle common names, because they destroy syntax in advance..." (xviii) For Foucault, the pipe in *The Treachery of Images* serves only to establish the relationship of similitude, not strict representation, to objects existing in the real world. Moreover, since heterotopias bear this exact same relationship to objects in the world, the central question raised in Magritte doesn't just concern "where and how pictures attach to the world" but also, "What kind of objects exist in that world?" Or, as McHale would have it, epistemological questions tip over into ontological questions. For if we cannot safely assume a relationship of identity (or even representation) between signifier and signified, then who is to say that there is one between mental images (which are themselves signifiers) and their objects? What, moreover, are we to make of the various stage props in *After Magritte*, which are also signifiers, albeit signifiers meant as much to draw attention to the artificiality of theatrical environments as to the lamps and ironing boards and fruit baskets they most superficially resemble.

Douglas Hofstadter remarks more explicitly on this specific characteristic of Magritte's work in his explanation of how an image which pur-

2. *Normalizing* Magritte *and Tumbling Philosophers*

ports to raise strictly linguistic issues also raises ontological questions: "The use-mention dichotomy, when pushed, turns into the philosophical problem of symbol object dualism, which links it to the mystery of the mind" (706). To defend his position, Hofstader quotes from comments Magritte made about his own painting, *The Human Condition*:

> I placed in front of a window, seen from a room, a painting representing exactly that part of the landscape which was hidden from view by the painting. Therefore, the tree represented in the painting hid from view the tree situated behind it, outside the room. It existed for the spectator, as it were, simultaneously in his mind, as both inside the room in the painting, and outside in the real landscape. Which is how we see the world: we see it as being outside ourselves even though it is only a mental representation of it that we experience inside ourselves [qtd in Hoftader 706].

Hofstader helps us see a synthesis within Magritte's work, as images from *The Treachery of Images* to *The Human Condition* are each seen to be questioning traditional ontological commitments, suggesting that material objects might simply exist as mental images.

Such a reading of Magritte is made most explicit in *La Lunette d'approche* ("The Field Glass"), which depicts a window looking out onto the horizon, a cloudy sky above a calm sea. However, the window opens inward, and it is slightly ajar. Through the opening, however, one doesn't see a continuation of the same image that is seen through the windowpane (as one might see in a more traditionally realistic painting), but, rather, one sees only blackness, no sky, no sea. The title makes Magritte's point even more suggestive. When we view something, as we might through a field glass (or even by use of cornea and optic nerve), what we see is never quite what exists.

While the paintings discussed by Hofstadter are different from the heterotopias discussed by Foucault, the effect is the same: "Heterotopias (such as those to be found so often in Borges) desiccate speech, stop words in their tracks, contest the very possibility of grammar at its source" (Foucault, *The Order of Things*, xviii). Thus, heterotopias such as *L'assasin menace* reject traditional epistemological and ontological perspectives about how knowledge can contribute to the realization of a unified whole since the knowledge presented in such paintings isn't ordered in a way that inspires confidence in the possibility that symbols reflect reality. *La Lunette d'approche* is, moreover, as antithetical to traditional ontological attitudes as it is to traditional epistemological attitudes, if not more so, since it rejects out of hand any utopia-preserving empirical data which traditionalists might gather in an attempt to reject the notion that heterotopias are as representative of the world as anything else might be. (How are we to trust any of our empirical tools if we can't trust our corneas and optic nerves?) Metanarratives which privilege a well-ordered and knowable universe are dismissed in favor of locally constructed truths; Magritte winks at us, and asks us to agree with his perspective of reality, becoming the artist's complement to what Hassan says happens to "ideas of author, audience, reading, writing, book, genre, critical theory ("Postmodernism to Postmodernity" 4) in the postmodern age.

If we try to make the case, however, that Stoppard's *After Magritte* presents a similar heterotopian attitude towards "openness, fragmentation, ambiguity, discontinuity, decenterment, heterodoxy, pluralism, deformation, all conducive to indeterminacy or under-determination" (Hassan 4) we run into trouble as soon as the play moves beyond its opening tableau. For as the play progresses, its heterotopian tensions are all too quickly resolved, as it is soon discovered that Thelma and Reginald have been preparing for a professional dancing competition, which explains their fancy dress, that Reginald is wearing waders in order to change the lightbulb above the waterfilled bathtub, and that Mother is lying on the ironing board so that Thelma, who must give Mother her daily massage, can more easily accomplish her task. The basket of fruit hangs as a counterbalance because the original balance of lead slugs from a .22 caliber pistol has fallen and spilled all over the floor. This, in turn, explains why all the furniture in the flat is stacked against the door: it has all been moved so that Thelma can search for the spilt slugs. And just as the constable disappears from his vantage point at the window to go inform The Inspector of the melee, the room quickly shifts back into a more "normal" state. Thus, by the time Inspector Foot has arrived at the door and cries out, "What is the meaning of this bizarre spectacle?" his words are met by a world that "makes sense" rather than by the heterotopian image of the opening tableau. At a loss, Inspector Foot confronts his constable: "Got the right house, have you?" (15).

Stoppard's response to Magritte's unique heterotopian perspective of the world is, therefore, to make sense of it. In Stoppard's ontology there is a place for everything and everything is in its place, and if we only stick

2. *Normalizing* Magritte *and Tumbling Philosophers*

around long enough, we will find out where everything goes. In contrast to Magritte — who makes for a nice fit with our working definition of postmodernism — Stoppard engages postmodern ideas only to subject them to scrutiny, before finally reinstating a very traditionally ontological understanding of the universe. In essence, Stoppard doesn't just reinforce traditional metanarratives but overtly rejects the idea that local narratives are (or should be) the dominant form, as the Inspector's very local narrative is shown to be false, replaced by a more universally shared narrative. *After Magritte* doesn't, therefore, simply privilege coherence, but also the idea that the empirical method is essential in establishing such coherence.

This tendency in Stoppard to discredit locally held beliefs ("little narratives" or "petit récits" in Lyotard) in favor of more universally shared ones helps to explain a number of similar nonsensical images found throughout the play. For instance, the collage which confronts the audience at the closing curtain is as equally Magrittean as that of the opening tableau, though its context makes it significantly less shocking since the audience knows in advance precisely what steps led up to this particular spectacle (104). Similarly, we find that a figure whom Thelma first described as a "one legged footballer" (70), and which Harris described as "an old man with one leg and a white beard, dressed in pyjamas, hopping along in the rain with a tortoise under his arm and brandishing a white stick" (77), was, in actuality, Inspector Foot himself, who had stopped in the middle of shaving in order to run out on the street and move his car:

> I couldn't move very fast because in my haste to pull up my pyjama trousers I put both feet into the same leg. So after hopping around a bit and nearly dropping the handbag into various puddles, I just thought to hell with it all and went back in the house. My wife claimed I'd broken her new white parasol [104].

If there is a moral to this play it would seem to be that if we only look deeply enough beneath any given heterotopian image, its mystery will reveal itself.

It would seem, then, that to the extent that Stoppard enjoys toying with heterotopias and other bizarre images, it is only so that he can see through them and, finally, feel comfortable that a coherent narrative about their nature persists. Moreover, rather than encouraging his audience to leave with widely different perspectives, Stoppard strives to instill a homogeneity of thought. Everyone in the audience is to agree that Inspector

Foot was the impetus behind the strange scene witnessed by Thelma and Harris. Everyone in the audience is also to agree that the opening and closing Magrittean images can be rationally explained. Thus, Stoppard doesn't encourage the factional disagreement that, for Lyotard, is the very mark of the postmodern era and is part and parcel of the proliferation of local narratives. Rather, after Magritte has left the building, Stoppard steps in to encourage his audience to leave the theater with epistemological and ontological attitudes that are so steeped in empiricism that they actually defy postmodernity.[2] According to this reading, *After Magritte* becomes a veritable guidebook, designed to help people see through heterotopias in such a way that they can make sense of them according to more traditional epistemological and ontological perspectives. (Ludwig Wittgenstein, similarly, hoped to cure philosophers of their overactive imaginations, but more on this below.) And as we will see, this theatrical technique will show up again in Stoppard's work, in *Jumpers*, but even more tellingly in *Arcadia* and *Indian Ink*, as situations that, on their surface entail empirical conundrums resolve themselves in such a way that epistemological stability is maintained.

Jumpers

Jumpers also contains many images and ideas which Stoppard attempts to normalize, most notably the bizarre discipline of analytic philosophy itself—which, as we will see, he likens to the discipline of acrobatics. However, it isn't until about one-third of the way into *Jumper* that the audience is presented with a scene which explicitly recalls the opening tableau of *After Magritte*:

> The door is opened to him [Bones] by a man [George] holding a bow-and-arrow in one hand and a tortoise in the other, his face covered in shaving foam. Bones recoils from the spectacle, and George is somewhat taken aback too [43].

Like the incredulous Inspector Foot of *After Magritte*, Bones is a police inspector. And while in *After Magritte* the joke of the play relies on the fact that the scene which Foot's constable has witnessed through the window—and decided must be indicative of a nefarious plot—is all too easily and eventually explained,[3] soon enough, George's appearance becomes practically irrelevant to the scope of Inspector Bones' investigation (if not

2. *Normalizing* Magritte *and Tumbling Philosophers*

to the scope of Stoppard's Investigation), as the spectacle which is George is quickly superseded by circumstances which Bones finds much more bizarre even than George's appearance; that is, the moral relativism of the "Orthodox mainstream" Radical Liberal (Rad Lib) party.

LOGICALLY POSITIVE MURDER

Interrogated on his doorstep by Bones, George eventually characterizes the moral philosophy of the Rad Lib logical positivists of his fellow university professors as follows:

> GEORGE: Oh. Well, in simple terms, he [McFee] believes that people on the whole should tell the truth all right, and keep their promises, and so on, but on the sole grounds that if everybody went around telling lies and breaking their word as a matter of course, normal life would be impossible. Of course, he is defining normality in terms of the truth being told and promises being kept, etcetera, so the definition is circular and not worth very much, but the point is it allows him to conclude that telling lies is not *sinful* but simply antisocial.

To George's expressed concern that perhaps the inspector wouldn't really want him "to go into this all" the inspector responds that he is "enthralled" (48). Just like Inspector Foot in *After Magritte*, Inspector Bones has sized up the situation and determined that something worth his attention is indeed amiss, albeit in this instance more because of the expressed moral relativism of the Rad Lib philosophy than because of George's appearance. We can only assume that just as the heterotopian image which confronts the audience of *After Magritte* is eventually normalized for Inspector Foot as he takes a closer look, so too will the image of Radical Liberalism be normalized as Inspector Bones takes a closer look.

John Fleming similarly finds the "disconnected [heterotopian] images" of the opening tableau of *Jumpers* to be a trope that is familiar in Stoppard's early work:

> *Jumpers* begins with a favorite device of Stoppard's early career: a mélange of provocative and seemingly disconnected images that jolt the audience. The succeeding action then proceeds to dispel the initial confusion as logical reason will be provided for the bizarre occurrences [86].

In mentioning Stoppard's early career, Fleming presumably is thinking of *After Magritte*, which, as we have seen, functions in just this fashion. However, Fleming does not take the opportunity to discuss any of Stoppard's early plays, and, in any case, while *Jumpers* does share notable features with *After Magritte*, it is important to note that such ontologically incongruous moments do not dominate the play in nearly the same way. Moreover, as long as we are making connections between the various early plays, it is well worth remembering that *Jumpers* also invokes *R & G* in its opening tableau, which Michael Hinden describes as follows:

> In *Rosencrantz and Guildenstern Are Dead* one of the pair in desperation asks: "Shouldn't we be doing something constructive?" "What did you have in mind." His friend replies, "A short, blunt, human pyramid?" In fact, a team of acrobats provides the opening image in Stoppard's post-absurdist play. By calling attention in this way to *Rosencrantz and Guildenstern Are Dead*, Stoppard seems to be suggesting that *Jumpers* can be considered a natural or logical outgrowth of the earlier work [5].

As mentioned in the Introduction, the way Jim Hunter describes the various philosophical principles raised by *R & G*[4] is also suggestive of the idea that the philosophical scope of *Jumpers* traverses the same postmodern landscape as *R & G*.

This larger landscape that Bones must familiarize himself with continues to prove ever more surprising. Even given the various advantages of being audience to that first third of the play which Bones is not privy to, it is easy to be as confused by what is going on as poor Bones. *Jumpers* opens with a party celebrating the landslide election victory of the Rad Libs, a fictitious political party which is based on a foundation of moral relativism of the logical positivist variety (logical positivists believed firmly — and exclusively — in the precepts of science and logic; thus, they held that all metaphysical speculation was nonsensical and that moral and value statements were merely emotive, and not morally binding). The party takes place in the home of George and Dorothy (Dotty) Moore, and much of the philosophy department is in attendance, composed as it is, predominantly, of logical positivists (with the ironic exception of George Moore himself).[5] Dotty used to be a famous singer, but quit after suffering a nervous breakdown. At the party she bungles her way through a poor rendition of "Blue Moon" before being followed on stage by a group of jumpers (acrobats) made up of logical positivists — led by the Vice Chancellor, Archibald Jumper (Archie). While in the form of a pyramid, one of the jumpers, McFee, is shot and killed. The audience is meant to believe that Dotty, apparently suffering from a relapse, has shot him. Archie is,

2. *Normalizing* Magritte *and Tumbling Philosophers*

among other things, a practicing psychologist who for some time has been attending to Dotty with what has all the appearance of a dubiously promiscuous bedside manner. When the scene breaks up, Archie tells Dotty, "Just keep the body out of sight till morning. I'll be back" (21).

All the while, George has been working in his study and so remains ignorant of McFee's murder. He doesn't subscribe to the Rad Lib philosophy and has been writing a paper which is meant as an attack against it. The paper is to be read in response to a paper by McFee in support of logical positivism. Much of the first act is taken up with George rewriting and rehearsing his ideas aloud for his secretary, unwittingly leaving Dotty to suffer through the crisis alone.

When Inspector Bones eventually arrives to investigate McFee's death, he turns out to be a fan of Dotty's, but is also convinced that she has committed murder and encourages her to cop to an insanity plea. Bones never discovers the body, however, which is eventually spirited away by Archie and the other jumpers while Bones searches another corner of the house. Unconvinced by the lack of evidence, he undertakes an interview with Dotty, whereupon she screams rape. In turn, Archie uses this compromising situation to coerce Bones into discontinuing his investigation.

Meanwhile, other possible solutions to the mystery of McFee's murder gain credibility: Archie might have shot him out of fear that McFee was going to leave the Rad Lib party; or, George's secretary might have shot him for fear that McFee (whom she was having a relationship with) was going to leave her. Beyond the striking image which confronts Bones at the door — and beyond the very strangeness of Rad Lib attitudes about murder — as audience members we are asked to take in this entire spectacle. Taking in the entire spectacle — and recognizing that the play in various ways is conscious of itself as spectacle — it is not hard to see why one might label the work postmodern for how it wears its constructivity on its sleeve. In *Jumpers*, the very act of engaging in philosophy is part and parcel of a constructed (and constructive) environment.

However, even while *Jumpers* may well traverse some of the same postmodern landscape as *R & G* and *Hound*, it is important to note that it embraces various traditional metanarratives in other ways, most notably in its critique of moral relativism. Indeed, Stoppard has been quite adamant about the fact that the play is sympathetic to the idea of God, and to the way in which God plays a necessary social function as an external point of reference for moral values. In an interview with Oleg Kerensky, he explained his thinking as follows:

> I've always felt that whether or not "God-given" means anything, there has to be an ultimate external reference for our actions. Our view of good behavior must not be relativist. The difference between moral rules and the rules of tennis is that the rules of tennis can be changed [86].

By contrast, logical positivism, the "orthodox mainstream" (49) position that serves as the philosophical terrain for much of *Jumpers'* investigation into contemporary philosophy, denies that any such point of reference is possible for moral claims and, moreover, that moral value judgments are no more than the expression of one's emotional opinion about something (according to this way of thinking, to say that murder is wrong is akin to saying "Boo to Murder!").[6] As we have seen, George's explanation of this philosophical attitude culminates in Bones' incredulous question about McFee: "He thinks there's nothing wrong with killing people?" (48).

Certainly, the play's attitude towards logical positivism is relevant to my own larger argument, especially given postmodernity's loose association with various forms of relativism. And to all accounts I would appear to be on especially solid ground here, given what Stoppard himself has said about moral relativism in interview: "I think it's a dangerous idea that what constitutes 'good behaviour' depends on social conventions" (Kerensky 86–87). For what are these "social conventions" that Stoppard is so quick to dismiss but just the sort of "local narratives" that Lyotard considers as having become so commonplace in the postmodern era. It would appear, then, that to reject logical positivism is to distance oneself from the sort of thinking which pervades postmodernism.

CRITICAL RESPONSES

That said, it would be well to keep in mind Fleming's observation that "the play's dazzling form has led to a wide variety of interpretations, some antithetical to Stoppard's professed values" (84). For even while it is clear among most critics that the work is meant to satirize various branches of philosophy, disagreement arises concerning who Stoppard's central target is. Tim Brassell focuses on Stoppard's desire to "illuminate the logical positivist in action, with all its attendant consequences" (118). Brassell con-

2. *Normalizing* Magritte *and Tumbling Philosophers*

cludes that the work is a condemnation of Logical Positivism's unique brand of moral relativism, as "Stoppard powerfully demonstrates the perversity of holding evaluation to be a matter of merely emotional significance, and suggests some of the deplorable values that might be shielded behind the philosophy's facade of rose-tinted logic" (132). Brassell finally concludes that George is "the play's hero" for the way that he confronts logical positivism (132). By contrast, Anthony Jenkins suggests that the brunt of Stoppard's satire serves, rather, to condemn George Moore's inability to act: "Stoppard pinpoints the weakness in George's moral position, for though he is disturbed by the Rad-Lib victory his concern is never strong enough to pull him away from his intellectual pursuits" (84). Thus, George is satirized for his inaction as he stands quietly by as first Dotty, and then his country, descend into chaos.

Perhaps as a way of avoiding this morass, Fleming reminds us that Stoppard isn't necessarily concerned about definitively capturing his ideas in words: "As long as one understands what a man means by a statement, what he really means, then his failure to put it into a precise capsule which has absolutely no ambiguity about it, in a sense, doesn't matter" (40). Barbara Kreps offers a typical if telling assessment:

> Clearly there is a strong prejudice, which we are meant to side with, toward what George has to say about God and Good and the way he knows them; but we are left, when all is done, with the uneasy recognition that the play talks in a direction that its action contradicts. In part, this contradiction is due to Stoppard's depiction of George as a decidedly flawed hero; but our perplexity is finally due, I think, to our perceptions not only of the several and contradictory ways knowledge relates to ethical behavior, but also to the revelation that all ways of "knowing" explored in the play can lead to error as well as to truth, while, in the realm of ethics, good intention counts for everything, but it can also count for nothing [188].

Kreps resolutely attempts to power through this bind by focusing on the way in which the play complicates epistemological certainty on numerous levels, thus making any uncertainty regarding Moore as hero just one example among many of such uncertainty in the text as a whole. The problem is that by the end of the essay, her assessment of George doesn't arrive at any deeper an understanding of this particular issue than she began with: "Thus in *Jumpers*, though his sympathies obviously lie with George and what he has to say about knowledge and morality, Stoppard went out of his way ... to demonstrate the weak spots both in George's character and in what George tells us" (206).[7] While I have certain sympathies with such a reading, at the end of the day I do think that Stoppard employs various "normalizing" techniques beyond satire and farce which indicate a preference for the more traditional epistemological and ontological attitudes espoused by George.

Perhaps Thomas Whitaker offers the most convincing interpretation of Stoppard's ethical vision when he recognizes, rather, that Stoppard is engaged in making a series of philosophical points:

> *Jumpers* repeatedly asks us, in fact, to experience the interplay of three modes of interpreting life: an agnostic empiricism that serves the will to power; an anxious religious demand or faith that can be practically and ethically blind; and a spontaneous and compassionate ethical response that helps to guide us through the play's actions. Each mode has its own kind of jumping — amoral, anxious, or theatrical — which contributes to the kaleidoscopic whirl of performance [102].

Thus, while Brassell argues that the play is primarily meant to reject the first of these modes, and Jenkins argues that it is meant to reject the second, Whitaker finds that the play's moral objective rejects both of them in favor of a third: "*Jumpers* has asked us to find in ourselves ... an enacted response to questions that must here remain without explicit answer" (106).

Notably, this perspective corresponds with what Stoppard later claimed to be the theoretical impulse of his television play, *Professional Foul*: that intuition itself, especially that of a child, was, perhaps, more relevant than the work of philosophers, who sometimes think too hard about things:

> If somebody came out of East Germany through the gate in the wall and wished to communicate the idea that life inside this wall was admirable or indeed platonically good, he'd have a reasonable chance of succeeding in this if he were addressing himself to a sophisticated person. But if you tried to do this to a child he'd blow it to smithereens. A child would say, "But the wall is there to keep people in, so there must be some reason why people want to get out" [Gollob and Roper 164].

This condemnation of fervent intellectualizing and defense of intuition persists throughout Stoppard's work; and because Stoppard had read extensively in analytic philosophy before writing *Jumpers*, analytic philosophy takes the brunt of his satire against excessive intellectualizing.[8]

2. *Normalizing* Magritte *and Tumbling Philosophers*

Stoppard's interviews are especially useful when attempting to understand his philosophical vision. In an interview with Mel Gussow he makes no secret of his thoughts about the absurdity of much of philosophy:

> Philosophy can be reduced to a small number of questions which are battled about in most bars most nights. Linguistic philosophy doesn't even have that distinction. That should occupy the position in life of collecting the labels of triangular pieces of cheese. There's a word for people who do that. And they trade cheese labels across continents. It doesn't do anybody any harm, but why would you want to have a professor in it? When I started reading books on moral philosophy, I was just amazed at how many people were writing the same book [74].

Even while Stoppard does occasionally express respect for particular philosophers (Wittgenstein, for instance), his tone is derisive of philosophy generally. And, upon closer inspection, similar complaints about the discipline can be found in *Jumpers* itself. That academic philosophers don't delve any deeper into moral questions than do laymen is apparent in how quickly Bones catches up to speed on the implications of the logical positivist's moral relativism once George explains the position to him:

> BONES: He thinks that there's nothing wrong with killing people?
> GEORGE: Well, put like that, of course.... But philosophically, he doesn't think it's actually inherently wrong in itself, no [*Jumpers* 48].

As it turns out, many of Stoppard's complaints against philosophy can be recognized in this passage. That Bones finds philosophy to be so counter-intuitive reinforces Stoppard's position that philosophers can convince themselves of any absurd belief if they pursue it diligently enough.[9] Indeed, George's proclamation that Archie's moral relativism is "Orthodox Mainstream" shows how narrowly focused and isolated philosophy is, as its practitioners simply cycle through the same old orthodox trivialities.

Conversely, George's own philosophical attitudes are also satirized, especially in that first conversation he holds with Bones, when George answers the door while "holding a bow and arrow in one hand and a tortoise in the other, his face covered in shaving foam" (43). And while we are immediately reminded of Inspector Foot from *After Magritte*, in this case we already know the strange circumstances that have compelled George to be so attired. George is, after all, a philosopher (in Stoppard, that is enough). The rabbit and tortoise are props for George's paper, which he means to use to refute Zeno's paradox. And while it is tempting to argue that here again Stoppard shows his epistemological conservatism — as he seeks to refute paradox through empirical research — this would presuppose that George is the hero of the play, a problematic assumption given the way in which George is satirized in the episode. In any case, Stoppard's point is that only a philosopher would have the time and energy to so attire himself, and the additional gall to call it work. The rest of us need not even go so far as throwing a pen against a wall to give the discussion a pass. We have thrown enough objects in our lifetimes that — like the child referenced in *Professional Fowl*— we know without even throwing the pen that the paradox is an exercise in overthinking.

Thus, it becomes apparent that *Jumpers* is primarily meant as satire of the entire philosophy industry, since even the pragmatically minded George is presented as too self-involved in theoretical concepts to see the simple truths that Bones does: not only that murder is, quite simply, wrong, but also that something needs to be done to keep it in check. Most damaging of all to philosophy is Stoppard's explanation that this satirization of analytic philosophy hardly required any effort on his part: "There are things in my play which people innocently suppose to be my kind of bizarre version of academic discourse, that I'm doing a Mel Brooks on it, when, in fact, occasionally, I hardly had to change a thing" (Gussow 75). When common sense trumps moral relativism, universal truths are privileged over local ones.

Philosophical Rebuttals

Perhaps it is this derisive rejection of philosophy generally that best explains the response to *Jumpers* by those who actually engage in philosophy for a living. After a fairly succinct account of *Jumpers*' various "thin and uninteresting" (5) allusions to analytic philosophy, Jonathan Bennett concludes that "*Jumpers*, in short, lacks structure, and lacks seriousness" and that "flattering as it may be to find our discipline represented on a West End stage, there is nothing here that deserves the attention of philosophers" (8). Strangely, Bennett avoids discussing Stoppard's attitude toward philosophy generally, leaving it an open question whether or not his rejection of philosophical inquiry more generally might itself be of significant philosophical import. Apparently, the mere possibility is ridiculous. As such, I suspect that it is only to avoid looking the vindictive spoilsport — rather than with the true "relief" that Bennett claims — that he finishes up

2. *Normalizing* Magritte *and Tumbling Philosophers*

by discussing how *R & G*, at least, contains "a display of conceptual interrelationships of the same logical kind as might occur in an academic work of analytic philosophy" (8).

A second philosopher within the analytic tradition, Henning Jensen, responds to Bennett's essay by recognizing that the true import of the work might, rather, lie in its satire of philosophers (Jensen notes that Wittgenstein similarly criticized philosophy), but dismisses it all the same, explaining that if this is Stoppard's intent, "such criticisms lose all point because of the gross inaccuracies in his reports of their views" (217). I suspect that as often as not Stoppard is inaccurate, just as are all those people who historicize events that lie outside their field of specialization (indeed, one wonders if these two philosophers have forgotten that the work is explicitly fictitious?). As such, I don't mean to quibble with the charge that Stoppard is unfair to analytic philosophy. In fact, I don't even mean to take on the role of Stoppard's defender. Instead, I mean to continue by examining how the way in which he satirizes philosophy fits together with other theoretical and aesthetic trends in his plays.

More to the point given my objectives, Roy W. Perret responded to this criticism in the preeminent analytic philosophy journal, *Philosophy*, by arguing that "Jumpers is indeed a philosophically significant play," most especially in how it uses farce and other theatrical techniques to explore its "appearance-reality" theme, which Perret understands is "fundamental to most of Stoppard's work" (373):

> Much of this comedy has dramatic point as a challenge to the audience's familiar assumptions about what is real and what is not. Hence in *Jumpers* Stoppard once again exploits the motif of a detective investigation and in his parody of this familiar literary form he also calls into question assumptions about the familiar form of what is supposed to be an investigation into reality [373].

I do think that this is a reasonable attempt to get the discussion back on track vis-à-vis Stoppard's philosophical concerns more generally. However, while I am sympathetic to Perrett's argument that giving the farcical elements in the play their due is central to unpacking the play's concern with "appearance-reality," I would add that there are more overtly metatheatrical components of the play (see below) which must be considered when teasing out what the play is trying to say about appearance and reality. And for all of Perrett's support for the play's philosophical seriousness, he does not finally find a theory of representation in the play. He argues instead for the importance of its literary style as a legitimate means for pursuing philosophical investigations:

> Coming to terms with the literary styles of the *Philosophical Investigations* and *Ulysses* involves a corresponding extension and rearrangement of our concepts of philosophy and literature. Similarly, Stoppard's use of farce to reinforce the central philosophical themes in *Jumpers* demands some extension and rearrangement of out concepts of philosophy and of farce to enable us to see how they can be dramatically presented as supportive of each other [381].

As useful a reminder as this is of the importance of making a connection between theme and content — especially in a work such as Stoppard's which experiments so freely with form — it is disappointing that, aside from what constitutes a throwaway comment on George's claim that "I know that something happened to poor Dotty and she somehow killed McFee, as sure as she killed my poor Thumper"— Perrett does not provide any specific examples of what he calls "philosophy as farce and farce as philosophy" (381) from the text, instead relying on various statements Stoppard has made in interviews.

Performing Philosophy

While Stoppard does go out of his way to criticize the very discipline of philosophy (a metaphilosophical practice that is far more common to continental philosophy than it is to analytic philosophy), this criticism is, however, very distinct from the way that postmodern theorists question the various disciplines. Remember that according to Foucault, knowledge is always and already explicitly tied to the reinforcement of existing power relations and to the oppression of the disempowered. By contrast, Stoppard doesn't preclude the possibility that knowledge might yet contribute to the accumulation of knowledge or the betterment of humanity (nor, even, that it doesn't continue to do so in fields outside of philosophy); rather, he is merely skeptical about some of the paths that the discipline of analytic philosophy has recently taken.

This fact is most apparent in Stoppard's use of satire and parody as a rhetorical device. In his essay "Postmodernism and Consumer Society," Fredric Jameson stresses that the use of parody marks a work as modern rather than postmodern since it retains a vestigial commitment to the idea that there remains a preferred mode of discourse:

2. *Normalizing* Magritte *and Tumbling Philosophers*

> In any case, a good or great parodist has to have some secret sympathy for the original, just as a great mimic has to have the capacity to put himself/herself in the place of the person imitated. Still, the general effect of parody is — whether in sympathy or with malice — to cast ridicule on the private nature of these stylistic mannerisms and their excessiveness and eccentricity with respect to the way people normally speak or write. So there remains somewhere behind all parody the feeling that there is a linguistic norm in contrast to which the styles of the great modernists can be mocked [114].

From this perspective, Stoppard's own satirical edge can be seen to presuppose a mode of philosophical discourse different from that which is practiced by either George or the Rad Libs. A philosophical mode that possesses all the characteristics that the current modes don't: one that is active rather than passive; one that makes moral claims that emancipate rather than morally bankrupt claims that can be easily appropriated to tyrannical exploitation; one whose moral claims would be in agreement with the common person's intuitions. Ironically, the one character who embodies all of these traits is Inspector Bones, a throwback to the mystery novel and to Scotland Yard, an era when investigative procedure still meant something — an era when nobody believed that investigative procedures resulted in a picture of reality which would ultimately prove as much "fragmentation, ambiguity, discontinuity, [and] decenterment" as a painting by Magritte ("From Postmodernism to Postmodernity," 4).

As convenient as this would be to my larger thesis, Bones, however, doesn't get the final word, as would be the case in a typical detective story. In fact, he is sent away in disgrace. The final word, rather, goes to Archie at the end of Act Two (or to Dottie, who breaks into song at the end of the dream sequence[10] Coda, just on the heels of a final monologue by Archie). And as it turns out, Archie's final words are more self-consciously reflective of the play as an artificial construct than is anything else in the entire play:

> ARCHIE: The truth to us philosophers, Mr. Crouch, is always an interim judgment. We will never even know for certain who did shoot McFee. Unlike mystery novels, life does not guarantee a denouement [*Jumpers* 81].

This epistemological uncertainty that Archie describes owes its skepticism to David Hume: scientific investigation, absolute proof from empirical evidence is simply not in the cards. And it is perhaps the single philosophical issue that Stoppard carries with him from this play to his later plays *Arcadia* and *Indian Ink* (about which more in their relevant chapters).

Most important at this juncture is the way in which the quotation speaks to *Jumpers'* inconclusive ending. For, of course, the lives of Archie and Crouch nicely fit the elements of a classic murder mystery. But Archie is also correct in pointing out that there is no denouement. Instead, all we get is the dreamscape Coda, where Archie's final monologue—with its reference to Beckett's *Waiting for Godot*—only ups the moral pessimism of the Rad Libs:

> Do not despair—many are happy much of the time. More eat than starve, more are healthy than sick, more curable than dying, not so many dying as dead—and one of the thieves was saved! [*Jumpers* 87].

Unsurprisingly, this very monologue has inspired numerous mutually exclusive readings of the play.[11] There is, however, a more important clue to the play's meaning in the Coda. For nothing speaks more clearly to the way in which all of George's monologues in preparation for his debate with McFee are something akin to the rehearsals for a performance than does the final dream sequence, wherein, after spouting several sentences of Joycean puns which amount to so much gibberish, the ushers in attendance hold up scorecards rating Archie's performance: "'9.7'—'9.9'—'9.8.'" It is a scene which speaks as clearly as any other to George's private anxieties about the performative nature of philosophical debate (just as, I might add, the rest of the Coda speaks to his various anxieties about the implications of moral relativism).

With this ending in mind the importance of earlier moments in the play comes into focus, such as when Bones picked up George's "script" (this is Stoppard's own word, from the stage directions) and George felt compelled to explain the significance of the forthcoming event to Bones:

> GEORGE: [I]t's a paper I am presenting to the symposium at the university.... It would be a great opportunity if only I could seize it.... I mean, it's really the event of the year (*Pause.*) In the world of moral philosophy, that is [46].

Indeed, when we first meet George in his study (having met him only briefly earlier, confronting Dotty about how her party is getting carried away and interrupting his work) there is much about George's movements which speaks to the fact that he is rehearsing for a performance rather than preparing for a lecture:

> *In dictating, GEORGE prefers to **address the large mirror in the fourth wall**. He does not take much notice of the SECRETARY. George now collects the pages*

2. Normalizing Magritte and Tumbling Philosophers

into a tidy sheaf, **takes a pace back from the mirror, assumes a suitable stance, and takes it from the top**... [*Jumpers* 23–24; italics in original, bolding is my own].

Most notable in these stage directions is the fact that while on the one hand he is dictating to his secretary, on the other he feels the need to find the right spot on stage and to assume a suitable stance, all while looking at himself in the mirror. Of course, the fact that there is no mirror—just an audience looking back at him through the mirror's empty frame—only draws attention to the way in which *the actor playing George* is in effect miming the act of looking in the mirror even as *George the character* is "rehearsing for his performance." Later, after reaching something of a crescendo in his speech—"the Necessary Being, the First Cause, the Unmoved Mover"—George "*takes a climactic drink from his tumbler which, however, contains only pencils*" (29). When he puts the tumbler down one of the pencils remains in his mouth. Presumably, he means to cover up one misfired affectation (i.e., that of taking a drink to emphasize a point) with another (i.e., I'm so comfortable with my position that I can add a little informality to my presentation by giving it while chewing on a pencil); this of course misfires as well, as he "Indistinctly" mumbles his next line, "St. Thomas Aquinas." Clearly, George needs all the rehearsal time he can get, a fact which is immediately apparent in the Coda. George's performative gestures are quickly upstaged when, after admitting to Archie that he had "spent weeks preparing my commentary," Archie, who because of the death of McFee will be responding to George's speech, resorts to the sort of "trash talking" more common to sporting events than to philosophical debates, bragging "We shall begin with a two-minute silence. That will give me a chance to prepare mine" [*Jumpers* 69].

It is also notable that George feels compelled to use props (a tortoise, a hare and a bow and arrow) in order to confront Zeno's distance paradoxes. George explains himself in this regard as follows:

> My method of enquiry this evening into aspects of this hardy perennial may strike some of you as overly engaging but experience has taught me that to attempt to sustain the attention of rival schools of academics by argument alone is tantamount to constructing a Gothic arch out of junket [*Jumpers* 27].

Notably, this points to another feature which Stoppard as playwright shares with George as performing philosopher—a tendency to use elements of

55

stagecraft, rather than argument, to confront whole schools of academics. In this instance, the bow and arrow are meant to provide experiential proof against Zeno's conclusion that an arrow should never reach its target. Indeed, George's preference for performative argumentative methods comes through most explicitly when, hearing Dotty yell "Fire" from the other room, he shoots the arrow before he means to (he will later determine that he has killed Thumper with this shot),[12] after which he "shouts furiously" at Dottie, "Thanks to you I have lost the element of surprise" (28). Accordingly, all of the different props employed in *Jumpers* are similarly meant to reject the moral relativism of the Rad Libs (if not also the philosophy industry more generally).

That Stoppard valued George's speeches perhaps as much for their strictly performative qualities as for the philosophical points he makes is apparent in a quote that John Fleming has culled from Stoppard's "Translator's Notes" for the play:

> George's long speeches would of course be much too long, regardless of their content, if it were not that in the way in which he talks is itself, to an English audience, a recognizable parody of a philosophical discourse; that the sentence structure has a built-in interest value, basically a humorous value [274].

This note to the translators suggests that this is a feature which Stoppard has consciously built into the work. Moreover, even George's difficulties with Dottie can be seen as part and parcel of the performative element of George's character, a fact which may explain why he is so quick to assume that Dottie's struggles with madness are little more than playacting, the absurdity of the situation reaching its pinnacle when, in response to some "Procession Music," he complains, "You are deliberately feigning an interest in brass band music to distract me from my lecture!"(26). George feels comfortable in his accusations given that only moments earlier Dottie had stood in as the boy who cried wolf by calling, "Murder — Rape — Wolves!" (26). Perhaps it is because so much of what George does is itself an act that when Dottie does engage in various manic actions at various points in the play George is all too quick to assume that she must be acting as well. Whether in charades (30) love (31), or false alarms (66), George never stops to ask himself what it really would have looked like if it had looked as if Dottie's anxieties were sincere. Despite George's greater commitment to belief in a known and knowable reality than is true of his peers, he yet appears to be especially ill-equipped at finding that reality, what with all

2. Normalizing Magritte *and Tumbling Philosophers*

of his grand rhetorical flourishes and overthinking of common sense and performing getting in the way.

In turn, a deeper understanding of what Stoppard is attempting to accomplish here necessitates treating George as a theatrical character; and one who, in many respects (most notably, in the lecture he means to offer), is as overtly artificial as Rosencrantz and Guildenstern — the implication being that making a performance of such beliefs (as George ends up doing) hardly helps George's case. Neil Sammels says of the performative features of the play that Stoppard is "deploying — performing with — an intellectual premise (a critique of Logical Positivisim and associated collectivist attitudes) rather than trying to promulgate a thesis" (116). But it is more than just this, for the artificiality of such events would seem to indicate the contingency or "relativity" of George's belief system rather than its universality. And while — just as we will see with Bernard (*Arcadia*) and Pike (*Indian Ink*), this does not so much mean George's ontology is wrong so much as is his approach — it yet serves to problematize George's comparatively grander narrative positions. As such *Jumpers* is, finally, a play which lets George's philosophical perspectives trump the sorts of local truths favored by the Rad Libs, even while its metatheatrical overtures mean that the play does not give itself over entirely to universal truths. George himself is too artificial a character for us to finally take too much comfort in the notion that his beliefs truly trump those of his peers. In any case, we are left with a play which, looked at one way (in its metatheatricalism) embraces the postmodern, and looked at another way (in its rejection of logical positivism) evades it.

3

Modernist Diversions

Travesties

As with his more famous play, *Rosencrantz and Guildenstern Are Dead*, in *Travesties* (1974) Stoppard once again employs a canonical text to serve as the template for his own work, only in this case his play isn't set so much in the space between literature and reality as it is rather, in a strange new intertextual/historical past, where Oscar Wilde's *The Importance of Being Earnest* (*Earnest*) intersects with the physical worlds of James Joyce, Tristan Tzara and Vladimir Lenin in Zurich during World War I, constructing a collage which eventually comments on everything from literary allusion and aesthetics to artistic and political revolution. Stoppard makes efficient use of Wilde's play, employing it both in *Travesties'* content — as we soon find out that Joyce himself is putting on a play of *Earnest* (just as the historical Joyce did in 1919 in Zurich, with Lieutenant Carr in the role of Algernon) — as well as in *Travesties'* form — as the action and dialogue of the various historical figures comes to resemble the action and dialogue of *The Importance of Being Earnest*, most notably in how Carr's actions in *Travesties* mimic those of Algernon. Additionally, Tristan Tzara fulfills the role of Jack and Joyce that of Lady Bracknell. Adding to the confusing collage of conflicting egos and ideas, Lenin, Tzara, and Joyce frequent the same library where, finally, a folder of Joyce's is switched with one of Lenin's, leading to an ending that closely mirrors *Earnest* (where switched handbags serve as a significant plot device).

Travesties is so self-consciously experimental that it isn't surprising that critics would refer to the play as postmodern. Richard Corballis, for instance, contends that it exhibits postmodernist tendencies in three ways, including: "a love of cryptic conundra, an emphasis on play, and an impulse toward allegory" (163). Of course Stoppard is always "playful," but how exactly this "playfulness" is "postmodern" Corballis never fully

3. Modernist Diversions

explains (although I'll have more to say about the playfulness of *Travesties* below), nor does he defend cryptic conundra as postmodern, an omission made more disconcerting given that one of Stoppard's intertextual touchstones for *Travesties* is the very modernist *Ulysses*, which employs so much cryptic conundra that its use by Stoppard makes the use of cryptic conundra in *Travesties* a virtual necessity. On its use of allegory, Corballis explains:

> [W]hat Stoppard (through Old Carr) gives us in Act One is in effect a series of snapshots of Joyce, some realistic, some quite bizarre.... These snapshots are assembled principally from the pages of *Ulysses* and Richard Ellmann's biography of Joyce. Unlike these two works, however, Stoppard's photomontage in no way evokes a "real" Joyce. His method may be described as allegorical insofar as he is "rewriting a primary text [James Joyce] in terms of its figural meaning" [158].

The argument that *Travesties* is postmodern because it is "allegorical" rather than "realistic" isn't very compelling, especially given how modernism itself was so given over to finding various non-realist (oftentimes even allegorical) methods of tapping into "the real" (an oversight on Corballis' part made especially odd by the fact that the Ithaca section of *Ulysses*—the very section Stoppard so freely alludes to in *Travesties*—is itself considered to be a milestone in modernist allegory.[1]

That said, I do think that with two of the three features Corballis considers he is looking in the right place when it comes to understanding how Stoppard's play sits right on what is generally agreed to be an ill-defined border between the modern and the postmodern: i.e., in its use of a rigorously postmodern playfulness (which to my mind often falls over into a rigorously modern seriousness) and in its intertextual pastiche (which comes with more than a small dose of what Jameson would characterize as modernist parody). I will argue, rather, that a more important feature than its allegorical properties is its overt use of Henry Carr—the play's narrator—as a framing device. This discussion is complicated, however, by the fact that while according to Brian McHale's theorization of postmodern fiction such a framing device ultimately situates the play as limit-modernist (See explanation of limit-modernist below), Linda Hutcheon argues that such framing devices are fully postmodern.

Joyce, Lenin, Tzara, Wilde and Aesthetic Preference

Fundamental to understanding how Stoppard is intrigued by postmodern ideals — even while ultimately rejecting them — is the work's overt consideration of aesthetics. The playful rigor with which Stoppard parodies Joyce, Lenin, and Tzara's aesthetic ideals in turn is perhaps best evidenced in the opening scene, where we meet the three in the library. When we first meet Tzara he is randomly pulling words from a hat, creating a poem as he goes: "Eel ate enormous appletzara key dairy chef's hat he'll learn oomparah! Ill raced alas whispers kill later nut east, noon avuncular ill day Clara!" (2).

Always as rigorous in his intellectual conceits as he is clever, Stoppard's resulting pastiche, while nominally in English, is meant to sound to the ear as if it is written in French. According to Jim Hunter the lines constitute "a limerick in French: "Il est un homme, s'appelle Tzara/ Qui des richesses a-t-il le nonpareil/ Il reste a la Suisse/ Parce qu'il est un artiste/ 'Nous n'avons que l'art,'/ il declara." Hunter translates this as follows: "[the] man called Tzara/ of unparalleled talents/ stays in Switzerland/ as an artist, declaring that all that matters is Art" (*Tom Stoppard* 135).

Immediately following Tzara's performance we hear Joyce dictating to his secretary as follows:

> Send us, bright one, light one, Horhorn, quickening and wombfruit. Send us, bright one, light one, Horhorn, quickening and wombfruit. Send us, bright one, light one, Horhorn, quickening and wombfruit [2].

The implication here is that Joyce's aesthetic is somehow similar to Tzara's — perhaps even inferior given that Tzara's words do make sense, albeit in a foreign language — a fact emphasized further as "Joyce begins walking up and down, searching his pockets for tiny scraps of paper on which he has previously written down things."[2] He reads them: "Morose delectation.... Aquinas tunbelly.... Frate porcospino" (3). As he reads, he discards some of the bits of paper and retains others. As it happens, the ones he retains can be found in *Ulysses*, while the ones he discards cannot (one way of reading this is that he, too, has been pulling words at random from a "hat").

Finally, Lenin's methodology is evidenced in a dropped bit of scrap paper, which Joyce then picks up: "G.E.C. (USA) 250 Million Marks." Lenin appears the most committed of the three to rhetorical precision in his approach, ultimately confronting Joyce and asking that his note be returned to him, while Joyce, in what is perhaps the most telling scene of the entire play, very nearly allows himself to be sucked into a similar mode of randomness as Tzara when he covets that bit of paper belonging to Lenin.

I am tempted to argue that the rigor apparent in *Travesties*—and the way in which its rigor ultimately links the work to Joyce (Stoppard simply could not have written what he did by pulling words from a hat; and, mind you, neither could Joyce have written *Ulysses* this way)—is itself sufficient to regard the work as modernist. But the issue is much more complicated than this. Numerous postmodern writers, from Thomas Pynchon to David Foster Wallace, are famous for having produced extremely rigorous works full of numerous intertextual surprises, suggesting that perhaps it is the *playfulness* of his rigor which differentiates Stoppard from Joyce. Terry Eagleton describes the playful in the postmodern as follows:

> There is perhaps a degree of consensus that the typical postmodernist artifact is playful, self-ironizing, and even schizoid; and that it reacts to the austere autonomy of high modernism by impudently embracing the language of commerce and the commodity. Its stance toward cultural tradition is one of irreverent pastiche, and its contrived depthlessness undermines all metaphysical solemnities, sometimes by a brutal aesthetics of squalor and shock [194].

And while there is perhaps something more playful—a contrived depthlessness, even—in *Travesties* than what is found in *Ulysses*, this line of thinking forgets that Joyce himself was extremely playful in his work (what with his puns and his red herrings meant to keep the critics busy for the next 100 years)—So, like Corballis, I have yet to fully differentiate the playful rigor of postmodernism from the more serious rigor of the modernist era.

Adding to the play's Joycean rigor, its use of *Earnest* as a template means that, as with *R & G*, Stoppard has once again given himself a very strict form within which to work, such that even as Carr and Tzara debate aesthetic theory, the very form of the play necessitates that the debate mirror the original dialogue of the opening scene of *Earnest*. It does with rather surprising results, as, for instance, when we find Tzara responding to Carr on the origins of World War I as follows:

TZARA: Oh, what nonsense you talk!
CARR: It may be nonsense, but at least it is clever nonsense.
TZARA: I am sick of cleverness. The clever people try to impose a design on the world and when it goes calamitously wrong they call it fate. In point of fact, everything is Chance, including design [20].

This replicates the following exchange from *Earnest* between Jack and Algernon about a bit of Algernon's own nonsense:

> JACK: Is that clever?
> ALGERNON: It is perfectly phrased! And quite as true as any observation in civilised life should be.
> JACK: I am sick to death of cleverness. Everybody is clever nowadays. You can't go anywhere without meeting clever people [136].

The literary contortions that Stoppard puts himself through are as playful in effect as they are rigorous in execution. It would be hard to ask for a swifter refutation of Tzara's claim that "everything is Chance, including design" than that which is provided by the very technique Stoppard employs so successfully here. When we give precedence to the rigor, it is hard not to think of Joyce. But when we note the playfulness it is hard not to think of another aesthete who looms large in the play, Oscar Wilde.

One way of sorting out the play's own aesthetic would involve determining which of the various characters comes in for the better treatment. In an interview he gave to Ross Wetzsteon, Stoppard explains where his own sympathies lie:

> Of course I don't want to give any of them shallow arguments and then knock them down. No, you have to give the best possible argument for each of them. It's like playing chess with yourself—you have to try to win just as hard at black as you do with white…. But while my sympathies may be divided in that sense, I find Joyce infinitely the most important [121].

If we are to believe Stoppard, his aesthetic preferences would appear to be modern. Apparently the rigorous playfulness of Joyce is meant even to trump the playfulness of Wilde. To be sure, one feels a lightness of effort in Wilde that one does not feel when reading Joyce or Stoppard (Wilde was famous for being able to speak quite brilliantly on any topic without preparation).

Finally, it is also worth noting that for four pages of the opening exchange, Stoppard adopts a strict verse form as the dialogue becomes a series of limericks, with the most telling coming from Joyce:

> An impromptu poet of Hibernia
> Rhymed himself into a hernia
> He became quite adept
> At the practice except
> For occasional anti-climaxes [*Travesties* 18].

3. Modernist Diversions

The self-reflexivity of this limerick in particular serves only to remind us that while Stoppard's sympathies might ultimately lie with the literary rigor of Joyce, he is not above referencing those very same contortions (and their consequent hernias) that one with such sympathies must put themselves through (and with how such rigor might anti-climactically fall short of its target). Despite Stoppard's apparent sympathy for Joyce, the parody cuts every which way as every bit of playfulness we discover also has an edge to it.

Parody and Intertextual Pastiche

Perhaps a better method for unpacking *Travesties'* postmodern playfulness is to consider what it means that Stoppard is parodying each of these figures in turn (including Joyce, what with his coveting of Lenin's random scrap of paper). To this end, of particular note is what Fredric Jameson has to say about the postmodern:

> [Postmodernity] is the moment at which pastiche appears and parody has become impossible. Pastiche is, like parody, the imitation of a peculiar or unique style, the wearing of a stylistic mask, speech in a dead language: but it is a neutral practice of such mimicry, without parody's ulterior motive, without the satirical impulse, without laughter, without the still latent feeling that there exists something normal compared to which what is being imitated is rather comic [*Postmodernism* 17].

The implication is that if Stoppard is indeed parodying each of these characters, then he is treating the issues at hand seriously rather than simply playfully. And as a consequence, what we are left with is the recognition that for all the work's playfulness, it also has a seriousness to it which, as Jameson explains it, necessarily puts it at odds with postmodern ideals (i.e., it presupposes a metanarrative position from which it critiques its subject). And just as we can assume that Joyce is to be preferred as an ideal to Tzara and Lenin, if Jameson is right we are also meant to conclude that there is some higher ideal which is perhaps even preferable to Joyce. Aesthetic truth would have crept into the play, pushing the relativistic attitudes about truth which come with the postmodern to the margins (although it may well prove that pastiche trumps parody in the play).

Or, to take yet another approach towards determining the play's relationship with postmodernity, it is worth recognizing that despite the fact that Stoppard is working with historical figures, each is as fully identified as a textual-theatrical construct as are the characters of *Rosencrantz and Guildenstern Are Dead*. In fact, there is much in the play that situates the work as postmodern according to McHale's explanation of how the postmodern historical novel subverts the concept that history is recoverable and tangible. McHale explains that while all historical novels involve "some violation of historical boundaries.... Traditional historical novels strive to suppress these violations, to hide the ontological seams between fictional projections and real world facts" (*Postmodernist Fiction* 17). This "suppression" typically involves an attempt by the author to make these works correspond to historical fact. As an example of how postmodernism subverts this tradition, McHale refers to Carlos Fuentes' *Terra Nostra*:

> *Terra Nostra*, by contrast, foregrounds its ontological seams by systematically transgressing these rules of its genre. Here familiar facts are tactlessly contradicted — Columbus discovers America a full century too late, Phillip II of Spain marries Elizabeth of England, and so on — and the projected world is governed by fantastic norms. Fuentes thus converts the historical novel into a medium for raising ontological issues, as do other postmodernist historical novelists, including Pynchon, Günter Grass, Robert Coover, Ishmael Reed, and Salman Rushdie [*Postmodernist Fiction* 17].

As a historical dramatist, Tom Stoppard might appear on this list as well. For while *Travesties* does give us four historical figures (Joyce, Lenin, Tzara, and Carr), and even correctly places these figures together in Zurich during World War I, in placing them into the various roles of *Earnest* he creates for them the most unlikely of scenarios.

Despite the focus on the aesthetics of Joyce, Tzara, and Lenin, the central character of the play actually turns out to be the aged Henry Carr, reminiscing on his deathbed about his years spent in Zurich during World War I. Apparently, Carr and Joyce eventually quarreled over the finances of their production of *Earnest* (while the resulting court case was something of a draw, Joyce got the last laugh, when he finally immortalized Carr as the abusive Private Carr in *Ulysses*). Stoppard, then, employs these few historical facts as a springboard for his own play, which unfolds on stage as Carr reminisces about and narrates the event. As such, Stoppard's use of historical characters has at least some affinity with how McHale describes Fuentes' use of them, as there is much in the play that is historically disingenuous. Jim Hunter points out a number of these "inaccuracies":

3. Modernist Diversions

Certain liberties with history were necessary (and indeed the play's title disclaims any attempt to portray the characters fairly). Carr became Consul, not assistant, and the name of the real Consul — Bennet — was transferred to his fictional subversive butler. More important, the *Earnest* production was brought forward at least a year, so that it could take place before Lenin left for Russia [*Tom Stoppard's Plays* 238].

One thing that is immediately obvious from Hunter's description, however, is that in comparison to Fuentes' *Terra Nostra,* the comparative triviality of these "liberties" to anyone who is not a Joycean deserves consideration. The inaccuracies are so minor, in fact, that it is questionable whether they are the sort that McHale considers as evidence of postmodernism. Consider, by final comparison, McHale's analysis of Robert Coover's *The Public Burning*, which revels in its historical inaccuracies: "He has Nixon try to seduce Ethel Rosenberg at Sing Sing prison on the eve of her execution ... and even more spectacularly when he has him sodomized by Uncle Sam himself in the novel's epilogue" (McHale, *Postmodernist Fiction* 89). A question arises: "How little leeway are we to grant the historical novelist before we invoke the label of 'postmodernity?'" From this perspective it is only fair to admit that while the work does engage in the sort of historical pastiche which is suggestive of the postmodern, it is at best only timidly so.

Perhaps of greater ontological consequence is Stoppard's use of Wilde, which functions to such affect that it is almost as if Stoppard, like Joyce before him, has staged a production of *Earnest*, but has done so by casting historical figures, rather than actors, in the leading roles. From this perspective it isn't so much the historical inaccuracies which work to foreground the work's ontological seams, as it is Stoppard's complete disdain for the rules of protocol that are typically followed when casting such a production. As Ira Nadel puts it, while historical inaccuracies mean nothing to Stoppard, "discrepancies, however, do matter" — (*Travesties* 482). Rather, Stoppard's creative casting would make it quite clear to most audience members that he has indeed disrupted the historical record, even if it is hardly common knowledge that Joyce actually put on his production of *Earnest* a year later than is evidenced in *Travesties*. In turn, the fixation on minutiae of your typical Joycean is mocked even while the play takes a unique tack in foreshadowing its ontological seams.

According to this perspective a perhaps more compelling understanding of *Travesties* comes in McHale's explanation of the relationship between intertextuality and postmodernity. According to McHale, the mixing of genres, of canonical texts, and even the importation of both literary characters and historical figures foregrounds ontological issues about intertextual space:

> [A]n intertextual space is constituted whenever we recognize the relations among two or more texts, or between specific texts and larger categories such as genre, school, period. There are a number of ways of foregrounding this intertextual space and integrating it in the text's structure, but none is more effective than the device of "borrowing" a character from another text [*Postmodernist Fiction* 57].

In *Travesties*, Stoppard goes well beyond the simple "borrowing" of characters — (which is certainly one way of looking at the appearance of Tzara, Joyce, and Lenin in the same text, even though they are figures from history rather than from literature. He also borrows the genres and aesthetic ideals of these same figures, so that at any point during the play we might, in quick succession, find a pastiche of character, genre, and form.

For his own part in the pastiche, we find the dadaist Tzara cutting up the poems of others in order to critique the very concept of literary genius. Tzara's prevailing aesthetic axiom is that all art is basically equivalent to that which can be created through the simple act of pulling words from a hat. Joyce's aesthetic vision, by contrast, proclaims the importance of literary allusion thus reaffirming the importance — even genius — of canonical figures: "I with my Dublin Odyssey will double that immortality, yes, by God *there's* a corpse that will dance for some time yet and *leave the world precisely as it finds it*" (42; the simultaneous parody of both Joyce and Joycean's goes without saying). Finally, Lenin proclaims that he has no patience for any non-propagandistic literature: "Today, literature must become party literature ... [and] must become part of the common cause of the proletariat..." (58). Moreover, Stoppard creates not only a pastiche of distinct aesthetic visions but also of different literary tropes. Lenin's rhetorical mode is most apparent in a long speech by Cecily at the beginning of Act Two (45), while Tzara's rhetorical premises reveal themselves most clearly, as we have seen, when he creates "poetry" by simply drawing words from a hat: "Clara avuncular!/ Whispers ill oomparah!/ Eel nut dairy day/ Appletzara.../ ... Hat!" (2). And then, in a most surprising passage late in Act One where Joyce is grilling Tzara about the nature of dada (38–

44), the literary modes of both Joyce and Wilde come at us simultaneously. Tzara embraces Gwen just as Joyce enters and confronts him: "Rise, sir, from that semi-recumbent posture" (37). This exactly mirrors a scene in *Earnest* where Lady Bracknell interrupts Jack and Gwendolyn. The pastiche continues in the interview that follows, which not only mirrors Lady Bracknell's interview of Jack, but also captures a passage from the "Ithaca" section of Joyce's *Ulysses* nearly word for word.[3] Thus, intertextual space is foregrounded as the trope of privilege even as the world of literary history is found to be ripe for ontological investigation. In "the zone," we are no longer certain where one text ends and another begins, with one implication being that this is the very nature of literary scholarship as well. It would seem, then, that the pastiche in the play trumps the parody.

The Unreliable Frame

The ontological disparities of the play notwithstanding, a further review of McHale's description of postmodernist fiction would appear to suggest that the ontological oddities of *Travesties* are finally normalized in such a way that the plays is at best limit-modernist (McHale's word for a work existing on the border between the modern and the postmodern). A "limit-modernist" work, as McHale explains it, occurs as a consequence of the fact that the distinction between the modern and the postmodern "is not linear and unidirectional, but bidirectional and reversible" (*Postmodernist Fiction* 11). McHale goes on to explain that all it takes for a text to remain essentially modernist even though it raises ontological questions is that the ontological dominant be recuperable as stemming from a more deeply relevant epistemological concern. As a result, what may well look like further forays into the postmodern on Stoppard's part in *Travesties*—because of the ontological questions raised when the play conflates historical and textual figures — might better be understood as limit-(post)modernism should all of the ontological mystification be prefigured by the problematic inclusion of an unreliable narrator.

And as it turns out, *Travesties'* Carr is just such a prototypically unreliable narrator, relating the play's events some decades after they have occurred, by which time he has become an old man with a faulty memory.[4] This unreliability is evidenced in Carr's attempt to describe Lenin: "What was he like, Lenin, I am often asked? (*He makes an effort*) To those of us who knew him Lenin's greatness was never in doubt. (*He gives up again*)" (8). As Carr continues to outwardly struggle with his memory it soon becomes clear that *Travesties'* most fundamental concerns are epistemological, concerning how we are to gauge the reliability of history, evidence, narrators, and witnesses, rather than questions about the stability of textual and dramatic worlds. Indeed, given his present circumstances it is no wonder that Carr confuses historical figures with textual ones from a play he had a role in so long ago. To be sure, by conflating Joyce with the shrill Lady Bracknell, Carr can be all the more at ease with his own role in that distant affair even as he revels in his selective memories of how poorly Joyce had treated him. Clearly, then, this is a work which looked at one way is postmodern, and looked at another is "limit-modernist" (or even "naturalist" for how it invokes an all too human failing in its normalizing of the play's more bizarre elements).[5]

However, this reading of *Travesties* wouldn't quite feel complete if one final turn of the screw didn't complicate the picture further still. And sure enough, when reading the framing of the play through Linda Hutcheon's understanding of postmodern historical fiction, the framing itself begins to look suspiciously postmodern for how it can be seen as drawing special attention to the process of narrating history—a constructive enterprise, to be sure. As Hutcheon explains its role in postmodern narrative,

> the narrativization of past events is not hidden; the events no longer speak for themselves, but are shown to be consciously composed into a narrative, whose constructed—not found—order is imposed upon them, often overtly by the narrating figure. The process of making stories out of chronicles, of constructing plots out of sequences, is what postmodern fiction underlines. This does not in any way deny the existence of the past real, but it focuses attention on the act of imposing order on that past, of encoding strategies of meaning-making through representation [63].

Hutcheon refers to fiction which draws attention to the way in which "events ... are shown to be consciously composed into a narrative" as historiographic metafiction, and her central argument is that such fiction ultimately serves to draw attention to the way in which "the non-fictional is as constructed and as narratively known as is fiction" (73). This seems a somewhat fitting description of what Carr manages to make out of his own history, which he simultaneously seeks to exploit—given the famous

3. Modernist Diversions

names he rubbed elbows with in Zurich — and to forget — given the ill-will and differences of opinion that marked those interactions:

> My memoirs, is it, then? Life and times, friend of the famous. Memories of James Joyce. James Joyce as I knew him. The James Joyce I Knew. Through the courts with James Joyce.... What was he like, James Joyce, I am often asked? It is true that I knew him well at the height of this powers, his genius in full flood in the making of *Ulysses* [*Travesties* 6].

He continues with notable irony directed at the public figure that Joyce became once "publication and fame turned him into a public monument for pilgrim cameras" (*Travesties* 6).

In turn, it is hard to ignore the possibility that with *Travesties* Stoppard intends to comment on what has become known in academic circles as the Joyce Industry. As a quick introduction to that industry, notable titles just from among Joyce's known associates which market on his fame include the article "The Joyce I Knew," by Oliver St. John Gogarty, as well as a number of books: *The Joyce We Knew: Memoirs of Joyce*, edited by Ulick O'Connor; Frank Budgen's *Further Recollections of James Joyce;* and his brother's (Stanislaus Joyce) *My Brother's Keeper: James Joyce's Early Years*. As such, one way of viewing the Joyce of *Travesties* is as a figure who has been constructed and reconstructed so many times that we need not blame Carr's memory alone for the version that eventually comes down to us through *Travesties*. To be sure, it is easy enough to imagine that Stoppard's own head, after reviewing all of the relevant material, would have been such a jumble of facts and fictions that the research led quite naturally to the resulting pastiche.

Perhaps equally notable is Hutcheon's discussion of how postmodern historical fiction rejects the totalizing impulse of traditional historiographical methodologies:

> Whether it be in historical or fictional representation, the familiar narrative form of beginning, middle, and end implies a structuring process that imparts meaning as well as order. The notion of this "end" suggests both teleology and closure and, of course, both of these are concepts that have come under considerable scrutiny in recent years, in philosophical and literary circles alike [59].

As we have seen, there is much about both the structure of the work and about how it takes an ironic attitude towards historical accuracy which decries the possibility of closure. More than anything else, it is this collage of characters — and its overt meddling with chronological and ontological norms — which draws attention to the work's constructivity and "highlights the areas in which interpretation enters the domain of historiographic representation" (Hutcheon 70).

Hutcheon's own description of Carlos Fuentes serves to highlight how much Hutcheon's position differs from McHale's:

> *Terra Nostra* deliberately and provocatively violates what is conventionally accepted as true about the events of the past: Elizabeth I gets married; Columbus is a century or so out in his discovery of America. But the facts of the warped history are no more — or less — fictionally constructed than are the overtly fictive and intertextual ones. [...] The realist notion of characters only being able to coexist legitimately if they belong to the same text is clearly challenged here in both historical and fictional terms. The facts of these fictional representations are as true — and false — as the facts of history-writing can be, for they always exist as facts, not events [73–74].

For Hutcheon, the interest in Fuentes is not so much about how he "foregrounds its seams by systematically transgressing these rules of its genre" (McHale) or even about historical distortion in itself, but rather about how such a narrative draws attention to what fiction shares with historiography: "Each is as true — and false — as the other."

This, then, makes for a better reading of *Travesties*; as a play "whose warped history" is meant to draw attention to how "[t]he facts of these fictional representations are as true — and false — as the facts of history-writing can be" (and whose very frame props up such an interpretation) or, as a play whose historical inaccuracies become "a medium for raising ontological issues" (albeit one where the frame serves to de-doxify those ontological issues).

The potential value of Hutcheon's understanding of postmodernism becomes increasingly useful for how it resonates with the fact that Carr isn't simply an old confused man but an old confused man with a grudge: "Irish lout. Not one to bear a grudge, however, not after all these years, and him dead in the cemetery up the hill, no hard feelings either side" (5). Consider Hutcheon:

> What is foregrounded in postmodern theory and practice is the self-conscious inscription within history of the existing, but usually concealed attitude of historians towards their material. Provisionality and undecidability, partisanship and even overt politics — these are what replace the pose of objectivity and disinterestedness that denies the interpretive and implicitly evaluative nature of historical representation [71].

3. Modernist Diversions

The extent of Carr's resentment couldn't be clearer, as, after first suffering through an attempt to be charitable during which he calls Joyce "A prudish, prudent man ... in no way profligate or vulgar, and yet convivial, without being spendthrift" (more "damning and contradictory praise" than "damning if faint praise"), he eventually lets his true feelings get the best of him, concluding: "In short a liar and hypocrite, a tight-fisted, sponging, fornicating drunk not worth the paper, that's that bit done" [6–7].

With this in mind, perhaps Carr's attempts at narrating the past are best seen as part of a more general critical attitude towards historiography generally, for who is to say that a historian would never let his emotions get the best of him. However, it should also be remembered that the simple act of conflating Carr's narration with the narration of your typical historian — and doing so in a way which problematizes historicization generally — puts a bit of strain on the text, as Carr is quite simply not involved in creating narration which is meant to be treated as history (i.e., he is not a historian). Moreover, he is also a fairly reliable unreliable narrator for how he points out his own biases and mistakes:

> CARR: Incidentally, you may not have noticed that I got my wires crossed a bit here and there, you know how it is when the old think-box gets stuck in a groove and before you know where you are you've jumped the points and suddenly you think, No, steady on, old chap [*Travesties* 43].

And yet it is this very strain which is, once again, symptomatic of a text at the crossroads, part modern, part postmodern. Or — more appropriately — it is this strain which is symptomatic of how Stoppard "traverses and occasionally arraigns" the postmodern (which is itself one reason why there are so many symptoms of the postmodern which never quite seem to fulfill themselves). Consequently, while it is impossible to precisely pinpoint *Travesties* on the modern-postmodern continuum, it is becoming increasingly clear that a transition from postmodernism to modernism is taking place, and also that, despite the new and various difficulties which arise, a further transition towards a more modernist aesthetic continues with his next play, *The Real Thing*.

The Real Thing

It perhaps shouldn't come as too great a surprise that Stoppard would follow up his work about how Joyce has been constructed by his critics by writing a second play along the same lines, this time about the fictional Henry, who continually reflects upon his own constructivity even while the metatheatrical structure of the play encourages the audience to consider Henry's constructed nature as well. As in *Hound*, *The Real Thing* (1982) begins with a mystification of ontological levels for its audience. The play opens on Max and Charlotte, just as Charlotte is returning from a "business trip." Max has proof that she has been elsewhere, however, and accuses her of having an affair based on his discovery of Charlotte's passport (she is meant to have been in Geneva). The scene ends with Charlotte storming off. In the next scene we meet Charlotte again, only now she is married to Henry (a playwright and Stoppard's apparent alter ego), and it soon becomes clear that the earlier scene was, in fact, merely a re-enactment of one of Henry's plays, with Charlotte in a starring role. This mystification of theatrical levels eventually becomes something of a pattern. For instance, near the end of Scene Two, Max and his wife, Annie, pay Charlotte and Henry a visit and we find out that Henry is having an affair with Annie; in turn, it quite naturally follows that in Scene Three we get something of a repeat of Scene One, with Max greeting Annie on her return from rehearsal with proof that she has been having an affair with Henry (this time, it is a bloody handkerchief that Henry had put in his pocket in the previous scene and which Max subsequently finds in their car). Apparently the two couples separate soon after this, as in Scene Four we find Henry living with Annie (setting the stage for additional repetitions of this same structure).

Chinese Box Worlds

We know from the discussion of *Hound* in the Introduction that McHale refers to such recursive structures as Chinese box worlds, and argues that they are common technique in both modernist ("Here recursive structure serves as a tool for exploring issues of narrative authority, reliability, and unreliability, the circulation of knowledge and so forth" [*Postmodernist Fiction* 113]) and postmodernist fiction ("one such strategy, the simplest of all, involves frequency: interrupting the primary diegesis not once or twice but often with secondary, hypodiegetic worlds, representations within representation" [*Postmodernist Fiction* 113]). Recognizing the "Chinese box" structure for what it is — and quoting Anthony Jenkins

3. Modernist Diversions

about how in the original production a "'portrait of Henry' which exactly reproduced the characteristically stooped shouldered stand of Roger Rees so that when he stood in front of it, there was an actor whose mannerisms inscribed Henry"—Fleming nicely explains its ontological impact on the audience:

> Like the written text, the stage design utilized a Chinese boxes' type of self referentiality, showing different levels of representation that have their own level of reality and that affect the perception of "reality" [160].

Given the concerns of the current project the structure is quite notable, and should not be too easily dismissed. And as McHale would have it, the very frequency with which Stoppard invokes the device is one means of distinguishing a work as postmodern:

> So if recursive structure is to function in a postmodernist poetics of ontology, strategies must be brought to bear on it which foreground its ontological dimension. One such strategy, the simplest of all, involves *frequency*: interrupting the primary diegesis not once or twice but *often* with secondary, hypodiegetic worlds, representations within representations [*Postmodernist Fiction* 113].

However, while Stoppard does repeat this technique with frequency, he does not employ the device to reach deeper ontological levels. Rather, it is almost as if the device serves as an occasional corrective to the way in which a life on the stage can ultimately dominate the lives of its key players, refocusing what has all the appearance of a theatrical concession to the incestuous relations endemic in the theater in such a way that again and again we are redirected towards the real (perhaps even "realist") center of human experience. As such, it is hardly the sort of recursive structure which continually disrupts "the primary diegesis" of the work given that while it may occasionally reach deeper levels of fictionality with the repetitions, it is also true that in each case we are able to quickly find our feet again (and, more importantly, that we are meant to). By contrast, *Hound* is a work which much more overtly "dupes the reader into mistaking a representation at one narrative level for a representation at a lower level or (more typically) higher level, producing an effect of *trompe-l'oeil*" (McHale 114).

Similar patterns play out as the work proceeds. In Scene Five we find Henry rewriting a script written by Brodie—a serviceman who Annie has taken a motherly interest in at least in part because she sees herself as a potential instigator to a fire that Brodie set at a national shrine during a protest against nuclear disarmament that Annie was involved in. As Stoppard is notorious for his own conservatism, this very composite description detailing Annie's attachment to Brodie is itself a kind of caricature of a relationship Stoppard would be both amused and troubled by. In turn, the dialogue of Brodie's play (which focuses on how Brodie met Annie and the events that follow) comes across as parody:

HENRY: They're on the train.
[*reading two parts*] "You're a strange boy, Billy. How old are you?"
"Twenty. But I've lived more than you'll ever live" [47].

Perturbed by what she sees as Henry's selectively negative focus, Annie requests that Henry read it from the beginning. However, as Henry reads, the stage directions suggest that Annie is "not quite certain whether he [Henry] is being wicked or not" (i.e., making fun of Brodie), although there is little doubt that Stoppard is, especially when Billy — Brodie's alter ego in Brodie's play — finally suggests to Annie (named Mary in Brodie's play), "You put me in mind of Mussolini, Mary. Yes, you look just like him, you've got the same eyes" (47). By this point Annie is fully aware of Henry's "wickedness" in mocking the play, and tells him that "If you're not to read it properly, don't bother" (47). Brodie's play is, in a word, contrived, pointing to one more way in which a work can deviate from "the real thing" (i.e., the types of plays which Henry and Stoppard write). Apparently, Henry has his work cut out for him if he hopes to turn Brodie's play into "the real thing" as well.

In Scene Six, this scene on the train appears again. And given the way in which "real" and "fictional" scenes shadow each other in what we have seen so far, we are meant to think that we are now witnessing Brodie's play. However, the audience is soon disabused of this notion — as once again Stoppard pulls the rug out from under his audience. Hersh Zeifman calls this strain in Stoppard the "Comedy of Ambush," and quotes Stoppard on this: "I tend to write through a series of small, large, and microscopic ambushes — which might consist of a body falling out of a cupboard, or simply an unexpected word in a sentence" (quoted in Zeifman 141).[6]

Initially, Annie is taken in by the ambush as well, before finally catching up: "Jesus, you gave me a shock./ *She looks at him. Pleased and amused/* You fool" (*The Real Thing* 55). We soon discover that Billy and

3. Modernist Diversions

Annie happen to be on the same train because they are both traveling to Glasgow for work, and that Billy is repeating lines from Brodie's play (Annie had given him a copy of the script with the hope that he might play Billy). It is irrelevant whether or not it is meant as coincidence that they share a name, or whether it is simple convenience on Stoppard's part since Billy will indeed be playing the Brodie character. In either case the incestuous social environment of theater, theater production, and playwriting is fully realized by Stoppard as a place in which the real and the artificial are once again at odds with each other. Finally, in Scene Ten, Billy and Annie put the scene up for real, and even on this occasion Stoppard doesn't fail us, adding a final twist, as at the end of the scene we find that what was meant to be a play — and looks to the audience to be a scene from a play — has fooled us once again, as the theater has been replaced by a television studio: "A light change reveals that the setting is a fake, in a TV studio" (73).

Stoppard finds one more outlet to conflate the real and the artificial in the play that Billy and Annie are working on in Glasgow, John Ford's *'Tis Pity She's a Whore*. For while Billy opens Scene Six by quoting from Brodie's play, he closes that scene by encouraging Annie to quote from Ford's. Eventually, his intentions for doing so become clear, as Billy uses them as a means to try and seduce Annie. However, even while Billy is seductively reciting Giovanni's lines from the play, Annie has been withholding Annabella's lines in a bid to fend off what she correctly recognizes as Billy's attempt to seduce her. However, the lines Annabella withholds are important even in their omission, concerned as they are with Giovanni's attempts to seduce Annabella (his own sister), as she asks "Are you in earnest?"

In Scene Eight there is brief bit of repetition of this same travestied exchange, as Billy and Annie rehearse their play. When the play asks that they kiss, "he kisses her lightly" before she "returns the kiss in earnest" (67). Aside from the way in which the intertextuality of the scene means that it would exist comfortably within McHale's zone of the postmodern — in that it borrows "a character from another text" (*Postmodernist Fiction* 57) — this borrowing is made all the more metatheatrically compelling for how it highlights the way in which the theater is identified as a medium in which artificial feelings for someone can grow into real feelings (providing one more conflation of the artificial with the real). Moreover, this scene also resonates nicely with the previous scene (Scene Seven) in which Henry met with Charlotte, who knowingly questions him about who is playing Giovanni to Annie's Annabella in Scotland. It turns out that Charlotte had played the same role herself at seventeen, and had lost her virginity to the lead actor. Charlotte's implication is clear. Eventually getting the hint, for the first time in the entire play Henry himself is finally struck by jealousy and goes home and searches through his wife's belongings for some sign of infidelity, such that when Annie returns home in Scene Nine, Henry's jealous questioning of Annie — and the fact that the house is in disarray from him having searched it — plays similarly to Scenes One and Three. Thus we find that the world of theater is a place where Henry's lack of jealousy can grow into the real thing even when all that it really has to nurture it is the rampant artificiality endemic to theatrical environments. The real in turn influences the artificial which influences the real, with no clear sense of whether chicken or egg came first.

Real Drama and Artificial Love

This "mystification" of ontological levels soon becomes a metaphor for many other sorts of disruption as well, eventually prompting the very types of questions which, as McHale would have it, make the work postmodern: How do we distinguish the real scenes from the artificial ones (or from the rehearsed ones)? Where does the world of the stage end, and the world of those actors — caught up as they are in rehearsing that play — begin? At what point in its production history does the play itself become real (as opposed to rehearsed)? And how are we meant to sort all this out given that everything we see — both the "real" scenes and the "artificial" ones — are themselves part of the very artificial environment which makes up *The Real Thing*?

As it turns out, much of the mystification is directed towards drawing an analogy between the real/unreal dichotomy of the theater, and in tracking the way in which a similar dichotomy exists concerning the nature of love, meaning that the play also asks the following questions: How do we distinguish real love from artificial love? When does love become real (as opposed to simply going through the motions)? And how are we supposed to sort all this out given that both the "real" exchanges of love as well as the "artificial" ones are part of the explicitly artificial environment of *The

3. Modernist Diversions

Real Thing, where Henry (remembering that he is Stoppard's likely alter ego) finally admits that "I don't know how to write love" (39). Hersh Zeifman discusses another clever way in which Stoppard uses the real-artificial dichotomy regarding aesthetics to mirror the same dichotomy regarding love:

> For Henry's teenage daughter, Debbie, for example, love has nothing to do with sexual fidelity: "Exclusive rights isn't love," she pontificates, "it's colonization." Henry's reply is instructive: "Christ almighty. Another ersatz masterpiece. Like Michelangelo working in polystyrene" (p. 63). The ersatz, the fake, the artificial, versus "the real thing": this is Stoppard's primary concern in the play, specifically in relation to the theme of love ["Ambush," 141].

Indeed, Zeifman's short essay on the way in which "the structure of his newest play — not simply its thematic content — dramatizes the difficulty inherent in determining precisely what 'the real thing' is" ("Ambush," 141), deserves more attention.

John Fleming notes that there are other significant ontological dichotomies under investigation as well, explaining that "the play broaches Stoppard's perception of the real thing not only in love but also art, politics, and writing" (157). We could also add the self to this list, given how the various dichotomies blend and overlap, one with the next, such that questions concerning the "artificiality" of the theater intersect with questions concerning the artificiality of the writer (and of writing and art). However, not since Wilde's own exploration of the importance of being earnest — or at least since Stoppard's use of Wilde's play in *Travesties*— has a play been more self-consciously concerned with where theatrical pretense ends and true earnestness begins (thus, the importance of Annie asking Billie "Are you in earnest?" when he first tries to seduce her) . For at every turn there is something akin to the "Bunburying" that Algernon and Jack engage in, in *The Importance of Being Earnest*:

> ALGERNON: [...] Well, go on! Tell me the whole thing. I may mention that I have always suspected you of being a confirmed and secret Bunburyist; and I am quite sure of it now. [...] I have Bunburyed all over Shropshire on two separate occasions. Now, go on. Why are you Ernest in town and Jack in the country?
> JACK: My dear Algy [...] in order to get up to town I have always pretended to have a younger brother of the name of Ernest, who lives in the Albany, and gets into the most dreadful scrapes. That, my dear Algy, is the whole truth pure and simple.

ALGERNON: [...] What you really are is a Bunburyist. I was quite right in saying you were a Bunburyist. You are one of the most advanced Bunburyists I know.

JACK: What on earth do you mean?

ALGERNON:[...] I have invented an invaluable permanent invalid called Bunbury, in order that I may be able to go down into the country whenever I choose. [...] If it wasn't for Bunbury's extraordinary bad health, for instance, I wouldn't be able to dine with you at Willis's to-night, for I have been really engaged to Aunt Augusta for more than a week [121–123].

Quite aside from the way in which the play repeats various narratives so as to draw attention to the blurring of lines between the real and the performed, the various characters of *The Real Thing* are each engaged in bunburying of their own. Notably, in trying to keep their affair hidden from Max and Charlotte, Henry and Anne — in the midst of a conversation about Brodie — perform a routine intended to suggest hostility towards each other:

MAX: He was stationed at the camp down the road. He was practically guarding the base where these rockets are making Little Barmouth into a sitting duck for the Russian counter-attack, should it ever come to that.

HENRY: (*To* ANNIE): I see what you mean.

ANNIE: Do you?

HENRY: Well, yes. Little Barmouth isn't going to declare war on Russia, so why should Little Barmouth be wiped out in a war not of Little Barmouth's making [31–32].

Even while Henry's remarks are equal parts flirtation and sarcasm, this charade also provides Annie with a bunburying ruse for meeting up with Henry later (Henry has his own, involving picking up his daughter from her riding course). However, the charade goes deeper than that, as Henry eventually suggests that he may well like to "join the Justice for Brodie committee" (32) himself.

There is a lot going on in this scene. Most notably, underneath Henry's mocking disdain for Annie's endeavor is the fact that agreeing to join her despite his own reservations would, of course, give them even more time together. Simultaneously, even while he pretends that his motivations for joining her are sincere, everyone will assume all the same that he is at least half-kidding. And yet, as a right-of-centre playwright in a theater environment chock full of left-of-center members, Henry may very well feel "that his image is getting a bit too right-of-center" even as he

3. Modernist Diversions

notes that "Public postures have the configuration of private derangement" (32). So too, no doubt, would Stoppard. One wonders whether the author is as artificial as everything else.

WHERE IS THE AUTHOR?

This is all made more confusing by the well-known fact that the play is Stoppard's most autobiographical work. Among other things, the central character, Henry, shares with Stoppard a strong distaste for both Marxist politics and bad grammar. In response to one of Max's ill-phrased statements, Henry admits, "I'm sorry, but it actually hurts." Stoppard's attitude has hardly changed over the years. In a recent interview with Mark Lawson about a new staging of *The Real Thing*, Stoppard admitted that when newspapers mistake "who" for "whom" "it still goes through me like a spear." And like Stoppard, Henry also resorts to writing television and movie scripts to support his lifestyle and to pay his alimony.[7] John Fleming provides a thorough account of the similarities, which include, among other things, that "both 'steal' another man's wife and find happiness in their second marriage. Both are lovers of pop music and neither, despite frequent exposure through their second wife's love of opera, can distinguish between one opera and another" (156). Because of these similarities, it is also generally assumed that the various infidelities in the play are thinly veiled references to Stoppard's own infidelities (he eventually left his wife Miriam Stoppard for the lead actress in the original production of *The Real Thing*: Felicity Kendal).

If we are to believe Stoppard, however, the resonance is simple serendipity for rumor-mongering critics, not that Stoppard feels too bad about such confusions.

> The whole thing was that it was supposedly to do with Felicity. In fact, *The Real Thing* was written two or three years earlier. I used to feel I should correct these things. Now, I think: if they want to think that about *The Real Thing*, then let it go.[8]

This is an especially interesting quotation considering that the play itself is concerned with the proactive role that authors occasionally play in attempting to influence their critics. If Stoppard really used to feel he could "correct these things," that must have been before completing *The Real Thing*, which goes out of its way to revel in how an author might mislead and misdirect his audience. In any case, the degree to which it mirrors his own life is practically irrelevant to the fact that for an audience member keeping up with the tabloids the difficulty in separating the artificiality of the stage from the social reality of those involved in its production would be compounded all the same and, at least to some degree, Stoppard is being disingenuous in denying he had a part in any potential resonances (although such denials can also be seen as part and parcel of the very mystification process).

While such mystification is specifically concerned with raising ontological questions about the nature of reality, it is also true that all of these questions come about as a result of certain forms of narrative unreliability. That unreliability itself is the crux of the disruption becomes apparent when Henry alludes to the many layers that build up between the writer of a text and the public figure of the author:

> I'm supposed to be one of your intellectual playwrights. I'm going to look a total prick, aren't I, going on the radio to announce that while I was telling Jean-Paul Sartre that he was essentially superficial, I was spending the whole time listening to the Crystals singing "Da Doo Ron Ron" [17].

Henry recognizes that his public persona is distinct from himself (the real thing), and, not wanting to upset this artificial construction which sustains his livelihood, undertakes various actions that explicitly add depth to these layers. And given that such disruption is part of the very content of the play itself (remember how Henry considered the benefit to his career of coming out in support of Brodie), it is reasonable to assume that this sort of disruption has become the aesthetic norm within the play in other ways as well. Why else, for instance, would Henry choose *Finnegans Wake* as his favorite novel for the Desert Island Disks interview even while admitting to his wife that the idea that he might have read it is "silly" (the joke being that the work is so notoriously difficult that it should be obvious to Charlotte that Henry would only have chosen it to buck up his intellectual credentials). Finally — in an amusing reversal which points to the volatile potential for information to go awry — Max reads Henry's professed preference for pop music as "Sheer Pretension" (24). As the characters strive to control the narrative of their own life, the unreliability of narratives generally presents itself as the primary disruptive force in the work, meaning that the play's fundamental thrust is epistemological (how do we trust that what has been narrated is true?).

Which leads us to one final way that an author — either real or

3. Modernist Diversions

fictional—can pack depth between himself and his public: by using his own plays to mystify his audience about himself. Viewed as perhaps one more means of mystifying his own fans, the fact that the opening scene serves as a disguised version of Henry's life—together with the fact that there are good reasons to believe that it (and the play in its entirety) is a disguised version of Stoppard's own life—means that the play in its entirety is an investigation not just of the unreliable *narrator*, but of the unreliable *author*. Thus, while opening with ontological mystification, *The Real Thing* becomes even more modernist than *Travesties* according to McHale's criterion, since all of the various overtures to ontological mystification can be recuperated as a commentary on epistemological uncertainty in the face of an overtly unreliable author: How do we know what we know in the face of an unreliable author, especially one so actively and explicitly disingenuous as Stoppard himself?

And Brodie, as it turns out, is just as much an unreliable author. For while the play presents Brodie as having set fire to the monument out of righteous indignation over the buildup of a nuclear arsenal, in the face of Brodie's blustering arrogance Annie eventually confesses that Brodies had been more about impressing her than anything else:

> He didn't know anything about a march. He didn't know anything about anything, except Rosie of the Royal Infirmary. By the time we got to London he would have followed me into the Ku Klux Klan. He tagged on. And when we were passing the war memorial he got his lighter out [79].

However, as concerns how important it is to nurture one's public perception—especially as a political writer—Brodie is a quick study, such that his public persona quickly becomes even more artificial than Henry's. But of course, he has much to learn about the act of writing itself, which Henry criticizes by saying it is as artificial as a "lump of wood" standing in for a cricket bat:

> This thing here, which looks like a wooden club, is actually several pieces of particular wood cunningly put together in a certain way so the whole thing is sprung, like a dance floor. It's for hitting cricket balls with. If you get it right, the cricket ball will travel two hundred yards in four seconds. [...] What we're trying to do is to write cricket bats, so that when we throw up an idea and give it a little knock, it might ... *travel* [...] Now, what we've got here is a lump of wood of roughly the same shape trying to be a cricket bat, and if you hit a ball with it, the ball will travel about ten feet and you will drop the bat and dance about shouting "Ouch!" with your hands stuck into your armpits. (*Indi-*

cates the cricket bat) This isn't better because someone says it's better, or because there's a conspiracy by the MCC to keep cudgels out of Lords. It's better because it's better. You don't believe me, so I suggest you go out to bat with this ([Brodie's] *script*) and see how you get on [*The Real Thing* 51].

This passage is deservedly famous. But to use Henry's own logic against him as John Fleming does — by pointing out that Henry's preference for "music such as 'Da Doo Ron Ron' and 'Um Um Um Um Um Um'" may well garner a similar response from a musicologist — is beside the point. For Henry never attempts to defend this music as classical music's equal. In fact, as we have seen he is rather embarrassed about this preference. The notable feature of this scene is how Stoppard identifies one more way in which the arts are consumed with various sorts of artificiality, including, in this case, lumps of wood which stand in as worthy pieces of literature simply because they employ the correct politics.

There are of course numerous reasons to avoid drawing associations between author and narrator — in fact, doing so in this case is to move in an interpretive direction which runs counter to the theme of *The Real Thing* itself. However, the terrible irony in this case is that this very theme comes into greater clarity even as such connections are made (or, rather, as we witness Stoppard the author building a narrative which he intends to obscure the reality of his own life). In an essay which also focuses on the interpretive and distancing layers built into the text, Susanne Arndt concludes that these distancing techniques ultimately serve a misogynist function in the play. Thus, while admitting that recovering "the real" from beneath various subjective façades is a difficult (if not impossible) procedure, Arndt concludes that Stoppard's tendency to get in the final word is epistemologically positivist: "Even though Stoppard's play constantly undermines the dichotomy of the 'real thing' versus the 'ersatz,' the distinctions between which are frequently blurred, in the end it affirms Henry's knowledge as the 'real thing'" (498). Thus, Arndt accuses Stoppard of providing a subject position (i.e., Henry's) from which masculinist truth and power emanate.

Whether or not this is a fair assessment of Stoppard's attitude towards women, Arntdt's final assessment of *The Real Thing*'s epistemological positivism does correspond with much of what I have to say about Stoppard in other chapters: that because Stoppard can't quite help pointing to the mystery behind the clockwork with one hand even while working towards

3. Modernist Diversions

understanding it with the other, this in itself means that he is fully engaged in addressing epistemological issues (and from a fairly traditional vantage point at that). As such it is certainly true that the play isn't very likely to be confused with the type of postmodern writing discussed by Hutcheon — which so often finds common cause in anti-epistemological attitudes and progressive politics — but as we will see in the coming chapters, Stoppard is an equal opportunity positivist, every bit as likely to attribute "real knowledge" to women (Ruth in *Night and Day,* Hapgood in *Hapgood,* Hannah in *Arcadia*) as to men.[9]

4

Intermission: *Night and Day*

If one's only introduction to Stoppard had been via his major plays, both the politics and realism of *Night and Day* (1978) would come as something of a surprise, just as it does within the arc of this volume. To be sure Stoppard's previous play, *Travesties,* does have a political element to it in the way that Lenin's political aesthetic is represented as suspect. Similarly, Henry, Stoppard's alter ego in *The Real Thing*, also expresses his displeasure with the aesthetics of the left. However, given the extraordinary theatrical innovations at play in *Travesties*—which dominates my discussion of that play—in the present context, at least, these connections appear threadbare at best. And while the arc of my argument is such that I do mean to ultimately make sense of the way in which Stoppard moves towards a fully realized realist aesthetic in his most recent plays—*The Coast of Utopia* and *Rock 'n' Roll*—this larger objective isn't especially useful in situating *Night and Day* as anything other than an intermission in Stoppard's career.

That said, I am committed to the task of situating it meaningfully within his career all the same, albeit in a marginally different way than I have situated the other chapters, focused as they are on how Stoppard is more and more given over to normalizing the ontologically and epistemologically strained attitudes of the various socio-cultural institutions which are part and parcel of the postmodern condition. In this instance, rather, I seek to characterize Stoppard as instead given over to normalizing postmodern conceptions of how various purveyors of modern culture (the media, the arts, the university) typically function so as to serve the interests of power—or, rather, play party to what Foucault means when he says that "'truth' is linked in a circular relation with systems of power which produce and sustain it, and to effects of power which it induces and which extend it. A 'regime' of truth" (133). There are, of course, both political and epistemological implications to such positions—and, as we will see,

4. *Intermission:* Night and Day

Stoppard is not shy about dismissing such attitudes outright in favor of objective and knowable truths.

Night and Day is set on the large African estate of Geoffrey and Ruth Carson in the fictional African country of Kimbawe. In addition to Geoffrey and Ruth, the play also focuses on three journalists, Dick Wagner, George Guthrie (who each work for the *Globe*), and Jacob Milne (an independent journalist), who are on assignment covering the events surrounding a socialist rebellion led by Colonel Shimu against the established government and its president, Mageeba. The dramatic tension of the play is further intensified by the fact that Wagner has recently spent a single night with Ruth in a London hotel room, and, moreover, by the additional complication that upon meeting Milne she is immediately smitten with him. Thus, while Ruth worries that Wagner's arrival might either lead to her husband finding out about her indiscretion — or (perhaps even worse) to Wagner's continued pursuit of her — Wagner, it seems, is more interested in acquiring a major scoop of his own than he is in reacquiring Ruth.

Meanwhile Milne, a "special correspondent," has just scooped the other journalists by getting an interview with Colonel Shimu that was published in *The Globe*. When Wagner discovers that Milne has had confrontations with the National Union of Journalists (NUJ) that resulted in his release from *The Grimsby Messenger* under dubious (at least to Wagner's way of thinking) circumstances, Wagner dubs him "The Grimsby Scab" (39) and takes it upon himself to inform his union brothers back in Britain about just who this "special correspondent" is. When Wagner finally gets his scoop — that President Mageeba will visit the Carson compound for a secret meeting with Colonel Shimu, he proceeds to crash the party. Ruth takes this opportunity to join in the resulting debate over freedom of expression. However, just on the heels of Wagner's interview with Mageeba, Guthrie returns from a trip to extend an invitation by Mageeba to Shimu with word that Milne has been shot and killed. It then becomes evident that Shimu will not make an appearance, and that war is imminent.

One of the more explicit themes of *Night and Day* is that the unionization of the press gives far too much power over media content to the union itself, while, conversely, the play comes across as far less concerned with the control that multinational corporations have in deciding media content. *Night and Day* is typical of the early Stoppard in that it employs its characters to debate these viewpoints (in this case Wagner argues the necessity of press unionization while Milne decries the way that unions inhibit freedom of the press). In an interview with David Gollob and David Roper, Stoppard admits that Milne best represents his own views: "Milne has my prejudice if you like. Somehow, unconsciously, I wanted him to be known to be speaking the truth" (8). The play's concluding moments clearly reflect Stoppard's attitude, as one of Wagner's own stories is suppressed because of the labor activities he himself put in motion when he informed his union partners about Milne's identity.

No doubt Stoppard was aware that in 1977, one year prior to the publication of *Night and Day*, *The Royal Commission on the Press* had issued a study concerning the various dangers that threatened the free exchange of information. The resulting report opened with a chapter that explained the importance of the free press to democracy:

> Newspapers and periodicals serve society in diverse ways. They inform their readers about the world and interpret it to them. They act both as watchdog for citizens, by scrutinizing concentrations of power, and as a means of communication among groups within the community, thus promoting social cohesion and social change [McGregor 8].

Notably, this parallels Milne's own idealization of the press, that it is to be "the last line of defense for all the other freedoms" (58). That Stoppard himself values a free press for these same reasons is clear from an interview with Melvyn Bragg: "I always felt like that no matter how dangerously closed a society looked like it was getting, as long as any newspaper was free to employ anybody it liked to say what it wished within the law, then any situation was correctable. And that without that any situation was concealable" (123).

For its part, the report of *The Royal Commission on the Press* looked primarily at the same two threats which stand at odds in *Night and Day*—corporate ownership and unionization. The commission's evaluation of the way in which the closed shop of unionization might interrupt freedom of the press opens with a suggestion that the issue has "been the subject of intense controversy during most of the lifetime of the Commission." The report continues by noting that "Many have feared the consequences of an increase in the potential capacity of the Union of Journalists to influence or control editorial policies" (McGregor 157). The Royal Commission recognized that the central dilemma resides in the fact that even while the Industrial Relations Act of 1971 had opened the door in favor of

4. Intermission: Night and Day

collective bargaining by unions throughout industry, this same act suddenly granted the National Union of Journalists (NUJ) more power than it once had:

> For the NUJ, the first priority is the freedom to improve the earnings and conditions of work of its members and to deploy its maximum strength for collective bargaining to this end. For those on the other side, what matters most is to secure the freedom of the press because they cannot "conceive of a civilised society that does not regard as its first priority the right of a man to express what he believes in whatever form he thinks appropriate [McGregor 160].

Even while the Royal Commission understood the nature of the dilemma — admitting that "to determine what is right must involve a balancing of valid but competing claims"— the commission finally decided that there is "an important distinction between production workers and journalists in relation to closed shops" (McGregor 160), explaining that "if a journalist is precluded from working in the press he is effectively silenced, and the public is deprived of the opportunity of reading what he writes" (McGregor 162). For this reason the commission suggested a number of legislative safeguards intended to protect editors and journalists from the power of the union.

Stoppard wrote *Night and Day* in the years immediately after the commission's report, so it is clear that Stoppard's view was that the commission had been too quick to appease the NUJ. However, even while Stoppard sides against the concerns of the NUJ, *Night and Day* isn't entirely oblivious to the counter concern of the commission: that multinational control can also inhibit the free expression and exchange of ideas. Soon enough this possibility is broached by President Mageeba himself, who expresses concern that multinational companies have too much control over press content: "So there we were, an independent country, and the only English newspaper was still part of a British Empire — a family empire — a chain of newspapers — a fleet of newspapers, shall I say" (80). Mageeba goes on to explain the way in which a corporate press controls the product it presents to its readers when he responds to a question from Wagner concerning whether he intended to lobby the British and the Americans to "get what you need to win the war" (80): "I know the British press is very attached to the lobby system. It lets the journalists and the politicians feel proud of their traditional freedoms while giving the reader as much of the truth as they think is good for him" (80). However, the fact that Mageeba uses this critique to defend his takeover of the press indicates just how fundamentally opposed Stoppard himself is to the possibility that the NUJ might serve as a meaningful check against abuse on the part of the corporate owners of the press. In essence, the NUJ's authoritarian control of the press is characterized as no better than Mageeba's control of the press. Moreover, this discussion with Mageeba speaks to an earlier point in the play, when Wagner related a story to Guthrie about a run-in that he had with a local government official concerning Milne's interview with Colonel Shimu in the *Globe*: "He wants to know which side the *Globe* thinks it's on. So I tell him, it's not on any side, stupid, it's an objective fact-gathering organization. And he says, yes. But is it objective-for or objective-against? (*Pause*) He may be stupid but he's not stupid" (28).

Wagner, then, even more than Mageeba, is most clearly sympathetic with the view that even a so-called objective press might be slanted one way or another, and eventually defends the union from just this perspective, noting that it works as a counterbalance to corporate bias:

> MAGEEBA: I realize of course that you are only an able-seaman on the flag-ship.
> WAGNER: Well, sir, we've come a long way since we were galley slaves. Northcliffe could sack a man for wearing the wrong hat. Literally. There was a thing called the Daily Mail hat and he expected his reporters to wear it. Until he got interested in something else. Aeroplanes or wholemeal bread.... Those days are gone.
> MAGEEBA: Indeed, Mr. Wagner, now the hat is metaphorical only.
> WAGNER: With respect, sir, you underestimate the strength of the organized workers — the journalists. I admit that even when I started in newspapers a proprietor could sack any reporter, who, as it were, insisted on wearing the wrong hat, but things are very different now [81].

This conversation, and Wagner's response, plays up this tension over which entity is more inhibitive of a free press, corporate control or union capitulation, a tension most explicitly evidenced in Ruth's interjection "Now the union can sack him instead" (82). Ruth's statement only elicits further discussion about which is the greater abuse of freedom of the press, during which time Wagner extols the virtues of union power ("I'm not talking about protecting my job but my freedom to report facts that may not be congenial to, let us say, an English millionaire" [82].), while Ruth defends the millionaire owners ("You don't have to be a millionaire to contradict one. It isn't the millionaires who are going to stop you, it's the Wagners who don't trust the public to choose the marked card" [83]).

4. Intermission: Night and Day

While Stoppard's attempt to present both sides of a debate equally is true to form, the case against the censorship potential of the owners is so poorly argued (and to be fair, it is meant more as parody than argument) by Mageeba and Wagner that the audience never hears how the potential for corporate abuse becomes even more problematic with monopolization (not to mention multinational monopolization). To be sure, the potential threat from corporatization is far more clearly evidenced in the commission's report,[1] which devotes an entire chapter to explaining how monopolization was influencing the industry. Monopolization's full effect on the demise of privately owned newspapers can be seen in some very telling statistics included within the report (21). We get a good picture of the sheer scale of the change by considering the following passage:

> At one end of the scale, Reed International has an annual turnover of over £1,000 million and its main activity is paper manufacture and paper products. [...] At the other end of the scale are family controlled companies which publish only a handful of weekly newspapers, perhaps with modest interests in contract and general printing and in newsagents shops [McGregor, 20].

It is evident, then, that increasing monopolization has resulted in the loss of the local press: "In 1961 there were about 460 publishers of weekly newspapers only; there are now some 180" (McGregor 22). The commission explains the potential consequences as follows:

> The fewer the companies owning papers in the provinces, the less the diversity of voices in the press as a whole, even though each is concerned mainly with local and regional issues. The ultimate danger is that if a company should fall into the hands of an irresponsible owner, the effects of his irresponsibility would be more dangerously widespread, the more newspapers he controlled [McGregor, 130].

The commission comes closest to making the point that multinational control might develop into a new and more dangerous form of censorship with its additional statement that "the credibility of the press will dwindle the more it comes to be owned by large corporations whose interests are inevitably remote from those of the localities which their provincial papers serve" (McGregor, 130). This, then, raises the inevitable question of how someone is supposed to stand up to the millionaire owners of the multinational press when there is no remaining public forum of any size from which to confront it. Needless to say, the effect of a company that kept a firm grip on what it thought to be newsworthy would indeed be magnified in such a way that even though the press was nominally free, the effect would be such that (to use Stoppard's own words) "any situation was concealable." To be sure, we can see how this issue has something in common with Baudrillard's fixation on the way in which the simulacrum obscures the real. By contrast, Stoppard believes a free press — no matter its size — is sufficient to avoid the sort of concealment which Baudrillard finds to be so endemic in postmodern society.

From this perspective, perhaps Mageeba's concerns about the corporate press are justifiable, especially since the corporate press's interests are even more remote from Kambawe than they are from Grimsby. Indeed, Mageeba's failure to establish this point would seem to indicate just how unconcerned Stoppard is with the efficacy of representability in the era of multinational business. In responding to *Night and Day* David Edgar explains the unfairness of the implicit bias as follows: "Tom Stoppard stacked the cards so grossly against his left-wing villains ... that if any of us had tried the same gambit the other way round, we would have been howled off the stage" (165). That time and again Stoppard simply equates a free press with democratic social justice, without once expressing concern that even a free press might yet marginalize certain stories which run counter to its interests — and, moreover, that such marginalization might be compounded when the press is monopolized at the multinational level — ultimately speaks to a fairly positivist attitude about the nature of representation; that the press can — and naturally does — provide its audiences with the truth.

Stoppard's uncritical attitude towards a multinational corporately controlled press becomes clearest in the final exchange of words that occurs between Ruth and Wagner before the conversation switches tracks to involve Mageeba and Wagner. Ruth states that freedom of the press is evidenced by the fact that "the country [Britain] is littered with papers pushing every political line from Mao to Mosley and back again." Wagner explains how little impact small newspapers have when competing with national papers, saying, "It's absurd to equate the freedom of the big battalions to the freedom of the pamphleteer to challenge them" (83). Ruth's unchallenged remark to this point (cited in brief above) is most telling:

> You are confusing freedom with ability. The *Flat Earth News* is *free* to sell a million copies. What it lacks is the ability to find a million people with four pence and a conviction that the earth is flat. Freedom is neutral. Free expression

4. *Intermission:* Night and Day

includes a state of affairs where any millionaire can have a national newspaper, if that's what it costs. A state of affairs where only a particular, approved, licensed and supervised non-millionaire can have a newspaper is called, for example, Russia [83].

Wagner isn't allowed an opportunity to respond because Mageeba interrupts to admit that the situation described by Ruth might, "of course, [refer to] Kambawe" (83). That Wagner doesn't respond indicates that Stoppard himself sees no legitimate response to Ruth's argument that the national press retains a large readership simply because it gives the public what it wants, while those forms of media which do not have a following fail simply because they don't provide that for the public.

That Ruth's sentiments correspond with Stoppard's own becomes clearer still when we compare the first edition, published in 1978 (from which I have been quoting), with the second edition, published a year later. In the second edition we find that the entire debate has been replaced by parody, with Ruth simply parroting a conversation that she claims to have had with her son wherein she plays the part that had been Wagner's in the previous version, while she gives to her son the role that she had played. That once again Ruth's ideas (now Alastair's) win the argument hands down only serves to further undercut Wagner's position, now so easily refuted by a mere schoolboy (New York Edition 83–85). Putting his own position into the "mouths of babes" is a rhetorical ploy that Stoppard has employed elsewhere, including both *Professional Foul* (1977) and *Every Good Boy Deserves Favour* (1978). John Fleming explicates the implication of this change similarly, explaining that it "only further skewers Wagner's views as now the suggestion is that even a child can see the "fallacy" of Wagner's leftist, union line" (147). Or, as Stoppard himself put it in an interview with Gollob and Roper about *Every Good Boy Deserves Favour*, even while you might be able to convince a "sophisticated person" that "life inside this wall [inside East Berlin] was admirable ... if you tried to do this to a child, he'd blow you to smithereens" (164).

The play's negative attitude towards unionization is, finally, most explicit in the conclusion, at which time Wagner himself is unable to publish the scoop he has received by interviewing Mageeba. For finally (and ironically), the *Globe* has been shut down for the week due to the labor dispute instigated by Wagner's own earlier message concerning the Grimsby scab (Milne). Certainly the implication of this final irony is that Wagner "had to learn the hard way" the dangers of collective bargaining. And while Wagner had planned on leaving Kimbawe with his scoop, after hearing of the strike he decides to stay on, which begs the rhetorical question from Ruth, "Aren't you supposed to be withdrawing your labour?" Apparently Wagner has given up his labor principles, as he snaps back, "Don't you get clever with me!" (92). Presumably, by this point in the play the audience is also expected to have given up its labor principles as well.

One way of drawing this more forcefully back to familiar ground given the arc of this book is to look at the extent to which Stoppard's attitude about the media corresponds with his attitudes about the theater. To this end — and given the theme of the work — it is hardly surprising to find that in the years following *Night and Day* Stoppard could not be counted on to support various social-political movements in support of the arts, especially if they were at all suggestive of the sort of organized labor which Stoppard believed to have potentially negative consequences for freedom of expression more generally. As a case in point, Stoppard was conspicuously absent from the scene in December 1988, when Clive Barker chaired a conference titled "Theater in Crisis" at London Goldsmith's College. One result of the conference was a declaration criticizing reductions in government support for the theater signed by notable players within the theatrical community, including Harold Pinter, David Edgar, and Caryl Churchill, among others. Numbered among the declaration's resolutions was a collection of distinct appeals for a return to pre–Thatcherite attitudes about the worth of the arts (that they are essential to "the full and free development of every individual"), the necessity for an apportionment of funds which would make the arts more "accessible to that diversity of needs and interests whether they be national, regional, local, community-based, gender-based, ethnic" and so on, and a proclamation that "a free market economy and private sponsorship cannot guarantee the necessary conditions for the theater to fulfill its many functions" (Lavender 211–213).

However, even while a number of playwrights (notably, Caryl Churchill in *Serious Money* [1987]) took it upon themselves to explore the impact that corporate power was having on the theater in the late 80s (under Prime Minister Margaret Thatcher), Stoppard refrained entirely from voicing his opinion on the matter (at least there is no public record of him having done so). This might easily enough be overlooked as irrel-

4. Intermission: Night and Day

evant vis-à-vis Stoppard's own commitment to the arts except for the fact that some ten years later Stoppard did join a second group of artists, the Shadow Arts Council, headed up in this instance by Peter Hall, which also advocated greater funding for the arts. And while this seeming discrepancy could perhaps be rationalized in any number of ways (e.g., as a simple oversight, or as in-fighting with his dramatist peers), upon closer inspection it becomes apparent that the aesthetic, economic, and ideological differences between the two movements are such that it not only provides poignant insight into Stoppard's own attitudes towards public funding for the arts, but is also consistent with his own long-held attitude towards organized lobbying campaigns and their potential impact on freedom of expression (especially as expressed in *Night and Day*).

The two movements were most different from each other due to the fact that it wasn't so much the amount of funding which concerned the Shadow Arts Council, but, rather, how current funding levels were being spent. For what truly worried the Shadow Arts Council was that Labour was much more committed to the more popular areas of mainstream music, radio, and television than with the more "elite" arts of theater and opera — not completely surprising given that the audience for the more popular arts largely comprised Labour's electoral base. Furthermore, while we do find Stoppard in an interview at this time explaining that he supported full funding for the arts, you really have to read between the lines here. As Ivan Hewitt puts it:

> The fact that everyone at the launch seemed to be nudging 60 gave a clue to the Shadow Arts Council's real aim. This is not to launch a debate, it is to return to the past.... To read these principles is to be taken back to a land far away and long ago, a land where the eternal verities of art and the personal taste of the ruling elite happily coincided. Art and culture were simply "the best that has been thought and said," in Arnold's phrase. The Council's resources were devoted "to the fine arts exclusively"; amateur and what later came to be known as "community arts" had to fend for themselves [1999].

It would seem, then, that what the Shadow Arts Council (and, by implication, Stoppard) actually supports is greater funding for the more established "elite arts" (e.g., those arts such as Stoppard himself was involved in), not the more community based ("philistine") arts such as the "Theater in Crisis" playwrights were fighting for. From this perspective, one reasonably persuasive explanation for Stoppard's apparent inconsistency is that it is simply indicative of his well-noted politically moderate conservatism. For while the "theater in crisis" conference involved "discussions held by a number of theater people on the left ... [of] the problems posed by 'Thatcher's Theater' and the national priorities it reflects" (Lavender 210), Peter Hall's Shadow Arts Council was comprised of figures of a much more moderate persuasion (with the notable exception of Caryl Churchill, who signed on to both).

At this juncture it is worth considering the full ramifications of Thatcher's legislation regarding how the arts should be funded which originally gave rise to the Theater in Crisis movement. Following on the heels of the above research into the fate of the regional press, the following description of the fate of the regional theater should come as no surprise:

> So in the first half of the 1990's the signs of a collapsing system appeared everywhere, ranging from the Royal Shakespeare Company closing the Barbican Theater for six months in a desperate attempt to reduce its growing deficit, to the Liverpool Playhouse appearing in court under the threat of receivership. Yet the economic misery was not evenly spread, as an acute contrast in financial performance between London's commercial theaters and the regional subsidized theaters demonstrates. There was a drastic 25% drop in total attendances at regional theater (12 to 9 million) between 1992 and 1995, while those for London's West end rose only slightly, but produced a 6% growth in box-office revenue. In this sector, government policies that "freed" the market seemed to be working. But despite efforts by the Arts Council to prevent it, the deterioration of regional theater continued throughout the decade, prompting even the ultra-conservative Whittaker's Almanac to pronounce in 1997 that "The days of a repertory rooted in its community and producing work which reflects that community appear to be numbered," and leading Peter Hall to claim in 1999 that "We're going to end up with almost no regional theater except for one or two centres, say Leeds and Birmingham" [Kershaw 280].

What we find, then, is that the consequence of the free market arts support system encouraged and supported by Thatcher's government so benefited the large production company at the expense of the small one that the theater, like the press before it, became dominated by fewer and fewer production companies, many of which had multinational connections. Consequently, Stoppard's refusal to comment on this situation — when considered against his implicit acceptance of press corporatization two decades earlier — comes across as at least tacit approval of the Thatcherite agenda and its consequences. The correlation is clear. We can almost hear Stoppard lecturing the Theater in Crisis movement similarly to how Ruth

4. Intermission: Night and Day

lectures Wagner in *Night and Day*: "[Even in the Thatcher era] the Flat Earth [community theater] is free to sell a million [tickets]. What it lacks is the ability to find a million people with four pence and a conviction that the earth is flat."

By contrast, the exploration of the corporatization of the theater that playwrights such as Caryl Churchill undertook (in plays such as *Serious Money*) couldn't be more different from what we find in Stoppard, not only politically — as Churchill does support a social structure which would redistribute funds in such a way as to serve as a counterbalance to monopoly control of the theater — but also in Churchill's perception of the role that she herself plays in determining the future of theater in Britain. For while in *Night and Day* Stoppard situates himself as an outsider capable of standing back from the goings-on between the NUJ and the corporate press and, consequently, able to objectively judge the situation for what it is, Churchill uses *Serious Money* to analyze her own role in the power/knowledge theatrical hierarchy. Moreover, while Stoppard conveniently ignores the fact that as a public figure his theater projects at least in part succeed or fail based on how they are reviewed in the press, Churchill's *Serious Money* is framed in a way that leaves no doubt that Churchill understands the relationship between the theatrical power structure and the success and/or failure of her own work.[2]

All things considered, one particularly poignant reading of Stoppard's failure to sign on to the "Theater in Crisis" manifesto is that just as Stoppard's sympathies in *Night and Day* explicitly favor the idea that the free exchange of information (in this case, news) enjoyed the most liberty in a free market economy unencumbered by the abuse which might arise if a powerful union of news-reporters has its way, consistency alone allowed that Stoppard might once again simply be favoring the idea that the free exchange of information (in this case, theater) would continue to enjoy the most liberty were it to remain unencumbered by the abuse which might arise were a powerful "union" of playwrights (i.e., the "theater in crisis playwrights") were to have its way.

One passage more than any other from *Night and Day* stands out as relevant in helping us to gauge Stoppard's attitude about the undue influence of corporate interests generally, and that is Ruth's rebuttal of Wagner's suggestion that the corporate press inhibits the proliferation of small newspapers:

WAGNER: I'm talking about national papers. It's absurd to compare the freedom of the big battalions with the freedom of a basement pamphleteer to challenge him.
RUTH: You are confusing freedom with ability. The Flat Earth News is free to sell a million copies. What it lacks is the ability to find a million people with four pence and a conviction that the earth is flat [83].

Ruth's argument is fairly straightforward, and is meant to win the day. Apparently Stoppard just isn't convinced that small institutions — be they community theaters or the local press — might have their voices marginalized according to the dictates of some more powerful institution. What's more, *Night and Day* very nearly stresses the opposite concern: that social protest movements are a much greater potential threat to freedom of expression than is corporate power.

Presumably, then, Stoppard believes that cutting-edge theater is supposed to compete with corporate-sponsored theater in the same way that the alternative press is supposed to compete with the multinational press. And yet one can't help but wonder what would have become of Stoppard's own *Rosencrantz and Guildenstern are Dead* had it not entered the marketplace in the comparatively hospitable environment of the late 60s, at a time when public funding for the arts was much more substantial than it was by the time of the Theater in Crisis movement. (The first two chapters of John Fleming's *Stoppard's Theater* puts this into proper perspective, as Fleming makes clear that *R & G* finally found its way into production more by chance and circumstance than by resolutely winning over those who read the script).

It is worth remembering that by the time of the Theater in Crisis Conference Stoppard would hardly have felt the pressure that Thatcher's agenda had on the theater more generally, as by this time his work had already found its way onto the international tourist map and, consequently, actually stood to benefit from the new system. Furthermore, given Stoppard's attitude about success simply being a consequence of producing good and timely material, by this late date in his career it would have been all too easy for him to assume that his own success had come about as a consequence of the simple fact that his work provides the public what it wants, while theater which fails does so only because it is, perhaps, all too intent on finding "a million people with four pence and a conviction that the earth is flat," or to be peddling some other such unmarketable nonsense.

4. *Intermission:* Night and Day

While this final observation is largely conjecture given Stoppard's silence on this issue, this particular reading of Stoppard's silence resonates in meaningful ways with the most fundamental distinction between playwrights such as Stoppard and Churchill (i.e., their differing epistemological values). For while in her own work Churchill focuses on how all knowledge — even that knowledge presented within her own plays — is constructed according to the dictates of the power elite, Stoppard's work (especially in such plays as *Arcadia* and *Hapgood*),[3] by contrast, suggests that knowledge is something sacred, whose free pursuit can lead to the recovery of truth and beauty, and to the reinvigoration of democracy. To imagine that his own success is, perhaps, dependent upon just how well he toes this very line of thought is, for Stoppard, unthinkable; his plays frequent the national theater because they belong there.

Which, of course, ultimately serves to situate this play within the larger argument of the work, in that Stoppard not only confronts — and rejects — postmodern ontological attitudes about how truth in representation is only a construct, but, moreover, also rejects the more explicitly ideological attitude that it is constructed "in a circular relation with systems of power which produce and sustain it, and to effects of power which it induces and which extend it." The surprise, then, isn't so much that it is so overtly political in its content (as its politics shares something within its epistemology), but, rather, that he can be read as having responded to Foucaldian ideas about truth and power so definitively (albeit unwittingly) at such an early stage in his career. For even while the plays we have discussed already track towards modernism for how they reject ontological anomalies in favor of epistemological doubt, this play rejects epistemological doubt for epistemological certainty (he will again embrace doubt in his next plays). From this perspective, perhaps it isn't so surprising that he chose dramatic realism to do so — a style that he only gradually returns to late in his career, and one, I will argue, that he employs at least in part for much the same reasons (i.e., that it allows for much more stable footing when critiquing power/knowledge than do more postmodern forms).

5

Normalizing Postmodern Science

In two of his more recent plays, Tom Stoppard takes contemporary science as his subject matter. In *Hapgood* (1988), he draws an analogy between quantum mechanics and international espionage, while in *Arcadia* (1993) he uses chaos theory to explain the difficulty that literary biographers confront when attempting to recover the past.[1] Although these plays are not as theatrically experimental as Stoppard's earlier work, they nonetheless engage the concerns of the postmodern era in their theatrical and metaphoric appropriation of twentieth-century theoretical science.

In *The Postmodern Condition: A Report on Knowledge*, Jean-François Lyotard helps to elucidate the implications of such an engagement with contemporary science, especially in his explanation of how quantum mechanics rejects any hope of formulating a universal scientific narrative of reality: "The modalization of the [quantum] scientist's statement reflects the fact that the effective, singular statement (the token) that nature will produce is unpredictable. All that can be calculated is the probability that the statement will say one thing rather than another" (57). In this and similar assertions, Lyotard recognizes both quantum mechanics and especially chaos theory as the postmodern theories par excellence, given their radical incredulity with the possibility of ever achieving a grand metanarrative description of physical reality.

For Lyotard, the postmodern era and its cultural artifacts (including the scientific theories noted here) are uniquely characterized by their "incredulity towards metanarratives" (xxiv), which raises the question of whether Stoppard's employment of quantum mechanics and chaos theory renders these plays postmodern. Indeed, given the radical implications of these theories, one might expect a playwright as innovative as Stoppard, who has so extensively explored nontraditional anti-narratives in such early works as *Rosencrantz and Guildenstern are Dead* and *The Real Inspector Hound*, to use quantum mechanics to postmodern effect — to create a work

5. Normalizing Postmodern Science

that is quantum-mechanically dubious about the possibility of narrative explicability. Such an assumption, however, would prove to be incorrect, as much of Stoppard's investigation into these theories seeks to normalize them by adopting classical interpretations of their more radical features rather than reveling in their radical ontological implications.[2]

Hapgood: *Quantum Metaphor, Classical Results*

Hapgood begins with an information exchange between secret government agents of Britain and the Soviet Union that has been specifically designed by the British to ferret out a double agent who has been slipping information to the Russians. When the exchange goes awry, the play takes on the shape of an espionage thriller with agents of the British government attempting to put the pieces back together in order to understand exactly how things went wrong. Betty Hapgood is the quick-thinking, businesslike "mother" of the operation; she is so good at keeping a complete mental picture of all the intricacies of a particular situation that she can play a game of chess with another agent without the luxury of a board. Joseph Kerner is a Russian physicist who had been sent to Britain as a "sleeper" years earlier, except that Hapgood has convinced him to work as a double agent (she also has a son, Joe, by him). Of all of Hapgood's associates — Blair (her boss), Ridley, Wates (an American agent), and Merryweather — Ridley is of particular note because he emerges as the double agent working for the Russians who is finally implicated in the act of espionage.

The mystery surrounding Ridley's espionage derives its complexity from the set itself, where the permutable possibilities for coming and going play themselves out to their full potential in the scene that follows, and it takes nearly three pages of stage directions to describe the intricacies of the exchange. Central to the scene, and to the mystery that follows, is the entrance of Ridley "from the lobby" with his briefcase in hand. Going "on a perambulation [he] moves around and through, in view and out of view, demonstrating that the place as a whole is variously circumnavigable in a way which will later recall, if not replicate, the problem of the bridges of Konigsberg" (2). After the scene plays itself out in its entirety, Hapgood is left to wonder what happened to the contents of the briefcase, which she had meant to intercept before it went into enemy hands; for even though things look to her as if they had gone as planned, when she opens the briefcase its contents — some film and a transmitter designed to help the operatives trace the bag — are missing.

In addition to Ridley, both Kerner and Hapgood are initially suspected of double-dealing with the Russians. The evidence against Kerner fails to be very convincing, however, since he proves to be clean of a special isotope that had been sprayed in the briefcase — proof that he could not have opened it. Hapgood does read positive, but this evidence against her proves nothing because she was the one who finally checked the briefcases' contents and would have encountered the isotope at that time. What does make her a suspect, however, is that she was holding the bag when the transmitter mysteriously quit sending a signal. Furthermore, it is discovered that she was Ridley's only alibi on a number of previous missions that also ended under mysterious circumstances. After the missing tracking device suddenly begins transmitting from Hapgood's office, Wates finally grows so suspicious of her that he has her followed. When finally given the opportunity, however, she easily enough explains away all of the evidence against her except for the fact that she had been an alibi for Ridley on so many occasions. It is this impasse that leads Kerner to propose the radical theory that Ridley could have been involved in each of the impossible scenarios if only he had a twin — a scenario which, in Hapgood's words, always creates "[i]ts own alibi" (41).

To catch Ridley and his twin in the act and prove their hypothesis, Hapgood pretends that she is still under suspicion and that the Russians have kidnapped her son, Joe. She talks Ridley into trying to retrieve the boy. For his part, Ridley has two reasons for assisting her: first, he genuinely seems to like Hapgood, and, second, retrieving the boy involves trading secrets to his Russian connections (or so he believes). The plan is to use Ridley's own tactics against him, with Hapgood pretending to have an identical twin sister of her own, Mrs. Newton — a tactic that is meant to give him confidence so that they can pursue their covert operations without Blair and Wates catching on. The "sister" is to impersonate Hapgood while she herself makes the exchange for her son. Ridley's role is to "babysit" and coach Mrs. Newton so that she makes an effective decoy — a task complicated by the fact that Mrs. Newton turns out to be such a pot-smoking, foul-mouthed version of Hapgood that Ridley has to bribe her to keep her in line. Ridley, however, is sufficiently fooled and goes along with the plan.

5. Normalizing Postmodern Science

After babysitting Mrs. Newton, his final task is to assist in the actual exchange, at which point he is shot and killed, and his twin is captured.

Significantly, the play's very genre suggests the postmodern. Fredric Jameson argues that "conspiracy theory (and its garish narrative manifestations) must be seen as a degraded attempt — through the figuration of advanced technology — to think the impossible totality of the contemporary world system" (*Postmodernism* 38). This play has all the necessary ingredients for a Jamesonian examination into the postmodern era's degraded faith in representation — international relations, espionage, conspiratorial complexity, and the realization that information exists as a market commodity. Consequently, Hapgood is confronted with just such an impossible totality in the confusion surrounding the disappearance of the briefcase, which grows especially pronounced once Kerner recognizes that Ridley's movements have their mathematical counterpart in "the problem of the bridges of Konigsberg":

> Well, in Immanuel Kant's Konigsberg there were seven bridges.... An ancient amusement of the people of Konigsberg was to try to cross all seven bridges without crossing any of them twice. It looked possible but nobody had solved it.... Euler [who eventually solved the puzzle] didn't waste his time walking around Konigsberg, he only needed the geometry [38].

When Kerner brings this same geometry to bear on Ridley's mysterious movements, traditional mathematics at first leaves him in a quantum quandary since there appears to be no classical solution to Ridley's movements:

> KERNER: When I looked at Wate's diagram I saw that Euler had already done the proof. It was the bridges of Konigsberg, only simpler.
> HAPGOOD: What did Euler prove?
> KERNER: It can't be done, you need two walkers. (*Pause*)
> HAPGOOD: Good old Euler [38–39].

Kerner realizes that for Ridley to have completed the pattern in question he would have had to make a quantum leap — to have gone "from here to there without going in between" (*Hapgood* 40). As such, a particularly compelling postmodern reading of this event would hold that quantum mechanics has come to the assistance of conspiracy theory in order to achieve a new means of thinking "the impossible totality of the contemporary world system."

To help in understanding how this solution to the mystery invokes a quantum metaphor and to fully appreciate the radical implications of this metaphor, consider the description of quantum phenomenon given to us by the physicist Richard Feynman — a description from the very lectures that Stoppard borrowed while creating Hapgood: "Electrons arrive in lumps, like particles, but the probability of arrival of these lumps is determined as the intensity of waves would be. It is in this sense that the electron behaves sometimes like a particle and sometimes like a wave. It behaves in two different ways at the same time" (138). Thus the quantum phenomenon defies traditional explication since light cannot be defined as either a particle or a wave. The radical aspects of quantum mechanics become even more apparent when Feynman explains that any attempt to track the path of a particle necessarily changes the path of that same particle: "You can, if you want, invent many ways to tell which hole the electron is going through, and then it turns out that it is going through one or the other." However, "if you try to make that instrument so that at the same time it does not disturb the motion of the electron, then what happens is that you can no longer tell which hole it goes through and you get the complicated result again" (143). Thus we find that for any empirical method that attempts to track each and every quantum particle deployed by a given source, the result will necessarily fulfill a particle pattern. Wave pattern, by contrast, will always and only result when empirical tracking methods are not employed. Hence it is almost as if quantum objects switch from exhibiting wave pattern to particle pattern only when they know that they are being watched. The quantum mechanical interpretation, which would explain Ridley's behavior, is that he switches his behavior because he is so closely watched and hence we no longer can tell which door he is going through. Instead we get a complicated result (and, I might add, one that is not at all dissimilar from those contemporary conspiracy theories Jameson speaks of which are so rife with paranoia).

The epistemological and ontological implications of quantum probabilities are profound. After explaining how quantum mechanics entails "that in the fundamental laws of physics [themselves] there are odds," Feynman explains its implications for any project designed to describe the physical world through science: "One theory is that the reason you cannot tell through which hole you are going to see the electron is that it is determined by some very complicated things back at the source." He continues the argument: "[P]hysics is incomplete and if we get a complete enough

5. Normalizing Postmodern Science

physics then we shall be able to predict through which hole it goes. That is called the hidden variable theory. That theory cannot be true; it is not due to lack of detailed knowledge that we cannot make a prediction" (145–46). Our inability to gauge a quantum particle's momentum and position simultaneously has nothing to do with the current state of knowledge but is a very fact of quantum behavior (i.e., it is not simply epistemological but thoroughly ontological). It cannot simply be attributed to a mathematical puzzle similar to the seven bridges. There is no solution that might make physics classical once again.

Lyotard argues, moreover, that quantum mechanics provides the ultimate incredulity towards metanarratives since the very patterns exhibited by quantum particles in controlled laboratory experiments — for instance, those described by Feynman — cannot be explained according to a coherent (classical) narrative. Indeed, what we have seen so far is that as soon as such a narrative is attempted — perhaps either by trying to measure the momentum or pinpointing the location of a quantum object so that we might tell its Newtonian narrative — the pattern changes. Thus it is a very tenet of quantum mechanics that the best we can ever hope for with regard to giving the life history of a quantum particle is to be able tell its story as a probability narrative. At best we can predict that a particular pattern will result, or express the odds against a particular particle traveling along a particular path. Contrary to Newton (whose mechanics imply that we might even predict the roll of dice if we knew all the necessary conditions involved), quantum physics asserts that no matter how much information we have about a particular system, prediction will always be a matter of probability.

Lyotard's point is that quantum mechanics is linked with postmodernity since scientists must admit that a grand narrative vision of the universe is unachievable. And it is to this characteristic that Arkady Plotnitsky refers when examining the similarity that exists between Niels Bohr's interpretation of quantum mechanics and such "anti-epistemologists"[3] as Friedrich Nietzsche, Georges Bataille, and Jacques Derrida, each of whom "may be seen as announcing the irreducible incompleteness of knowledge (as classically understood) in [its] respective fields" (4).

Such an anti-epistemological interpretation of the event in question is refused, however, as soon as Kerner sees his way through to a classical interpretation of Ridley's behavior by positing the existence of twins. Hapgood is finally pleased with "Good old Euler" not because she thinks the quantum analogy holds (and that Ridley has been making quantum leaps) but because she realizes that she now has her *men*: for Ridley must have a twin. When Kerner makes the analogy to quantum mechanics explicit by imagining how it must have been a Russian physicist trained in quantum mechanics who realized the possible benefits of using twins as agents, he provides the necessary contextual narrative which only serves to normalize the situation further:

> One day! Constantin Belov jumped out of his bathtub and shouted "Eureka!" Maybe he was asleep in the bath. The particle world is the dream world of the intelligence officer. An electron can be here or there at the same moment. You can choose. It can go from here to there without going in between; it can pass through two doors at the same time, or from one door to another by a path which is there for all to see until someone looks, and then the act of looking has made it take a different path. Its movements cannot be anticipated because it has no reasons. It defeats surveillance because when you know what it's doing you can't be certain where it is, and when you know where it is you can't be certain what it's doing: Heisenberg's uncertainty principle [40].

Apparently Belov thought that twins would be the next best thing to quantum particles because they might help defeat the best surveillance operations of the enemy, just as quantum particles defeat the surveillance operations of the quantum physicist. Ridley and his twin come to fulfill this possibility in how they appear to "go from here to there without going in between."

As a result, instead of embracing either the radical ontology or the apparent anti-epistemology of quantum mechanics in such a way as to link his work to such figures as Nietzsche and Derrida, Stoppard, rather, can be seen as offering a thoroughly classical interpretation of quantum mechanics. In this strategy Stoppard is in good company. Einstein, for instance, was never satisfied with the idea that "God might play dice with the universe"—a statement with which Stoppard perhaps agrees, for Kerner quotes Einstein to this effect in *Hapgood* (41). Along the same lines, J. S. Bell explains how some physicists continue to believe that quantum mysteries are the result of incomplete knowledge. In this view, the apparent randomness of quantum behavior is founded on "hidden variables."[4] David Bohm, for example, postulated that a (hidden) "guiding wave" or "radio transmitter/receiver" serves to communicate data from one particle to another in such a manner that quantum indeterminacies result. Bohm's

5. Normalizing Postmodern Science

theory, however, is inconsistent with Einstein's theory of relativity because, in Plotnitsky's words, "[t]he theory acquires signals that propagate instantaneously. Thus, it violates the finite limit upon all interactions in actual space, established by Einstein's relativity — the speed of light, one of the most fundamental experimental constants in all physics" (171).

Like these hidden variable proponents, Kerner posits that a hidden variable theory explains away the quantum conundrums of the opening sequence when he suggests that there must be two Ridleys, not just one; and, moreover, that each twin carries a "small radio transmitter/receiver." That these are hidden "gadgets [which] are going to get quite a lot of use" (*Hapgood* 5) only makes the analogy more explicit — and a classical parallel is provided to the "guiding wave" of Bohm's theory. Thus each time one of the Ridleys sees that he is being watched, the two can split up, the first to be seen by Hapgood et al., and the second to be told by the first (via radio transmitter/receiver) where to go so as to produce the quantum result. Stoppard, like Einstein and Bohm before him, imagines that a classical scenario that normalizes non-classical behavior still persists. Stoppard thus actively avoids using quantum mechanics to its full postmodern potential and, moreover, even appears to side with Einstein in his desire for a more explicable quantum world. Or, as John Bull puts it, "The apparent uncertainty is thus carefully orchestrated by a dramatist who is always securely in control of the theatrical tricks and sleight of hand" (203).

A second analogy to quantum mechanics which contains more promising connections to postmodernism occurs when Kerner is forced to explain to Blair how the prototypical double agent is in a much more ambiguous position than is suspected by either side: "Oh, you think there's a what's-what? Your joe. Their sleeper. Paul, what's-what is for zoologists: Oh yes — definitely a giraffe. But a double agent is not what's-what like a giraffe, a double agent is more like a trick of the light" (9). Like all double agents, Kerner remains under suspicion; as a double agent, there may be reason to believe he could be a triple or even a quadruple agent. The analogy is that light, similarly, is always under suspicion since it can be recognized as consisting of either particles or waves. Kerner says, "When you shine light through a gap in the wall, it's particles. Unfortunately, when you shine the light through two little gaps, side by side, you don't get particle pattern like for bullets, you get wave pattern like for water. The two beams of light mix together and–" (9). At this point Blair, still wanting to know definitively whether Kerner is "ours or theirs," interrupts. However, he is missing Kerner's point, which is that he, like a quantum object, is neither (or, perhaps, both). Kerner later explains to Hapgood just how difficult resolving this question has actually become: "Paul thinks I was a triple, but I was definitely not, I was past that, quadruple at least, maybe quintuple" (76). If finally Blair can't determine Kerner's allegiance, it is because, like the quantum observer, he always gets just "what [he] interrogate[s] for" (10). If Kerner himself can't determine his own allegiance, it is because he recognizes that he is a complex mix of double, triple, quadruple, and so forth. The two dilemmas are related in that even Kerner's best goodwill gesture would fail to help Blair with his determination. As in quantum mechanics, there is no hidden variable theory that might help to determine the situation.

This particular mystery concerning Kerner's allegiance will go unsolved by the British investigators. Moreover, the mystery is complicated in a number of ways that do invoke postmodern sensibilities: Blair, for instance, gets only what he interrogates for; Kerner himself is ultimately uncertain about his own intentions because he has vested interests on both sides; complicating matters still further is the conspiratorial intrigue which finds Kerner being played with by both sides, each trying to maintain the validity of its position by feeding just enough information through him to maintain his credibility as either Russian sleeper or British joe. Kerner says:

> Somehow light is continuous and also discontinuous. The experimenter makes the choice. You get what you interrogate for. And you want to know if I'm a wave or a particle. Every month at the pool, I and my friend Georgi exchange material. When the experiment is over, you have a result. I am your joe. But they also have a result: because you have put in my briefcase enough information to keep me credible as a Russian sleeper activated by my KGB control; which is what Georgi thinks he is. So naturally he gives me enough information to keep me credible as a British joe. Frankly, I can't remember which side I'm supposed to be working for, and it is not in fact necessary for me to know [10].

Ridley, summing up the complex predicament, explains that for all of Hapgood's efforts to keep her team's efforts in the black, "She's lucky if she comes out better than even, that's the edge she's in it for" (70).

We might take the resulting ambiguity as indication that *Hapgood* is, finally, dubious about the possibility of representation in the contemporary world. Indeed, Kerner's plight might best be explained by citing Jameson's description of the postmodern conspiracy thriller. "[I]n representations

5. Normalizing Postmodern Science

like these," he says, "the operative effect is confusion rather than articulation," since a "point" is reached where "we give up and are no longer able to remember which side the characters are on" or in what way "they have been revealed to be hooked up with the other ones." This, in turn, has larger ramifications, for we are thus led "presumably [to have] grasped the deeper truth of the world system (certainly no one will have been astonished or enlightened to discover that the head of the CIA, the Vice President, the Secretary of State, or even the President himself, was secretly behind everything in the first place)" (Jameson *The Geopolitical Aesthetic* 16). Similarly, Kerner is himself confused about just "which side" he is on. Moreover, similar doubts crop up about Hapgood as well when it is revealed in the play that she has a child by Kerner.

However, the mysterious forces at work behind the scenes in this situation simply involve the private human drama of everyday social relations, not first-world conspiratorial intrigue. Thus, as complicated as the depiction of Kerner is, the effect of the play in its entirety does not approach Jameson's view of postmodern conspiracy since the level of complexity fails to encompass Hapgood's immediate superiors (Blair's motives for using Hapgood's son as bait, for instance, are easily understood — as is the final outcome of the situation), let alone to imagine the "deeper complexity of the world system." Suspicions end at the text's margins as well as at the end of the stage. There is no final, lingering conspiracy, since each conspiracy is ultimately placed under control as soon as the complexity dissolves with the convenient death of Ridley and the capture of his brother. This is much different from the effect described by Jameson, wherein further conspiracy theory always derives from complexity itself.[5] Thus, whereas quantum complexities invoke the proliferation of radical conspiracy theories that implicate everyone involved, Stoppard, by contrast, ties things up rather neatly (of course, the effect might be very different if the play had a metatheatrical structure similar to *Hound*).

A better understanding of some of the postmodern opportunities Stoppard avoids may be achieved by coming at this from another angle. To this end, Lyotard's view of the postmodern as consisting of "incredulity towards metanarratives" needs to be understood within in the larger context of the two definitions he provides: one, epistemological, in the primary essay in *The Postmodern Condition*, and two, aesthetic, from his essay "Answering the Question: What Is Postmodernism?" And while it is perhaps easier to recognize quantum mechanics as postmodern according to the epistemological description (as we have already done), fully appreciating the anti-epistemological potential that quantum mechanics holds for the artist necessitates that we proceed by looking at Lyotard's aesthetic definition: "The postmodern would be that which, in the modern, puts forward the unpresentable in presentation itself; that which denies itself the solace of good forms, the consensus of taste which would make it possible to share collectively the nostalgia for the unattainable; that which searches for new representations, not in order to enjoy them but in order to impart a stronger sense of the unpresentable" (*The Postmodern Condition* 81). Lyotard explains by way of example that James Joyce fulfills this definition when he puts "the whole range of available narrative and even stylistic operations into play without concern for the unity of the whole" (80). What Lyotard finds relevant is the way in which coherence at the larger narrative level is sacrificed in favor of the coherence of smaller narratives.

This aesthetic definition still relates to quantum theory, as we will see if we adapt the first sentence that I have quoted above: "[P]ostmodern [physics] would be that which, in [classical physics], puts forward the unpresentable in presentation itself." Indeed, how better to put forward "the unpresentable" than to appropriate a theory that suggests that determinability is always, even inherently, a matter of probability? Continuing our revision, we might point out that quantum theorists (such as Bohr) are those theorists who "[search] for new [quantum] representations, not in order to enjoy them but in order to impart a stronger sense of the unpresentable [nature of quantum behavior]." This presents a poignant adaptation of Lyotard's words and helps to explain the years Bohr spent contending with Einstein's attempts to make quantum mechanics classical once again. Finally, note that all of this quantum mechanical finagling is generally done "without concern for the unity of the [scientific] whole." In other words, classical physics is out the window.

How better, then, to encourage radical anti-epistemological perspectives (if this were one's intent) than through the adoption of the radical anti-epistemologies already implicit in quantum mechanics? Plotnitsky, for instance, helps to underline the radical anti-epistemological nature of one of Derrida's theses — the thesis which suggests that the signifier loses meaning with the loss of its context — when he suggests that its elucidation would benefit from the employment of a quantum mechanical analogy.

5. Normalizing Postmodern Science

Plotnitsky argues that the epistemological doubt that arises in such instances is more analogous to the epistemological indeterminacy that occurs in quantum behavior than it is to undecidability (209–10). In making his case he explains how Derrida's use of Kurt Gödel's incompleteness theorem has less radical anti-epistemological implications than does an analogy to quantum mechanics and indeterminacy:

> It may be that one will have to abandon or extend and radicalize "deconstruction" if "deconstruction" is incompatible with some economies of indeterminacy. At the very least, we need a metaphorical and conceptual field that allows for more complementary engagements of undecidable and indeterminate configurations. The approaches based on complementarity may be more open to such possibilities than those based on undecidability. Perhaps, in the final account, even at their most anti-epistemological, differance and accompanying Derridean structures and efficacities remain too determinate and are, thus, not radical enough to account with sufficient effectiveness and richness for the practice of interpretation or theory [216].

Here the metaphor of undecidability is faulted for not entirely elucidating the full degree of unintelligibility that is suffered by those signifiers that are left devoid of context. As an example of such radical indeterminacy, Plotnitsky examines Derrida's own consideration of the phrase "I forgot my umbrella," which Derrida admits has been "abandoned like an island among the unpublished writings of Nietzsche" so that a "thousand possibilities will always remain open even if one understands something in this phrase." Derrida goes on to list possibilities (the beginning of a novel? a proverb?). Plotnitsky, however, suggests that interpretability suffers much more than even Derrida's thesis admits that if "we look ... beyond Derrida's even if," for "the economy transpiring here would complicate even further and finally limit and disable not only all possible decidable determinations, but also those defined by undecidable determinability or determinate undecidability. The description suggests something much closer to multiple indeterminate play, similar to that of quantum field theory, rather than (only) Gödelian undecidability, although the latter can and must be engaged along the way"(Plotnitsky 219–20).[6]

Imagine, then, the difficulty that would ensue if investigators such as those in *Hapgood* could only determine the probability that a particular crime might occur, but could never be there to stop it, or even be able to reconstruct the event in such a way that they could assign the crime to the culprit beyond all reasonable doubt. In such an event, the culprit would always (necessarily) be one step ahead of the investigator as the very investigative actions would cause the criminal act to revise itself so that the investigator's description would never match the crime. We would be left with something similar to the investigative dilemmas of Oedipa Maas in Thomas Pynchon's *The Crying of Lot 49*, whose whole reality reconstructs itself in direct response to her investigation into the Trystero System. Hapgood's investigation of Ridley, by contrast, yields much more coherent results.

Michael Frayn's play *Copenhagen* provides a more explicitly quantum example of the literary potential implicit in quantum mechanics. Here the mystery in question concerns the motivation that caused Nazi collaborator Werner Heisenberg to visit his old mentor, Bohr, in German-occupied Copenhagen. Both the motivation for the visit and what was discussed remain historical mysteries; in Frayn's play, however, these mysteries become quantum. Just when Heisenberg himself gets a glimpse of why he might have visited Bohr, he "turned to look" and "it went away." The final answer to the mystery is that there is no answer. The uncertainty of human nature is always compounded in ways that are far more difficult to track even than quantum particles. Heisenberg explains the predicament:

> I'm your enemy; I'm also your friend. I'm a danger to mankind; I'm also your guest. I'm a particle; I'm also a wave. We have one set of obligations to the world in general, and we have other sets, never to be reconciled, to our fellow-countrymen, to our neighbours, to our friends, to our family, to our children. We have to go through not two slits at the same time but twenty-two. All we can do is to look afterwards, and see what happened [78].

Frayn gives us only this, only an approximation of the events of 1941, together with an examination of why approximation is the best that can be achieved. Moreover, the conspiratorial inclinations inspired by *Copenhagen* in its audience are never contained as they are in *Hapgood*. Rather, the quantum mysteries investigated in Frayn's play continue to propagate at the multinational level, especially in questioning the very means of scientific legitimation. It is an important fact that Heisenberg's place in the annals of scientific history will always be colored by his political allegiances, and one that the play makes note of.

A similarly inspired attempt at pushing quantum analogies to their anti-epistemological conclusions would have resulted in an espionage thriller much different from what we get in *Hapgood*, for it would be a

5. Normalizing Postmodern Science

thriller in which all mysteries are ultimately left unresolved; in which Kerner's theory about Ridley does not turn out to be true; in which criminal investigation would not proceed according to the classic Sherlock Holmesian idea that we can use a crime's traces to solve the crime (at least not in the sense that Holmes conceived of and practiced it). In such an instance, Ridley might either go free — as the very investigation into his behavior would have interfered with the results — or, at best, he might be captured by mere chance. There would be a final rejection of coherency in one form or another — and, at last, a lingering doubt about whether the scope of the conspiracy had been fully recognized and contained. For one so inclined, quantum mechanics, with its ties to nuclear science, would provide a postmodern author with the perfect platform for an investigation into science's ideological agendas.

This is not to say that Stoppard has misunderstood quantum mechanics, or even that postmodernists have a better understanding of quantum mechanics than does the playwright.[7] Indeed, quantum mechanics does not deny that very accurate prediction can yet occur or that scientific work can yet be accomplished. The difference between Stoppard and a typical postmodernist is that, rightly or wrongly, a thoroughgoing postmodernist would likely focus on the changing epistemological attitude that comes with the advent of quantum mechanics, embracing the idea that while philosophers and scientists of previous generations assumed that we might eventually move beyond predictions which were, at best, probable — after quantum mechanics it has become certain that no matter how much we know about a particular system, probability is the best we can ever hope to achieve. A postmodernist would embrace this change as significant. Stoppard does not.

Anti-epistemological Metaphor in Arcadia

That *Arcadia* uses chaos theory as a metaphor for the difficulties faced by those involved in biographical/bibliographical literary research is, at least on its surface, decidedly contemporary (perhaps even postmodern) for the way in which it suggests that such work is as likely to result in the construction of its subject as in its recovery. That the play shares certain thematic concerns with *Hapgood* (both, for instance, question the likelihood of achieving accurate forensic results through empirical investigation) makes it worth investigating to see whether the later play employs scientific theory to postmodern effect in ways that *Hapgood* does not. It is important to begin, however, with the simple observation that chaos theory is much more a "classical" science than quantum mechanics, for it suggests that empirical investigations into chaotic systems are only practically impossible rather than theoretically impossible. Hence, the extent to which *Arcadia* is postmodern is dependent on the extent to which it emphasizes the theory's assertion of practical impossibility to significant anti-epistemological effect. In any case, it is a promising beginning for my larger thesis that even while he continues to be interested in the odd and the anomalous, Stoppard is continually on the move towards ever more traditional and straightforward theories.

Arcadia tracks the archaeological efforts of two American literary critics, Hannah Jarvis and Bernard Nightingale, as they attempt to piece together the events that occurred at a large country house in Derbyshire in April 1809. Bernard numbers among his "discoveries" not only Lord Byron's presence at the country house on the date in question, but also "proof" that Byron left for Europe after a duel he fought at the manor resulted in the death of the third-rate poet Ezra Chater. Bernard's certainty in this matter relies on a number of historical documents that have come into his possession. These include two letters from Chater challenging their unnamed addressee to a duel for "insulting" his wife. Because Bernard has found these letters in a book of poems that had once been in the possession of Byron, he assumes that they were addressed to Byron. Additionally, the book in question is *The Couch of Eros*, written by the same Ezra Chater who penned the letters. Bernard also has discovered the existence of two reviews of Chater's work, both scathing, written anonymously. Further, the review of *The Couch of Eros* cites many of the same passages that are underlined in the book — an indication that it had been written by someone who had once been in possession of the book, which also bears an inscription: "To my friend Septimus Hodge, who stood up and gave his best on behalf of the Author — Ezra Chater, at Sidley Park, Derbyshire, April 10th, 1809" (9). Bernard assumes that Byron had borrowed the book from Septimus (who could not himself have written so scathingly, given the pleasantries in the inscription) when he wrote the second review. Finally, Bernard has found that there is no other mention

5. Normalizing Postmodern Science

of Chater after the publication of *The Couch of Eros*. His theory is that Byron, after seducing Chater's wife and after being challenged by the husband to a duel, shot and killed him, with the result being a self-imposed exile to the Continent. (Part of the coup of Bernard's discovery stems from the fact that this removal of the famous poet from England had yet to be satisfactorily explained in the biographical literature.)

Theory in hand, Bernard ventures to Sidley Park to find out more about the people in question. He discovers that within a year of the date in question Mrs. Chater remarried, corroborating the belief that her husband had died around the time of the alleged duel. When he finds that Septimus and Byron were contemporaries at Cambridge and that Byron had visited Sidley Park on the date in question (hunting records indicate that he shot a hare on that date), he feels that he has all the proof he needs to publish his findings.

However, because the play dramatizes both the biographical investigation undertaken in the current era as well as the events of 1809 which Bernard and Hannah are intent on investigating, the audience soon sees the mistakes Bernard makes while constructing his "proof." Much of the confusion stems from the inscription that Chater wrote to Septimus. The members of the audience, however, know the disingenuous circumstances under which the inscription was written, since they have witnessed the scene where, when confronted, Septimus admits to Chater that he is to be the reviewer of Chater's latest work, which he has called a work of genius. Chater is placated enough to write the favorable inscription until he hears that Septimus had scorned him in an earlier review. This compels the challenge of the second letter.

Even in the face of legitimate skepticism from Hannah, Bernard remains obstinate: "Proof? Proof? You'd have to be there, you silly bitch!" (49). Bernard refuses to accept Hannah's compelling case for restraint: "Nobody would kill a man and then pan his book. I mean, not in that order. So he must have borrowed the book, written the review, posted it, seduced Mrs. Chater, fought a duel and departed, all in the space of three days. Who would do that?" But Bernard's response is, quite simply, irrefutable: "Byron" (59). Given the reverence with which he holds Byron, everything easily fits his theory — especially that Byron might have so quickly seduced Mrs. Chater. And it is no wonder that everything must fit since Bernard has already committed himself to a conference

113

on the following day at which he plans to present his theory. His legacy awaits.

Upon returning from his lecture, however, Hannah finally presents him with the evidence that causes his house of cards to collapse — proof that Ezra Chater died in Martinique in 1910. Humbled but obstinate, Bernard bitterly proclaims, "I've proved Byron was here and as far as I'm concerned he wrote those lines as sure as he shot that hare. If only I hadn't somehow ... made it all about killing Chater. Why didn't you stop me?!" (90). Suddenly, even Bernard is attuned to the construction and admits distress at the fact that he has "made it all about killing Chater." However, his remaining obstinacy over the author of the reviews and about who shot the hare only further emphasizes the way in which constructions are created by interpretive excess. For the audience knows that even Byron's shooting of the hare is debatable since Augustus claims that the hare was his own. Thus Stoppard satirizes the scholarly tendency to make a mountain of criticism out of a molehill of evidence merely in order to publish. The final implication is that the records that result from such investigations are untrustworthy. That the ravages of time and chaos on the bibliographical/biographical record finally prove too great to overcome; hence everything Bernard pieces together is composed of red herrings and ambition. At its very core the play is about the practical impossibility of doing historical research, since all the hidden variables make such research infinitely difficult.

Indeed, as James Gleick explains it in *Chaos: Making a New Science*, which Stoppard admits to having read before writing *Arcadia*, a central tenet of chaos theory is that predicting the behavior of physical objects is complicated by the fact that even small events (those suspect molehills, for instance) can have very large effects: "Tiny differences in input could quickly become overwhelming differences in output — a phenomenon given the name 'sensitive dependence' on initial conditions. In weather, for example, this translates into what is half-jokingly known as the Butterfly Effect — the notion that a butterfly stirring the air today in Peking can transform stormy systems next month in New York" (8). Susanne Vees-Gulani, appropriating this concept to explain why Stoppard would use chaos theory to disrupt the possibility of bibliographical recovery, points out that it increases the difficulty not only of predicting the future, but also of describing the past. She sees the "consequence of sensitive depend-

5. Normalizing Postmodern Science

ence on initial conditions" as "the irreversibility of chaotic systems." Hence she asserts the impossibility of speculation "not only about the future of the system, but also about its past. Even though the output of a system is determined by its input, it is impossible to reconstruct this input exactly" (413). This theory stands behind Stoppard's depiction of the difficulty that Bernard and Hannah experience in recovering the past.[8] When Septimus, for instance, lends his book to Byron, it travels a complex path that becomes impossible for the investigator to trace so many years later.

By implication, chaos theory would appear to complement those contemporary theories which suggest that biographical interpretation results in the construction of its subject, since true recovery is impossible. As such, Bernard's actions become describable according to a wide range of contemporary constructionist (some would even call them "postmodern") theories of truth from W. K. Wimsatt, Jr., and Monroe C. Beardsley's "The Intentional Fallacy,"[9] to Michel Foucault's concerns about the subjective identity of the author,[10] to the interpretive theories of Stanley Fish, who argues "that all objects are made and not found, and that they are made by the interpretive strategies we set in motion" (331). Apparently what has set Bernard in motion is the "interpretive strategy" of "publish or perish," which, together with a system too complex to describe, motivates Bernard and leads him to his false narrative. The implications are, at least on the surface, more radically anti-epistemological than *Hapgood*, which never suggests that Hapgood's conclusions about Ridley are similarly constructed.

Much of the critical theory that defends the thesis that truth is constructed can be loosely categorized as postmodern according to Lyotard's description of the postmodern era as having become "incredulous of metanarratives," having instead developed a preference for "the little (or local) narrative." According to this view, constructivist theories of truth are postmodern since they no longer accept the belief that biographical research yields accurate grand narratives about those issues under investigation; instead, constructivists believe that such research only provides "local narratives" such as those created by Bernard. It appears, then, that Stoppard's implementation of chaos theory creates a postmodern effect.

However, as tempting as it might be to simply label *Arcadia* "postmodern" because of its suggestion that literary critics create the truths that they publish, the issue grows more complicated when we examine *Arcadia* according to Jameson's explanation that parody has been replaced by pastiche in the postmodern era. As Jameson explains it, "Pastiche is, like parody, the imitation of a peculiar or unique style, the wearing of a stylistic mask, speech in a dead language: but it is a neutral practice of such mimicry, without parody's ulterior motive, without the satirical impulse, without laughter, without the still latent feeling that there exists something normal compared to which what is being imitated is rather comic" ("Postmodernism and Consumer Society" 114). As Jameson explains it, because Stoppard's treatment of Bernard is in fact more suggestive of parody than pastiche, we are left with the distinct impression that there is a normal way of doing biographical research — a way that might yield more accurate results — according to which Bernard comes across as "rather comic." That this characteristic is, moreover, inconsistent with Lyotard's understanding of postmodernism becomes clear in that its satirical edge works to reject the validity of local and private beliefs in favor of normal and universally shared ones.

Clearly, identifying the norms that Stoppard's satire presupposes is complicated by the fact that the play exists at a number of epistemological and aesthetic crossroads. This is most explicitly true in its content, since both the setting of 1809 and that of the early 1990s are each eras when the epistemological dominant was in a state of transition, from Enlightenment to romanticism and from modernism to postmodernism respectively. It is not surprising, then, that the play's own attitude about the state of knowledge and the nature of truth fluctuates between nostalgia for both Enlightenment and romantic theories of knowledge and a reveling in the anti-epistemological theories that denote postmodernism. In order to better understand those epistemological norms to which *Arcadia* subscribes, I will look first at its treatment of Enlightenment norms before moving on to examine its treatment of romantic and, finally, chaotic and/or postmodern norms.

Enlightenment epistemologies commit to rationality as the means by which truth is discovered. Thus, *Arcadia* portrays an Enlightenment attitude whenever it suggests that rationality might be able to assist Bernard and Hannah in their recovery of the past. In fact, such instances are numerous. For even while the work critically satirizes their efforts, the satire often suggests that if they only worked in a careful enough manner they might do a better job of recovering the truth than they do. Hannah sums up the

5. Normalizing Postmodern Science

preferred method quite nicely when she explains that Bernard's theory about Byron "[c]an't prove to be true, it can only not prove to be false yet" (74). Valentine, explaining that this is "[j]ust like science," recognizes in her statement the scientific method that is ultimately privileged as a central norm by both Bernard and Hannah.[11] Finally, it is according to the scientific method that Bernard's theory is proven false when Hannah eventually discovers how Chater really died. Moreover, even while Bernard yet holds firm to an erroneous theory, that Byron wrote the two reviews in question, the scientific method is further validated as a norm since now his theory is a closer approximation of the truth (that is, it more closely matches that "truth" which the audience witnesses and which exists as the general standard of truth for all of the contemporary investigation). Progress has been made.

Moreover, the scientific method is privileged once again as Hannah's own theory about the true identity of the hermit grows more and more refined. True to form, her theory that it was Septimus is initially regarded as tenuous, and Valentine, challenging her on it, asks, "Did Bernard bite you in the leg?" (66). However, her theory is soon corroborated by the discovery of a drawing of Septimus with Plautus, the turtle, for the hermit was already in fact known to have owned a turtle by this name. Thus false theories are disproven, while those that correspond with the reality of the scenes from 1809 gain credibility. The grand narrative that scientific progress can be achieved by continually subjecting our best theories to a method of conjecture and refutation is alive and well. Knowledge as construction is at least partially rebutted since theories that began as interpretive constructions are reconstructed to mirror the truth more accurately. Or, as Paul Edwards puts it, "[t]he promise, then, (however questionable it is in reality) is that information and, by extension, nature itself, can overcome the tendency to an increase in entropy." Edwards also notes that "at the end of the story, after all of the research, and despite entropy, just about everything has been recovered" (181). Edwards, however, goes on to suggest that "the overcoming of time at the conclusion of *Arcadia* is a triumph of art, not of science" (183), seemingly ignoring the fact that while it might not precisely be science which turns back time and makes the past recoverable, it is the scientific method.[12]

Plenty of romantic attitudes are, however, prevalent in the work as well. Perhaps in partial defense of the leap of faith required to believe his

Byron theory, Bernard is the staunchest defender of a romantic epistemology. In response to Valentine's accusation that his research questions are trivial and that "[w]hat matters is the calculus. Scientific progress. Knowledge," Bernard is quick to cite "the bomb and aerosols" as part of his rationale for espousing such an epistemology and concludes by summing up his preference for romantic ideals:

> If knowledge isn't self-knowledge, it isn't doing much, mate. Is the universe expanding? Is it contracting? Is it standing on one leg and singing "When Father Painted the Parlour"? Leave me out. I can expand my universe without you. "She walks in Beauty, like the night of cloudless climes and starry skies, and all that's best of dark and bright meet in her aspect and her eyes." There you are, he wrote it after coming home from a party [61].

According to this perspective, truths not only are privately constructed, they are also to be pursued for their own sake rather than with the intent of accurately describing the world at large.

Another concept from romanticism that persists is the idea of the hero who toils alone and in obscurity while creating works of genius. Bernard no doubt would like to fill this role, but he fails miserably, as does the hack Chater. However, the play does include characters who are prototypes of the hero, first and most obviously the hermit, who compelled Hannah's research for her forthcoming book, *The Genius of the Place*. However, we soon learn that the true genius was Thomasina. When Valentine finally admits that even while "[s]he didn't have the maths, not even remotely," "she saw what things meant, way ahead, like seeing a picture" (93), Thomasina's kinship with Byron as a personality type is assured. Her brilliance has allowed her to come to an intuitive understanding of the fundamental principles both of chaos theory and of the second law of thermodynamics—no small feat. The first is especially surprising, since, as Valentine had already mentioned:

> There wasn't enough time before. There weren't enough pencils! ... Now she'd only have to press a button, the same button over and over. Iteration. A few minutes. And what I've done in a couple months, with only a pencil the calculations would take me the rest of my life to do again — thousands of pages — tens of thousands! And so boring [51].

Indeed, Thomasina's "picture" is hardly a rationally explicated and rigorously tested proof of chaos. This is why at first glance Septimus responds, "This is not science. This is story-telling" (93), and it is why

5. Normalizing Postmodern Science

Valentine is so slow to recognize her genius. Thomasina, the true genius of Sidley Park, is, then, in every sense the true romantic hero-genius, toiling alone and in obscurity, creating success with limited means.

In addition to the play's investigation of constructivism, *Arcadia* also makes overtures to postmodernism even as Stoppard draws attention to what chaos theory shares with romanticism. Stoppard's understanding of chaos theory, as noted above, relies primarily on James Gleick's *Chaos: Making a New Science*. The many direct points of contact with Gleick's work have been noted by Prapassaree and Jeffrey Kramer, who have pointed out Stoppard's use of loose quotations, topical commonalities (including chaos' implications for population theory), and even the idea of using changes in the aesthetics of gardening to represent metaphorically the larger ideological shift from the Enlightenment to the romantic (1–10). They also note that Gleick himself had stressed the importance of chaos theory for its elimination of "the Laplacian fantasy of deterministic predictability."[13]

Yet while this final connection to Gleick's work suggests why Stoppard might have chosen to seek such an encounter between Enlightenment era thought and chaos theory, Prapassaree and Kramer neglect something more significant. For Mitchell Feigenbaum (who, in Gleick's view, emerges as the key figure in chaos theory) might not have persevered with the anti-epistemological ideas that culminated in chaos theory had he not been "listening to Mahler and reading Goethe" and thereby "immersing himself in their high Romantic attitudes. Inevitably it was Goethe's *Faust* he most reveled in, soaking up its combination of the most passionate ideas about the world with the most intellectual" (Gleick 163). These works, according to Gleick, inspired "romantic inclinations" and encouraged Feigenbaum to notice phenomena he might otherwise have missed. He also began reading Goethe's scientific works, including his treatise on color, which has largely been forgotten in the wake of Newton's optics. Gleick observes that for all of Newton's acceptability within the scientific establishment, "Feigenbaum persuaded himself that Goethe had been right about color" (165). The implication is that the Enlightenment never really ended with the rise of romanticism, and that contemporary chaos theorists such as Feigenbaum have found themselves waging similar epistemological battles against Enlightenment-minded holders of the torch.

Thus, Gleick implies that between the romantic era and chaos theory there exists a similarity of anti-epistemological thought, and that a chasm exists between the romantic/chaotic and the traditionally epistemological Enlightenment. An epistemological kinship between romanticism and postmodernism itself can be recognized if we remember Lyotard's own comments on chaos theory, which he recognizes as uniquely postmodern and also as a better example than quantum mechanics of a theory that is incredulous of any and all grand deterministic narratives:

> It will be argued that these problems (the predictive limitations of quantum mechanics) concern microphysics and that they do not prevent the establishment of continuous functions exact enough to form the basis of probabilistic predictions for the evolution of a given system. This is the reasoning systems theorists-who are also the theorists of legitimization by performance — use to try to regain their rights. There is, however, a current in contemporary mathematics that questions the very possibility of precise measurement and thus the prediction of the behavior of objects even on the human scale [57].

Lyotard does not refer to this "current in contemporary mathematics" specifically as chaos theory, but he does attribute it to Benoît Mandelbrot, who, according to Gleick, was one of chaos theory's key figures for his investigation of fractal figures that "lie intuitively between a line and a flat surface" (58). Precise measurements of such objects become problematic for Mandelbrot because they are infinite in length and so defy the narrative explication that comes with measurement.

This particular understanding of the kinship between romantic-era epistemology and chaos theory explains much about Stoppard's *Arcadia*. For why else would Stoppard portray these two distinct eras simultaneously except that he saw, as did Feigenbaum, a common thread between the two? Stoppard takes from Gleick the idea that a commitment to chaos theory brought with it a dismissal of Enlightenment era thinking. Not surprisingly, in an interview with Nigel Hawkes about *Arcadia*, Stoppard explained how anti–Enlightenment ideas are recycled in different eras. "In any age, including the period around the year 1800, we had a kind of reaction against scientism by the poets of the time," he explained, "so you find that Blake and Wordsworth and Coleridge as young men are resisting the thinking of that time that science was rapidly finding out all the answers, and would solve all the mysteries. The sense, or illusion, that science is doing exactly that seems to accompany every age, and creates an opposing force" (Hawkes 268). Given the context of the discussion, Stoppard's implication would appear to be that romanticism has been recycled in the con-

5. *Normalizing Postmodern Science*

temporary era in the form of chaos theory. At odds with the way that *Arcadia* privileges the scientific method, the play also uses chaos theory to reject the idea that biographical recovery might ever result in absolute accuracy. Moreover, it is also clear that Stoppard understands that between the second law of thermodynamics (because of the fact that the culture which gave us the plays will track towards greater disorder) and chaos theory (because of the fact that once this disorder arrives, it is practically impossible to sort out again) "[t]he missing plays of Sophocles [won't] turn up piece by piece," (38) as Septimus once believed. Additionally, since "the Improved Newtonian Universe" that Thomasina has discovered "must cease and grow cold," (93) there is no reason to believe that Sophocles' plays might be "written again in another language" (38). Given this rejection of the Enlightenment belief that knowledge accumulates, perhaps it is worth exploring the possibility that postmodernism is the play's epistemological norm after all, and that Jameson's assertion that satire precludes this possibility is simply wrong (not to mention the apparent privileging of the scientific method).

Chaos theory is not, however, as postmodern as Lyotard believes, nor is it even as romantic as is suggested by Gleick and Stoppard. Indeed, in many respects it remains a prototypically classical science that, for all its caveats about the inherent difficulty of predicting complex systems, yet purports to describe the world. For while chaos theory concedes that complete description becomes a practical impossibility given the complexity of the equations that are necessary to track chaotic systems and the endlessness of the relevant data, determinability yet remains a theoretical possibility. As such, this characteristic of chaos theory means that its epistemological valency is a far cry from quantum mechanics, where, as we have seen, indeterminability is so endemic that probability is not simply a necessary (practical) default but the rule. Moreover, chaos theory does not, then, preclude the possibility that the scientific method might provide more accurate descriptions over time; while, by contrast, the anti-epistemological elements of quantum mechanics (the inability to know both the speed and position of a quantum particle isn't simply a matter of missing information) go all the way through. Perhaps it is in recognition of this very characteristic of chaos theory that Stoppard lets biographical recovery run the semi-determinable course that it does, seemingly at odds with the anti-epistemological sentiment of chaos theory generally.

This is not to say that one could not use chaos theory to postmodern effect, nor is it to say that Lyotard is completely wrong in recognizing in it a disruption of the Laplacian dream. My main point, rather, is that in a truly postmodern work we should expect a celebration of those chaotic disruptions that inhibit the biographer rather than satirical nostalgia for what has been lost. To this end, the chaotic ramifications of the feedback loop would provide a particularly suitable analogy for postmodern experimentation. Weather prediction, for instance, is as complex as it is because any single error that gets fed into the system goes through a feedback loop which instantaneously presents predictions that are vastly different than reality. Gleick observes:

> But suppose the earth could be covered with sensors spaced one foot apart, rising at one-foot intervals all the way to the top of the atmosphere. Suppose every sensor gives perfectly accurate readings of temperature, pressure, humidity, and any other quantity a meteorologist would want.... The computer will still be unable to predict whether Princeton, New Jersey, will have sun or rain on a day a month away. At noon the spaces between the sensors will hide fluctuations that the computer will not know about, tiny deviations from the average. By 12:01, those fluctuations will already have created small errors one foot away. Soon the errors will have multiplied to the ten-foot scale, and so on up to the size of the globe [21].

That chaotic systems are hard to predict, then, is in part because of the feedback loop. No matter how small the original error, eventually its effects are enormous, like the boy who asked for a single grain of rice to be doubled for each space on a chessboard and thereby bankrupted a kingdom.

In *At Swim-Two-Birds*, Flann O'Brien provides a particularly cogent example of how a feedback loop might complicate traditional narrative. O'Brien writes of a fictional novelist, Trellis, whose characters take on consciousness and, unhappy with their plight, proceed to drug their author so that he will no longer be able to interfere with their lives. Further, they employ yet another character to write a fiction about Trellis in which he becomes the victim of torture as well as a defendant in a court proceeding on the charge of unfair treatment of his characters. The work's radical ontology is evident in how it emphasizes the constructed nature of reality by allowing a narrative about a given reality to have ontological power over that very reality for which it serves as narrative.[14] Imagine the antiepistemological implications that would result if Thomasina's era similarly changed shape to match the very narrative that Bernard is telling. If that were the case, the work might even have played up the chaos analogy in

5. Normalizing Postmodern Science

particular by invoking a metanarrative iterative (or feedback) function.

Gleick describes a relevant scenario in which "a microphone, amplifier, and speakers" are being positioned "in an auditorium," with the possibility of "the squeal of sonic feedback. If the microphone picks up a loud enough noise, the amplified sound from the speakers will feed back into the microphone in an endless, ever louder, loop" (223). It is this very feedback loop that is more than partly responsible for the difficulty involved in tracking chaotic systems. (How is one to determine what goes into the feedback loop and what doesn't?) Consider, by contrast, the radical anti-epistemological message that develops in a work wherein the biographical narrative changes the past in such a way that the present itself changes — a process that causes the past to again be reinterpreted so that it once again changes, and there again changes the present in an ever deafening loop.

The sonic squeal that would result from such self-conscious meta-criticism is that same postmodern squeal of metanarrative feedback that denies Trellis the narrative voice he needs to defend himself when he is on trial for his own metanarrative crimes ("but, unfortunately, as a result of his being unable to rise or, for that matter, to raise his voice above the level of a whisper, nobody in the court was aware that he had spoken at all") (298–299). Neil Murphy notes another means of magnification which results as the feedback loop comes full circle in *At Swim-Two-Birds*, which is that even as "the invented bastard son Orlick tells his story, Trellis and many of his characters are duplicated, so we now have different versions of the same characters at different ontological levels in the text" (14). By comparison, the set which makes up *Arcadia*— and even the desk which collects a collage of items from each century — is downright tidy.

Jameson provides a similar account of the gesture contained in Edvard Munch's *The Scream*, which "subtly but elaborately disconnects its own aesthetic of expression. [...] Yet the absent scream returns, as it were, in a dialectic of loops and spirals, circling ever more closely toward that even more absent experience of atrocious solitude and anxiety which the scream was itself to express" (*Postmodernism* 14). And as we have already seen, a similar reverberation inspires the inevitable crying of Lot 49 as Oedipa's efforts cloud her investigation and thus change both the future and the past. Similar examples appear elsewhere, as in Caryl Churchill's *Serious Money* when — even as Scilla pursues the cause of her brother's mysterious death — as she tracks her target she herself becomes implicated in the crime.

This only further complicates the mystery, of course. For how can she hope to separate the true conspiracy from the reverberation that results from her own feedback? Especially when the work not only rejects epistemological certainty but also points to the ideological agendas implicit in such investigations?

By comparison, Stoppard's narrative is decidedly traditional. The reverberations that result from the various chaotic deteriorations are simple enough that careful application of the scientific method can result in progress. It is almost as if Stoppard refuses to experience any of "the atrocious solitude and anxiety" which is the postmodern product of such feedback (and so he turns his back on the recursive forms of *Hound* and *The Real Thing*). A thoroughly postmodern work might, by contrast, simultaneously raise ontological questions about the nature of the past and epistemological questions about how we are to know that past—and remain incredulous about that past's grand metanarrative.[15] Indeed, that a postmodern squeal is the end result of such biographical investigation is evident in the critical treatment of such authors as Joyce and Shakespeare, whose works have spawned interpretive industries where the squeal is so deafening that it is impossible to get a word in edgewise (although Stoppard himself does so with great panache in *Travesties*). And while Stoppard is dismissive of the excesses of critical investigation,[16] his treatment of such excess does not exemplify the resulting postmodern squeal; instead, Bernard's falsehoods about Byron prove so small in the face of conjecture and refutation that they die away to nothing as Stoppard once again refuses to accept postmodern incredulity.

Because Stoppard's use of chaos theory is not especially antiepistemological, it might even be argued that Stoppard delves into chaos theory only because he is convinced that chaos theorists really have seen "what things meant"—and that if the universe happens to be so complex that it fails to be deterministic, so be it. At least we know the "truth."[17] As a matter of fact, Stoppard's portrayal of Thomasina replicates Gleick's assessment of the chaos theorists he valorizes in his book: that people like them "saw what things meant, way ahead, like seeing a picture." In turn, Thomasina's distant cousin, the mute Gus, sees things with romantic clarity, except when there is too much noise.

This celebration of genius points to another way that one norm of *Arcadia* works at cross purposes with the rest. For while the romantic era

5. Normalizing Postmodern Science

privileged individual truths over scientifically determined ones, the metanarrative status of those truths for people like Bernard who accept them is equal to those who accepted the norms of the Enlightenment, for each serves the same function as grand narratives. By contrast, a postmodern attitude rejects the hero-genius grand narrative as fully as it does Enlightenment grand narratives. This complication is compounded by the fact that the romantic genius trope would likely have functioned ideologically as well. And yet, when Stoppard characterizes the genius, he never undertakes an investigation of this possibility. What, for instance, are we to make of the pre–Victorian regime which conspired in such a way that Thomasina was finally consumed by flames rather than by marriage? As it turns out, there are plenty of similar occasions where Stoppard might have chosen to reflect upon the way that ideology shapes knowledge. For Stoppard, however, chaos theory either is or is not true. Thomasina either discovered it, or she didn't. The possibility that chaos theory became true only once the patriarchal establishment found a use for it is never even considered. Truths are universal in Stoppard's conception of what arcadia would look like.

Moreover, Stoppard never suggests that chaos theory might initially have been refused for ideological reasons (the fault lies all too simply with technology), or that it might finally have gained credence for ideological reasons when the world had finally created the necessary technology. This refusal to examine the way that ideology establishes truth is especially pronounced in *Hapgood*, for there is much that might yet be said about nuclear theory's (and, indirectly, quantum mechanics') legitimation at the hands of those who saw the benefits of nuclear power. Stoppard's sentiments on these issues, however, prove far removed from the sort of postmodern writers Linda Hutcheon focuses on, for instance, who never pass up the opportunity to use the anti-epistmological implications of their work to simultaneously question the ideological impulses that have turned international espionage into a legitimate means of pursuing nuclear research, or to question the "old boy" network that continues to be a legitimating force within mathematics.

That Stoppard goes out of his way to normalize what might be employed to radical ontological, epistemological, and even ideological effect means that these plays fit within the trajectory of a career which, as we have seen, has become increasingly committed to known and knowable realities. As such, I am very nearly tempted to argue that these are Stoppard's most traditional plays, as Stoppard has taken it upon himself to normalize the anti-epistemological attitudes within the must cutting edge fields of contemporary science, even while remaining fully committed to a very traditional scientific methodology of conjecture and refutation — a methodology he will continue to invoke in his next two plays, *Indian Ink* and *The Invention of Love*.

6

Metahistorical Detectives

"I want it to be as inaccurate as possible."
— Tom Stoppard on his forthcoming biography

Stoppard first started working on *In the Native State*, the radio drama precursor to *Indian Ink*, in 1988, and it was broadcast in 1991. He began working on *Arcadia* in 1989 and it was first staged in 1993. *Indian Ink* was finally staged in 1995, followed by *The Invention of Love* in 1997. The plays share a common theme, as they each track the successes and failures of literary critics engaged in historiographic research. In *Arcadia* and *Indian Ink*, the work of these critics (each one a fictional character) is largely derided as both prone to error and potentially "trivial." In *The Invention of Love*, however, Stoppard proves to be much more sympathetic to the famous classicist A. E. Housman than he is to the fictional critics he satirizes in *Arcadia* and *Indian Ink*, seemingly coming around to the opinion that, trivial or not, the pursuit of "useless knowledge" is "where we're nearest to our humanness" (71). Despite their differences, each place is ultimately concerned with the knowability of history. As such, the central issue of each of these plays is epistemological, concerning how it is that we know the physical world.

Of course Stoppard had made intellectuals and academics the targets of his satirical broadsides before. In *Jumpers* George Moore is characterized as so obsessed with defending an objective morality that his mental absenteeism means that he is clueless about the ethical dilemmas confronting him in his own home. In *Travesties* Joyce, Lenin and Tzara each have their aesthetic principles satirized as either too abstruse (Joyce), lacking in intellectual rigor (Tzara) or hypocritical and morally bankrupt (Lenin). However, in these more recent plays there is such a consistency to his concern with the veracity and value of what the literary critic accomplishes that it is hard to ignore the possibility that Stoppard may well be responding to events in his own life.

According to this line of thought the issue is somehow related to the collapse of his marriage to Miriam Stoppard and his subsequent relationship with Felicity Kendal (Stoppard was legally separated from Miriam in 1990). In his biography on Tom Stoppard (of which Stoppard famously quipped that he hoped "it would be as inaccurate as possible"), Ira Nadel explains the media circus which sprung up around his attachment to Felicity Kendal (Stoppard's favorite actress throughout the 80s and 90s):

> Stoppard and Kendal had been seen together frequently that autumn [1990]. The papers loved the story and tabloid reporters would camp out in front of Kendal's house with tape recorders and cameras at the ready. Contradictory headlines soon appeared, like "Why I Won't Be Marrying Tom," or "Playing for Real" [384].

Stoppard had already had a go at the press's obsession with rumor-mongering in *Night and Day* (where Ruth decries the "slavering minions of a Philistine press lord (48) "which pursued her at the commencement of her affair with her current husband, Carson) — and, moreover, had already dealt with infidelity in *The Real Thing* (which many a critic has assumed was biographical given his eventual affair with Felicity Kendal, who was the leading lady in the premiere London production) — and so, presumably, it would hardly do to go down either of those paths again under such transparent circumstances.

In the intervening years, however, Stoppard had also become quite the target for American academics in the mold of *Indian Ink*'s Eldon Pike who were "doing Tom Stoppard" (all too familiar words to the ears of this Stoppard scholar) the way Pike was "doing Flora Crewe" (26). And while his own biography would not be published until 2002, the fact that he put his manuscript archive up for sale in 1990 through Sotheby's — together with the fallout in the press when it was announced that he had passed on selling the archive to the British Library in favor of the Harry Ransom Center at the University of Texas at Austin (Nadel 393 — 394) — would very naturally have had him thinking about how his papers were likely to be read (and misread) by American academics out to make a name for themselves. One need only note Pike's fixation on the more salacious details of Flora's life — when hearing that Modigliani had painted her in the nude he responds "(reverently) A nude!" (*Indian Ink* 10) — to see the potential in reading *Indian Ink* in this fashion.

6. Metahistorical Detectives

Stoppard's eventual attitude towards Nadel's biography is telling, most notably the fact that Nadel stops just short of thanking Stoppard, writing that "Tom Stoppard has been from the first a skeptical but supportive witness to the entire project, who surprised me at one of our encounters with the question, "So, when is it to be done?" (595). Soon enough Nadel proves himself to have the perfect disposition to be the biographer for a playwright such as Stoppard who had shown such contempt for academics in the past. He was well aware of the fact that *Arcadia* and *Indian Ink* serve as potential indictments of any shoddy work on his behalf, and even quoted Stoppard in an *Irish Times* interview as saying, about misinformation in the media about his private life, "I never demand corrections. I quite like it really. If enough things that are untrue are said about you, no one will know what really is true" (xiii). Quoting Hanna (from *Arcadia*) that "It's wanting to know that makes us matter" (a sentiment shared by Housman, of which more below), Nadel defends his work in a manner which he believes Stoppard would approve of:

> So even if Stoppard unintentionally misleads, setting false traps for his biographer and offering explanations that don't quite match with the record or with other statements of his, it is nonetheless the effort of getting it right that matters. When he jested that he hoped the would-be biography would be as inaccurate as possible, he also added that he knew he was behaving badly [xiii].

A fair enough — if somewhat optimistic — response to the dilemma posed by writing such a biography. For I find it hard to believe that the same person who so clearly privileges the idea that certain facts are best kept within the family — as Mrs. Swan does in *Indian Ink* in her explanation to Anish about why she did not divulge her possession of the erotic watercolor which the Rajah had given to Flora, saying that "I didn't tell Eldon. He's not family." — would stop at "unintentionally mislead[ing]" Nadel when, rather, the sort of intentional misleading such as can be found in *Indian Ink* could prove to be so much more effective at covering up what "really is true." In any case, whether or not Stoppard went out of his way to mislead his biographer — and the extent to which these three plays comment on that fact — is largely beside the point. For as we shall see, the ways in which *Arcadia*, *Indian Ink*, and *The Invention of Love* challenge standard (and not-so-standard) research methods speaks for themselves.

Another Look at Arcadia

In Stoppard's hands, the way in which *Arcadia* and *Indian Ink* focus on the historiographic pursuits of literary critics means that the plays have something in common with the detective genre, as Bernard seeks to uncover evidence which would prove his theory that Lord Byron shot and killed Chater in a duel (quite the detective mystery, one must admit), and Pike seeks evidence which would prove his theory that Flora had been painted in the nude by an Indian painter (which would have been something of a scandal in 1930s India). As was discussed in Chapter 1's treatment of *The Real Inspector Hound*, Brian McHale sees detective novels as the quintessential modernist genre for how they "revolve around problems of the accessibility of knowledge, the individual mind's grappling with an elusive or occluded reality" (*Constructing Postmodernism* 147). However, unlike *The Real Inspector Hound*, which I argue shares more with what McHale refers to as "anti-detective" stories in how it "foregrounds its own ontological status," in the discussion which follows I will aim to show not only that both *Arcadia*'s and *Indian Ink*'s "quest[s] for a missing hidden item of knowledge" are more or less successfully concluded — a fact which not only identifies them as modernist texts according to McHale's definition — but that they are fairly traditional modernist texts at that.

What this means is that in addition to the way in which *Arcadia* normalizes postmodern science (as discussed in the previous chapter), there is yet another way in which the play appropriates a modernist aesthetic, as the play shifts from investigating what authors do in the construction of their public personae (see my chapter on *The Real Thing*), to investigating the role that literary critics play in the creation of an author's persona. For even as Hannah and Bernard attempt to piece together the various events that occurred at the Coverly Estate in April 1809, because the play dramatizes both the biographical investigation undertaken in the current era, as well as the events of 1809 which they are investigating, the audience soon sees how Bernard's "proof" is constructed rather than recovered.

Indeed, such construction is commented upon fairly explicitly in the opening scene of *Arcadia*, where we find one of the characters from 1809, Thomasina Coverly, at her studies with her tutor, Septimus, who encourages her to formulate a proof of Fermat's last theorem. Thomasina realizes, however, that "Fermat's Last Theorem" is only a red herring:

6. *Metahistorical Detectives*

SEPTIMUS: My lady, take Fermat into the music room. There will be an extra spoonful of jam if you find his proof.
THOMASINA: There is no proof, Septimus. The thing that is perfectly obvious is that the note in the margin was a joke to make you all mad [*Arcadia* 6].

This moment becomes prophetic, for as we have seen it neatly sums up the implications of Bernard's biographical work as well. Apparently, there are numerous other bits and pieces in the historical record which serve no other purpose than to make the Bernard's of the world mad, and that Bernard's own critical imagination had been working overtime as he examined every marginal clue he could find, before finally proclaiming:

I've proved Byron was here and as far as I'm concerned he wrote those lines as sure as he shot that hare. If only I hadn't somehow ... made it all about *killing Chater*. Why didn't you stop me?! [*Arcadia* 89].

Finally, then, "the thing that is perfectly obvious" is that "there is no proof" for any of Bernard's biographical discoveries, except for that "proof" which he himself has constructed. The audience knows that Byron wasn't even at the country house on the date in question and, therefore, that he couldn't have shot the hare, let alone have shot Chater. Thus, Stoppard nicely satirizes the tendency scholars have of making a mountain of criticism out of a molehill of evidence merely in order to publish. Moreover, Stoppard implies not only that authors are constructed objects, but also that they are constructed through the biographical/bibliographical work of their critics.

At this point, the critic might be tempted to conclude that because of the play's overt investigation of the way in which literary critics and historians construct rather than discover their subject, this means that the play shares its ontological premises with a wide range of postmodern fiction which similarly privileges ontological constructivism. However, it is my position that while a prototypical postmodern author may well go out of his way to continually problematize his audience's perspective of the way in which narrative constructs reality — in turn, constructivism itself would become a poorly understood phenomenon (think of the way in which Oedipa Maas in Thomas Pynchon's *The Crying of Lot 49* is at a complete loss at the end of the novel as to whether her detective work has discovered a conspiracy or merely "projected" one) — Stoppard, rather, goes out of his way to clarify (or, rather, to "normalize") the systematic mistakes which Bernard followed in constructing his version of reality. Consequently, while readers of Pynchon leave a novel such as *The Crying of Lot 49* with their worldview in ontological turmoil—perhaps asking at every turn whether or not the way they witness reality is a product of their own imagination or, rather, whether it is some sort of local narrative—Stoppard's audience leaves the theater comfortable in the knowledge that even while the occasional critic may go out of his way to construct a version of reality which will get him published, at the end of the day these constructions are both of little consequence and likely to "normalize" themselves over time into mutually shared truths which have been subjected to an objective method of conjecture and refutation. At the end of the day, even while *Arcadia* does raise important epistemological questions concerning the validity of research methods and the reliability of what is accepted as knowledge, Stoppard's epistemological conservatism means that ontological reality is seen as a tangible, stable, and, even, knowable phenomenon.[1] Consequently, perhaps the most traditional aspect of the play is the way in which it defends Karl Popper's scientific method of conjecture and refutation (see note 3 of Chapter5)—a method which, while making appearances in *Arcadia* and *Indian Ink* as a useful tool in historiographic research, is most explicitly legitimated as the proper method of historiographical research in *The Invention of Love*.

Indian Ink

Indian Ink is similarly concerned with how literary critics construct their subjects. And, like *Arcadia*, the play ultimately "normalizes" this process, albeit with the added caveat that the personal passions of those who are subjected to historiographic scrutiny may well disrupt this historical record in a way which only further complicates the job of the historiographer (and, apparently, more power to them). Moreover, *Indian Ink* is also set in two time periods, a fact which once again serves the thematic purposes of the work by allowing the audience to witness the mistakes that Eldon Pike makes as he researches his subject, Flora Crewe.

The sections of *Indian Ink* that are set in 1930s colonial India follow the exploits of Flora Crewe, a British poet who, because of her health, has been sent to India to recover. While there Flora meets an Indian painter, Nirad Das, who undertakes a portrait of her. Much of this part of the play

6. Metahistorical Detectives

details the conversations which occur between Nirad and Flora as he paints her, conversations which are frequently disrupted by Flora reading from her latest poems and from her letters to her sister. The letters fill us in on various details of her Indian experience and provide the audience with her opinions on those experiences. Eventually, Flora admits her distaste for Nirad's painting, explaining that she had "thought [Nirad would] be an *Indian* artist" (43). Nirad is hurt by Flora's criticism, and, after insults all around during which Flora continually tells Nirad to "stick up for yourself," Flora nearly faints from the heat and Nirad has to help her off with her clothes and into bed. This episode inspires him to paint Flora nude and in more of an Indian style.

PIKE'S CONSTRUCTED SUBJECT

During the sections of the play set in 1980s postcolonial London and India, we find that Flora Crewe has become the subject of bibliographical/biographical research undertaken by Eldon Pike, an American academic. The play tracks the difficulty Pike faces in acquiring accurate records about her experiences in India. Flora is long since dead (dying soon after Nirad finished the painting), so Eldon consults with Flora's sister, Mrs. Swann, to help him with his biographical research. When we first meet Pike he is working on Flora's collected letters, which he intends to edit and publish. In his interview with Mrs. Swann he "discovers" the first painting of Flora by Nirad, which he then uses as the cover illustration for her collected letters. Consequently, Nirad's son, Das, now living in London, upon seeing the book on display in a bookstore and recognizing that the painting must be his father's, undertakes to visit Mrs. Swan, at which point he shows her the nude which has, since its creation, been in his family's possession. However, even without the backdrop of chaos theory, this scene makes it strikingly clear just how difficult the biographer's job can be, as Mrs. Swan and Das conspire to keep the truth from Eldon — Mrs. Swan, at least partly out of imperialist prudishness (indeed, she refuses, to the last, to believe that there might have been anything sexual about the relationship between Flora and Nirad), and Das, because he hesitates to let his father be relegated to a footnote in Pike's biography.

The criticism of academia's bibliographical excesses that occurs in *Indian Ink* is similar to that found in *Arcadia*. Pike, like Bernard, seems as much driven by his career as he does by the inherent importance of the subject he is engaged in researching, as becomes clear in his conversations with Mrs. Swan:

> PIKE: The University of Texas has Flora Crewe indexed across twenty-two separate collections! And I still have the Bibliothèque Nationale next week. The Collected Letters are going to be a year of my life!
> MRS. SWAN: A whole year just to collect them?
> PIKE: (Gaily) The notes, the notes! The notes is where the fun is! ...Which you might call a sacred trust. Edited by E. Cooper Pike [4].

Of course, given that Stoppard's own papers were purchased and archived by the University of Texas, this would appear to suggest that at least some of the satire of an industry — which is at least equally concerned with publication for publication's sake as it is with fulfilling a "sacred trust" — is directed at himself for having been complicit in such an enterprise.[2] And, of course, it is just these notes that Mrs. Swan finds so cumbersome in reading *The Collected Letters*: "Far too much of a good thing, in my opinion, the footnotes: to be constantly interrupted by someone telling you things you already know or don't need to know at that moment" (25). No doubt, we would also find Eldon Pike's editorial interruptions of *Indian Ink* itself similarly intrusive except that they are elevated to the level of comic farce, as, for instance, when Flora suggests that it "was ten years ago almost to the day" since she had last seen the Raja's Daimler (which had then belonged to a former suitor), and Pike cannot help butting in to both correct Flora and hype one of his essays: "In fact, nine. See 'The Woman Who Wrote What She Knew,' E. C. Pike, *Modern Language Review*, Spring, 1979" (51).

Also like Bernard, Pike becomes similarly obsessed with a theory about his subject (that Das painted a nude of Flora) on the slimmest of evidence. However, while the difficulties Bernard has in reconstructing the events of 1809 are largely attributed to the effects of entropy and chaos, Pike's difficulties, by contrast, are at least partly a result of the fact that Mrs. Swan and Das Anish collude to undermine his agenda. Pike's primary piece of evidence is a letter from Flora to Mrs. Swan:

> PIKE: Here. "In an empty house..." — "Perhaps my soul will stay behind as a smudge of paint on paper, as if I'd been here, like... Radha?" [...] "—the most beautiful of the herdswomen, undressed —" [9].

Mrs. Swan is dismissive of Pike's argument that this is proof that Flora must have sat for a nude painting in India, suggesting instead that the letter can

6. Metahistorical Detectives

be read to mean what one wants it to "Isn't that the point of being a poet?" (9). Pike, however, is unconvinced by her reasoning, and, what's more, begins to develop a theory that perhaps Flora's relationship with Das extended beyond the painting of a nude. Pike pursues his theory as he continues his research in India, where he has the following exchange with his guide, Dilip:

> PIKE: Do you think he had a relationship with Flora Crewe?
> DILIP: But of course — a portrait is a relationship.
> PIKE: No, a *relationship*.
> DILIP: I don't understand.
> PIKE: He painted her nude.
> DILIP: I don't think so [59].

It would appear that Mrs. Swan and Das Anish are right to be concerned. Apparently, there is nothing which will turn both of their works into footnotes faster than to have one's history appropriated by the scandalmongering which Pike passes off as literary criticism.

However, just as Bernard's wild speculations concerning Byron come crashing down around him upon the discovery of the fact that Mr. Chater died of a monkey bite in Martinique, Pike's comes crashing down as well when it is discovered that Flora had been given a watercolor by the rajah. Soon enough, Pike comes to the assumption that this was the nude watercolor mentioned in Flora's letters:

> PIKE: Thank you. That was thoughtful of you. The Gita Govinda ... would that be anything to do with a herdswoman, Radha?
> RAJAH: But absolutely. It is the story of Radha and Krishna.
> PIKE: Yes. And ... erotic? She could have been nude?
> RAJAH: Well, let us say, knowing His Highness, the paintings would have been appropriate to the occasion.
> PIKE: A watercolour of course. On paper [*Indian Ink* 65].

Pike is barely able to hide his disappointment, finally responding to the Rajah's hope that he has "been of some service" to Pike's biography of Miss Crewe by responding "Yes. You could say that. But thanks anyway" (66). Of course, the wonderful irony of this moment — which would be all the more compelling to those audience members familiar with *Arcadia*— is that in this instance, Pike's original (albeit unpublished) assumptions about both a nude watercolor and a relationship between Flora and Das happen to be correct (not that Pike really has the evidence to prove things either way). Fleming compares this instance in the two plays as follows:

> Bernard demonstrates his intelligence only to be brought down by his hubris; in contrast, Pike is rather dimwitted, a likable oaf who provides many good laughs, but who is too stoogelike to offer any serious commentary on the difficulty historians have in trying to interpret the past. Stoppard's ironic touch is that Pike is actually correct in his speculation that Das painted a nude portrait [221].

And while the fact that the more dim-witted of the pair also turns out to be correct (albeit without ever knowing it) may well be seen by a student of McHale as a sign that the play has surely "evacuate[d] the detective story of its epistemological thematic," I'm not sure how much we should make of this intertextual in-joke to those familiar enough with *Arcadia* to make the connection, especially given that part of the reason Pike is so continually driven down wrong paths has to do with the fact that Mrs. Swan and Dilip actively conspire against him to conceal the truth.

> MRS. SWAN: If you decide to tell Mr. Pike about the watercolour, I'm sure Flora wouldn't mind.
> ANISH: No. Thank you, but it's my father I'm thinking of. He really wouldn't want it, not even in a footnote. So we'll say nothing to Mr. Pike.
> MRS. SWAN: Good for you. I don't tell Mr. Pike everything either [80].

It is as a consequence of this disingenuousness that Pike finally fails so completely in recovering Flora's "deep motive" or "creative power" that he must finally construct Flora according to his own needs, eventually going so far afield that his assistant, Dilip, feels compelled to rebuke Pike's suggestion that Flora might have sat nude for Nirad.

> DILIP: Well, we will never know. You are constructing an edifice of speculation on a smudge of paint on paper, which no longer exists.
> PIKE: It must exist — look how far I've come to find it" [59].

To be sure, the tale that Pike eventually fabricates proves once again that necessity is the mother of invention, and that there is no greater necessity than publication for one who has been provided with research funds (For how else could a literature professor afford such a trip to India!) with the expectation that he will publish and eventually seek tenure. Ironically, Stoppard leaves it to Pike himself to explain this very phenomenon: "This is why God made poets and novelists, so the rest of us can get published" (4).

Ultimately, *Arcadia* and *Indian Ink* both suggest that biographical criticism doesn't so much serve the reconstruction of truth as it does the empowerment of critics within the academic community. Moreover, it is

6. Metahistorical Detectives

also worth noting the degree to which the plays emphasize how Bernard's and Pike's biographies marginalize the opinions of others in the process. Bernard, for instance, seeks to place himself at the center of a bibliographical maelstrom of criticism about Lord Byron's motivations for leaving England, never caring who he disenfranchises in the process. Pike, meanwhile, so manages to marginalize those who are the very subject of his study, as well as their immediate kin, that Mrs. Swan feels that her memories of her sister are being limited, excluded, and chosen for her by Pike's bibliographical study: "There are pages where Flora can hardly get a word in sideways. Mr. Pike teaches Flora Crewe. It makes her sound like a subject, doesn't it, like biology. Or in her case, botany" (26). We see, then, that because of Pike's construction Flora is no longer the sister whom Mrs. Swan knew and is in danger of becoming nothing more than a series of bibliographical entries in the academic record, one more subject to be studied by the literary establishment. Thus, the narrative that was Flora's life has been replaced by another that may be true for Pike and his students, but is false for Mrs. Swan and, more especially, for Flora herself.

It is notable that Anish's own investigation into his father's painting is not so easily confounded. In a scene meant to mirror Pike's querying of Mrs. Swan about the possible existence of a nude watercolor, Anish shows her the actual nude painted by his father and begins to query her about the possibility that Flora and his father might have been lovers, a possibility substantiated by a line in one of Flora's letters where Flora coyly refers to an illicit encounter by saying "Guess what — you won't approve." In the collected letters Pike has footnoted the entry with the suggestion that it refers to Captain Durance, but Anish presents an alternate theory:

> ANISH: I don't mean any offence.
> MRS. SWAN: Then you must care not to give it.
> ANISH: But would you have disapproved of a British Army Officer, Mrs. Swan? More than of an Indian painter? [79].

Unable to accommodate this final possibility, Mrs. Swan is emphatic: "Certainly. Mr. Pike is spot-on there" (79). Even still, the truth yet proves to make itself more readily available to Mrs. Swan and Anish than it ever does to Pike. For *Indian Ink* gives every indication that Das and Flora did have an affair, and, if not that, that they shared a much deeper emotional connection than did Flora with Captain Durance, a fact which Das is able to read in his father's painting: "This was painted with love. The vine embraces the dark of the tree" (68). And despite her protestations, Mrs. Swan comes to a fundamental truth of her own, admitting that "Flora's weakness was always romance" and that she "quite possibly had a romance with Das. Or with Captain Durance. Or his highness the Rajah of Jummapur. Or someone else entirely. It hardly matters, looking back" (79). Suddenly, Mrs. Swan sounds suspiciously like Valentine: "Well, it's all trivial anyway. [...] The questions you're asking don't matter, you see. It's like arguing who got there first with the calculus. The English say Newton, the Germans say Leibnitz. But it doesn't *matter*. Personalities. What matters is the calculus. Scientific progress. Knowledge" (60). By implication, how Flora loved is trivial. What matters are the poems.

Furthermore, while *Indian Ink* is critical of the means by which academics attempt to know their subject, it implicitly approves of the way that drama attempts to know this same subject given that Stoppard criticizes the Pikes and Bernards of the world for their constructions, all the while unselfconsciously creating constructions of his own, including the construction of these same buffoonish critics (Pike and Bernard), all too polite Indians (Das and Nirad), and self-satisfied colonials all too concerned about Indian sovereignty (Flora), not to mention inconsistent Marxists (Lenin in *Travesties*), pretentious poets (Tzara in *Travesties*), incredibly astute intelligence agents (*Hapgood*), admirable news reporters (Jacob Milne in *Night and Day*), and writers of unsurpassed genius (Joyce in *Travesties*). Perhaps Stoppard is postmodern despite himself. For while Bernard's and Pike's constructions are clearly the result of poor scholarship — and, as such, draw attention to epistemological issues regarding proper methods of doing historiographic research — the way in which Stoppard knowingly constructs some objects (for instance, his own public persona) while unknowingly constructing others (all too polite Indians) problematizes any attempt to pin down the play's postmodernity regardless of our opinion on the relationship between the political and the postmodern.

Postcolonial Politics

As noted several times throughout this volume, Stoppard's occasional forays into politics necessarily complicate any attempt to distinguish his modernity from his postmodernity, especially when his investigation of the artificial/real dichotomy is considered in conjunction with the role

6. Metahistorical Detectives

power plays vis-à-vis this dichotomy. What does it mean that in *Night and Day* Stoppard explicitly rejects the idea that the corporate press constructs narratives to suit its purposes, while the academics of *Indian Ink* and *Arcadi* are called out as corrupt for doing the same? In noting that political rumblings often exist only in the background to Stoppard's plays, Jim Hunter explains, "It's typical of Stoppard to sketch political confrontation somewhere at the margins of a play, rather as if writing always from Zurich during the First World War" (85). However, the consequent rumblings about Stoppard's politics from academics are especially hard to ignore in the case of *Indian Ink*, even for one inclined to ignore the way in which the play's politics may or may not affect our reading of the play's various modern and postmodern elements. Indeed, the very fact that its politics has loomed large in most treatments of the play makes sweeping this difficult issue under the rug more difficult than it is with the rest of Stoppard's plays.

As Josephine Lee puts it, the very fact that Stoppard approaches the subject of India as if it is just "another one of [his] dramatized debates" has drawn attention to what appears to be:

> [a] series of positions on the "ethics of empire" [wherein the] colonial history of India can be traced, beginning with the conflicting perspectives articulated by Anish Das and Mrs. Swan. Anish's heroic romanticization of the struggle for Indian nationhood and independence is juxtaposed with Mrs. Swan's insistence that "We made you a proper country! And when we left you fell straight to pieces like Humpty Dumpty" [39].[3]

Indeed, it is hard to believe that Stoppard would have been entirely unaware of the potential maelstrom which can result simply by choosing India as one's setting. John Fleming provides what is perhaps a typically postcolonial indictment of the plays treatment of India:

> The fact that the loquacious and strong-minded Flora, the one who urged Das to take back his country, is so meek and inarticulate when directly confronted with the arrogant, domineering, invasive attitude and practices of the British colonizers is disturbing — offering himself the opportunity to critique the ethos of empire, Stoppard has seemingly passed [217].

Oddly enough, Fleming fails to recognize that *had* Das listened to Flora, this might have made her into the equally problematic great white hero of the cause (which reminds us that it is hard to win for losing when it comes to engaging postcolonial issues).

Laurie Kaplan's essay on this issue — "*In the Native State / Indian Ink*: Footnoting the Footnotes on Empire" — offers a notably mixed opinion of the play's postcolonial attitude, arguing that a scene in which Pike expresses horror at the way in which a woman put the stump of her arm up against the window of a car Pike is riding in — "It was ... raw ... so when the light changed, the stump left this ... smear (59)" — is indicative of the debate over the play for how it can read in two very distinct ways. "This addition to the stage play could seem gratuitous postcolonial local color, but it could also be pictorial evidence that the playwright has chosen not to be the great comforter of the middle class" (343). Apparently, if it is read as local color it is morally suspect, while if it is read as Stoppard refusing "to be the great comforter of the middle class," then it is acceptably progressive.

Remembering that Stoppard had spent time in India as a child, a third — and potentially more damning — possibility, however, is that the image speaks directly to Stoppard's own colonial nostalgia, as expressed in interview to Paul Allen:

> The experience I had, as I say, after writing the play was one which was not particularly surprising to me. I was vaguely aware of its existence. That's the phenomenon of quite a lot of Indians of the older generation — having their own nostalgia for the British India days. I met several people who spoke in these terms, you know, that it had all started to go wrong when the British left [241].

To be sure, there is much in *Indian Ink* that can be read as nostalgia for the colonial era, at least some of which is suggestive of the idea that India is worse off without the British. Mrs. Swan, moreover, dogmatically argues just this position. Kaplan, for all her bibliographical research, fails to notice that such scenes are even more common in *Indian Ink* (which was written after Stoppard's visit, while *In the Native State* was written before), which points to the fact that the trip very well might have further confirmed Stoppard to this position. Moreover, the fact that Stoppard may have been privy to such comments from indigenous Indians only speaks to the fact that Indians would have long since learned to say all the right things to their British visitors (is Stoppard really that naive?). In any case, to this reader it would seem that such statements are — along with the favorable representations of British subjects such as we see in Flora — the true comforters of the middle class? (One begins to wonder what has become of this "refusal of comfort" Kaplan speaks of.)

6. Metahistorical Detectives

Certainly Mrs. Swan would expect no less than to hear that "it had all started to go wrong when the British left" if she were to visit India. In fact, while not quite bending to the force of her argument that India "fell straight to pieces like Humpty Dumpty!" when the British left, Anish Das does collect his anger, finally responding to her statement that he "should feel nothing but shame" at India having fallen apart by apologizing, "Oh yes ... I am a guest here and I have been..." And while Mrs. Swan also tempers her own position by cutting him off to say that he has only been provocative (18), the passage once again asks us to consider the irony in the fact that while the play's central theme is concerned with how critics create rather than discover their subject, Stoppard fails to realize just how true that is of playwrights as well. Perhaps, then, there is more subtlety to this passage than we were prepared for. Perhaps we are to determine that Mrs. Swan has been too bold. And that Das Anish has been too quick to apologize. And, in turn, recognize that Stoppard is drawing attention to the possibility that his own nostalgia is also problematic.

Josephine Lee provides an engaging defense of Stoppard that speaks nicely to just this issue, noting that the play includes "a series of positions on the ethics of empire" and finally deciding that while the play certainly "evokes 'India' as incomprehensible, erotic, irrational, unsophisticated, and childlike, and England as central, stable, and coherent ... happily, Stoppard's plays do not rely on these problematic identifications" (48). Central to Lee's discussion is the following much quoted passage from an interview Stoppard gave to Paul Allen about the difficulty of writing *In the Native State*:

> The difficulty, particularly in this decade by the way, is not to write Indians who sound like Indians, which is hard enough, but to avoid writing characters who appear to have already appeared in *The Jewel in the Crown* and *Passage to India*. I mean the whole Anglo Indian world has been so raked over and presented and re-presented by quite a small company of actors who appear in all of them ... and so I mean there is this slight embarrassment about actually not really knowing much about how to write an Indian character and really merely mimicking the Indian characters in other people's work. Because my own memory of living in India really hasn't been that much help because my conscious knowledge of how Indians speak and behave has actually been derived from other people's fictions [242–243].

Lee correctly recognizes that Stoppard's use of stereotypes isn't so much indicative of imperial bias on his part but, rather, "becomes a key question for Stoppard, for whom the 'real' India is inseparable from the fictions" (42). A reasonable implication of Lee's reading of Stoppard would have it that even as Stoppard "creates characters who are not beings autonomous of culture but who are pointedly products of the real and imaginary spaces they inhabit" (50), Stoppard self-consciously identifies himself as part and parcel of these same "real and imaginary spaces." This would mean that Stoppard is cognizant of his own role in constructing the hybrid culture which constitutes British-Indian relations.

Thus it is just this consciousness — such as it is — which serves to normalize the presumed imperial bias of the play. Linda Hutcheon usefully explains the politically de-doxifying effect of works which are cognizant about their constructivity:

> The narrativization of past events is not hidden; the events no longer speak for themselves, but are shown to be consciously composed into a narrative, whose constructed — not found — order is imposed upon them, often overtly by the narrating figure. The process of making stories out of chronicles, of constructing plots out of sequences, is what postmodern fiction underlines. This does not in any way deny the existence of the past real, but it focuses attention on the act of imposing order on that past, of encoding strategies of meaning-making through representation [63].

The implication of the effect being that if we can only correctly identify constructivism as it occurs, then seeing through the construction to the truth remains a distinct possibility. Which is, of course, why Stoppard is so quick to target his own role in constructing his literary personae with playful references to the fact that he has left his own papers to his biographers' mercy by handing them over to UT Austin.

However, given just how muted Stoppard's acknowledgment of his own role in constructing and contributing to Indian stereotypes is, it would hardly be sufficient to suggest that it means that the work is postmodern, even if I were employing Hutcheon's theory as my theoretical touchstone. India for Stoppard is a known and knowable locale, despite whatever he does or doesn't construct in his own treatment of it. Equally knowable is his own role in fostering his legacy. What we don't get is something in between: an unknowable India — wherein Stoppard admits his own ambiguous part in its inevitable construction; an unknowable Stoppard, wherein Stoppard ignores completely his own part in his own self-construction (consider the fact that he both "hoped the would-be biography would be as inaccurate as possible" but also had the good sense to admit that he "knew he was behaving badly"). In the end we are comforted with the knowledge that perhaps just enough of who Stoppard is will make itself apparent (through his self-conscious allusions in his plays, through his interviews, and through his essays) that academics will eventually be able to move beyond the cartoonish versions supplied by figures such as Bernard and Pike (and perhaps myself) and eventually come to terms with the real Stoppard.

The Invention of Love

In many respects, *The Invention of Love* picks up where *Arcadia* and *Indian Ink* leave off, at least for how it, too, focuses on the research exploits of literary critics, which is the focus of this discussion of the play. However, as we will see, the nature of literary scholarship has important parallels with the nature of love and aesthetics, such that it is impossible to talk about the one without also considering the others.

The play opens on A. E. Housman looking out across the river Styx, awaiting the ferryman to take him to the other side. The ferryman, however, is expecting two passengers:

> CHARON: A poet and scholar is what I was told.
> AEH: I think that must be me.
> CHARON: Both of them?
> AEH: I am afraid so.
> CHARON: It sounded like two different people [2].

And so we are introduced to the dual nature of the central character: one part reserved classical scholar, one part repressed romantic poet, who suffered through years of unrequited love for his heterosexual classmate Mo Jackson. To stage this dual nature, Stoppard creates two distinct characters, AEH (whom we have already met) and Housman (AEH's younger self, who soon stumbles onto stage as if a product of AEH's memory).

A DIFFERENT TYPE OF SCHOLAR

To be sure, the play shares something of its form with *Travesties*, and it eventually becomes apparent that rather than standing at the river Styx AEH is on his deathbed. As such, all of the play is something akin to witnessing Housman's life flashing before his eyes at the moment of his death. And while Stoppard does have occasional fun with his structure — three separate times we are witnesses to a scene where Housman, Jackson and Pollard row a boat onto the stage, and each time we receive a bit more of the context such that meaning shifts in substantial ways — there is nothing of the ontological theatricalism of *Travesties*. For while we might have reason to suspect that AEH's version of events does not comport with reality, unlike in *Travesties* such epistemological skepticism is hardly necessary for explaining away any excessive ontological incongruities, as there are none. Indeed, the subsequent monologue from AEH is perhaps meant to be reassuring on this point if for no other reason than that he is upfront about his degree of uncertainty (although this, too, is something he shares with Carr from *Travesties*).[4]

As for AEH's professed uncertainty regarding the event, it is also worth considering how the play differs from *Arcadia* and *Indian Ink*. For while Bernard and Pike are each characterized as overly-ambitious fools obsessed with making names for themselves through their academic work despite the fact that the historical record is at best mute about their bold predictions about Byron and Flora Crewe respectively, A. E. Housman is so patient in his critical endeavors that, even after having failed out of university for being too single-minded in his research,[5] he suffers in anonymity as secretary at a patent office while slowly building his name through patient careful scrutiny of the Latin of Ovid, Juvenal and Lucan, eventually becoming lecturer at University College London and then professor at Cambridge. One way of reading this is that after the parodic exegeses of Bernard and Pike, Stoppard follows up by delivering a play focused on a character who exemplifies what he takes to be a better mode of literary scholarship.

This perspective hopefully puts to rest an exchange of letters between Daniel Mendelsohn (a classics scholar at Bard College) and Stoppard in the *New York Review of Books* instigated by Daniel Mendelsohn's review of the play, in which he criticizes the play for "making Housman into the (unattractive) representative of timid, thwarted, dry-as-dust 'scholarship' and 'science.'" This charge led to a response from Stoppard, who countered that "I do not disdain Housman for his devotion to the recovery of ancient texts, I revere him for it. It is puzzling, therefore, to be told that my wish is to make Housman 'an object for fun' on that account." The exchange goes

6. Metahistorical Detectives

a few more rounds, escalating in tone, with Mendelsohn writing that while the "playwright may 'revere' intellectuals, he likes to punish them, too."

I would argue, rather, that while Stoppard does like to punish particular types of intellectuals for refusing to follow a suitable research method (those in the mold of Bernard and Pike, for example), Mendelsohn — while aware of Stoppard's past treatment of such characters — seems unable to differentiate between Bernard and Housman, despite the fact that the differences are substantial. As such, I find that a better summation of Stoppard's attitude towards Housman comes from Kenneth Reckford (also a classics scholar, at UNC Chapel Hill), who writes, "We see something of the passion of mind and heart that will last a lifetime, transcend failure and disappointment, and even outlast, if only for a little while, the human life on whose limits Stoppard's play, like Housman's poetry, so powerfully insists" (110).

Not that the play is empty of the sort of mocking of intellectuals Stoppard first became famous for in *Jumpers*, where the textual knots philosophers will tie themselves in while making their points is likened to so much acrobatics. Reckford draws our attention to the implications of the fact that in this case the audience is witness to a famous group of scholars (Pattison, Pater, Jowett and Ruskin) playing at croquet: "Stoppard's notion, of course, going back, again, to *Jumpers* and to *Rosencrantz and Guildenstern Are Dead*, is that donnish discourse even at its best can still be seen as a kind of highly competitive game or sport" (119). However, while in *Jumpers* the acrobatics of the Rad Libs are only marginally tempered by the blindly dogmatic materialism of George, Housman is put forth as a very reasonable sort of intellectual to stand in contrast to Pattison, Pater, Jowett and Ruskin.

This perspective also provides an answer to those critics who have expressed some degree of surprise at Stoppard's choice of subject matter. John Fleming describes John Wood's evolving opinion as follows:

> When actor John Wood heard that Stoppard was writing a play about Alfred E. Housman, he thought: "There's an unpromising subject, a minor poet who lived like a hermit and was staggeringly rude" (Gussow, "So Rude"). By the time Wood read the play and accepted the leading role, he found Stoppard's Housman to be a fascinating character [224].

Wood's change of heart is certainly a consequence of the fact that Stoppard makes such a charming character our of Housman, but this hardly takes away from the fact that Wood wouldn't have found him so charming if Stoppard hadn't been charmed enough by him in the first place to craft him into a compelling character. And after Bernard and Pike, it is easy to see how someone so serious-minded in his research as Housman would have come as something of a relief to Stoppard.

Quoting Stoppard's explanation that he was attracted to "the two sides of him. The romantic mind of the poet and the analytical mind of the classical scholar," Fleming explains that "the duality of the human temperament" is a metaphor that is of longstanding interest for Stoppard. He notes that it also "undergirds both *Arcadia* and *Indian Ink*" (226). However, I think that Fleming is onto a much more meaningful understanding of Stoppard's interest in Housman as subject matter when — after quoting AEH's defense of knowledge for its own sake as something "that you can't have too much of" and "there is no little too little to be worth having" (*Invention* 37) — Fleming explains that "This defense of ivory-tower scholarship is the intellectual/academic corollary to art for art's sake" (233). For while we know that Stoppard admired Wilde's aestheticism, and has often been accused of being too much in the same mold in producing work which refused to embrace socio-political agendas, I would argue that it should hardly be surprising that he might be inclined to embrace a similar mode of literary scholarship (i.e., one not in the service of publication, but merely in service of itself).

While explaining Housman's caustic wit, Fleming very nearly makes the case himself, without ever fully connecting the dots:

> He was so good in his field that even one of the scholars he ridiculed remarks: "Mr. Housman is applying for the post at my urging. He is, in my view, very likely the best classical scholar in England" [84]. In a discipline rife with egos and personal politics, Housman spared none of his colleagues in his critiques yet still managed to reach the pinnacle of his profession [239].

It is my contention that it is this aspect of Housman — perhaps even more than Housman's duality — which drew Stoppard to him, for politically he is the counter opposite to Bernard and Pike, who would stop at nothing to establish a tenured career in academia. By contrast, in a development which serves to answer the great mystery of why it is that the foremost classical scholar of his era failed out of university, Stoppard presents Housman as driven more by his love for Jackson than by his career. No doubt, as a playwright who discontinued his education after his Cambridge

6. Metahistorical Detectives

O levels, Stoppard couldn't help but to admire a man who had reached the pinnacle of his career on sheer hard work and talent. Moreover, it is also worth noting that just as Stoppard privileges both art and criticism devoid of politics (i.e., art in the mode of Oscar Wilde), he very well may have favored Housman for the purity and privacy of his love for Jackson over, perhaps, the more ostentatiously public affairs of Oscar Wilde.

Scholarship for Its Own Sake

According to Nadel, as early as 1961 Stoppard is quoted as expressing his sympathies with the aestheticism of Wilde by exclaiming that "art is necessary for itself." Nadel goes on to suggest that the quote "hint[ed] at a position he will develop in the first ten years of his playwriting. The Wildean emphasis on style is enough justification for writing" (80). Apparently, these first ten years would include *Hound, After Magritte, Jumpers,* and *Travesties,* and only come to an end with the politically charged *Night and Day*. Similarly, Jim Hunter explains of the young Stoppard, "He admired the deft style of Evelyn Waugh and — the most famous dandy in English letters — Oscar Wilde, who hovers ambivalently behind much of his work and actually appears on stage in *The Invention of Love*" (19). Clearly, Wilde looms large among Stoppard's many influences; in my own discussion of *Travesties* — a play which uses *The Importance of Being Earnest* as its frame — I ultimately argue that while Stoppard very well favors Joyce's aesthetic to Lenin's and Tzara's, there are good reasons to believe that he has an even stronger preference for Wilde.

Wilde's appearance in *Invention* suggests the same possibility with this play, with some critics deciding that Wilde is Stoppard's preference in this case as well. In his *Review of New York Books* article reviewing the play, Mendelsohn argues that the play values Wilde's outrageous aestheticism more than it did Housman's considered seriousness. Similarly, Jim Hunter, after quoting Wilde explaining to Housman in the play's conclusion that "your life is a terrible thing. A chronological error," writes that "in Wilde's view, and Stoppard's, the life to be pitied is Housman's" (96).

However, I would argue that the answer to the question of Stoppard's preference lies in the fact that Housman's literary critical ideals share something with those of the even-handed Hannah Jarvis, who puts Bernard's flights of fancy in their place. She argues that his theory about Byron "can't prove to be true, it can only prove not to be false yet" (*Arcadia* 74). Valentine explains that this is "just like science," recognizing in Hannah's statement the scientific method that is ultimately privileged as a central norm by both Bernard and Hannah. Notably, it is also the method that AEH commits his life to:

> By taking out a comma and putting it back in a different place, sense is made out of nonsense in a poem that has been read continuously since it was first misprinted four hundred years ago. A small victory over ignorance and error. A scrap of knowledge to add to our stock. What does this remind you of? Science, of course. Textual criticism is a science whose subject is literature, as botany is the science of flowers and zoology of animals and geology of rocks [38].

Clearly, AEH is just the sort of critic who has already been identified by Stoppard in *Arcadia* as representing his preference. For Reckford, what differentiates Housman from his peers is that he was a professional: "But an equally important suggestion is that the dons of that earlier time were amateurs, not professionals. This is how Housman would have seen them. Jowett, the great popularizer of Greek literature, didn't really know his Greek. Pater and Ruskin were all style and no substance" (121). This seems about right, except that Bernard and Pike, perhaps, are not so much professionals as members of a self-selecting profession, too dedicated to their own profession as a profession in itself to give proper attention to scholarship for its own sake. Housman's obsession with commas is later used to comic effect when he fails to get Wilde's joke (relayed to him by Pollard) that "I have worked hard all day, in the morning, I put in a comma, and in the afternoon I took it out again!" (47). As Reckford explains it, "Housman doesn't get the joke. Punctuation, for him, is a serious business. His scholarship is at the furthest pole from Wilde's irresponsible art, his creative frivolity" (125).

AEH's aspirations, moreover, should remind us of the scene in *Arcadia* when Thomasina has only just begun to come to terms with the implications of her glimpse into chaos theory; she pessimistically wonders out loud "how we can sleep for grief," and Septimus provides the following optimistic reply which, I would argue, is at least part and parcel of Stoppard's own:

> We shed as we pick up, like travelers who must carry everything in their arms, and what we let fall will be picked up by those behind. The procession is very long and life is very short. We die on the march. But there is nothing outside the march so nothing can be lost to it. The missing plays of Sophocles will

6. Metahistorical Detectives

turn up piece by piece, or be written again in another language. Ancient cures for diseases will reveal themselves once more. Mathematical discoveries glimpsed and lost to view will have their time again. You do not suppose, my lady, that if all of Archimedes had been hiding in the great library of Alexandria, we would be at a loss for a corkscrew? [*Arcadia* 38].

In his textual criticism, Housman is clearly engaged in the science of turning up the plays of Sophocles "piece by piece."

Notably, while we also find both Bernard and Housman in the position of needing to defend the research that they do against skeptics, their response to these skeptics is very different. In response to Valentine's accusation that Bernard's research questions are "all trivial anyway" and that "What matters is the calculus. Scientific progress. Knowledge," Bernard is quick to cite "the bomb and aerosols" as reasons for preferring a romantic epistemology. Bernard sums up his preference as follows:

> If knowledge isn't self-knowledge, it isn't doing much, mate. Is the universe expanding? Is it contracting? Is it standing on one leg and singing "When Father Painted the Parlour"? Leave me out. I can expand my universe without you. "She walks in Beauty, like the night of cloudless climes and starry skies, and all that's best of dark and bright meet in her aspect and her eyes." There you are, he wrote it after coming home from a party [*Arcadia* 61].

According to this perspective, truths are privately constructed and, as such, they are to be pursued for their own sake, rather than with the intent of accurately describing the world at large. However, while Bernard defends romantic ideals over scientific ones, he never really responds to Valentine's critique that what he does as a critic is trivial. Instead he defends Byron, a bait and switch on Bernard's part that goes unnoticed in the following discussion. A similar exchange occurs between Housman and Chamberlain over how we are to determine between two competing theories concerning the provenance of a particular passage:

> HOUSMAN: One of them always makes the better sense if you can get into the writer's mind, without prejudices.
> POLLARD: And then you publish your article insisting it was really "Lashing it up."
> CHAMBERLAIN: Why?
> POLLARD: Why? So that the other people can write articles insisting it was "mashing it up" or "washing it up."
> CHAMBERLAIN: Toss a coin — I would.
> POLLARD: That's another good method. [I'm] only teasing, Housman, don't look so down in the mouth [70].

Housman refuses to be baited into the exchange, defending himself in private to Pollard later: "It's where we're nearest to our humanness. Useless knowledge for its own sake. Useful knowledge is good, too, but it's for the faint-hearted" (73). Housman may as well be an aesthete defending purity in artistic endeavors, as later, he says of knowledge more generally: "It does not have to look good or sound good or even do good. It is good just by being knowledge. And the only thing that makes it knowledge is that it is true" (37). Knowledge for its own sake would appear to share much with "Art for its own sake," with the primary distinction being that for an aesthete the only thing that makes it art is that it is beautiful.

To be sure, Théophile Gautier's aesthetic slogan *L'art pour l'art*, which would have been translated and come down to Wilde via Walter Pater as "Art for art's sake," wasn't for the faint-hearted either, as it faced withering criticism from the likes of George Bernard Shaw, who famously responded to *The Importance of Being Earnest* by writing, "Unless comedy touches me as well as amuses me, it leaves me with a sense of having wasted my evening. I go to the theater to be moved to laughter, not to be tickled or bustled into it" (250). So too failing out of school to be closer to the one you love is not for the faint-hearted, at least not when one's aspirations are equally split between love for one's best friend and love for the classics. And what, moreover, are we to make of the fact that Housman would pursue a subject matter as obscure as Propertius, who becomes something of a running joke in the play, with everyone expressing surprise at Housman's interest, which Housman finally explains as follows: "Propertius looked to me like a garden gone to wilderness, and not a very interesting garden either, but what an opportunity!— it was begging to be put back in order" (72). What better way to show one's commitment to classical scholarship for its own sake than pursuing the work of someone so obscure, and about whom nobody could ever claim you were putting on airs (perhaps this tells us something of choosing the unattainable Mo Jackson, as well). This, of course, means that Housman shares more with Wilde than Reckman recognizes when he explains that "His scholarship is at the furthest pole from Wilde's irresponsible art, his creative frivolity." Yes, scholarship — unlike art — is to be pursued with great care. But the endgame is the same. They are both pursued for their own sake. Finally, then, the most significant difference between Housman and Wilde is that Housman would leave the pursuit of style and society for its own sake to Wilde.

6. Metahistorical Detectives

LOVE FOR ITS OWN SAKE

That love holds a similarly idealized position in the play is evident in how much Housman is willing to give himself over to love for its own sake, even when the pursuit of this love means working in obscurity as a secretary in a patent office just so he can keep house with the heterosexual Jackson, even as Jackson, unawares, seeks advice on his own romantic affairs from Housman. This leads, perhaps, to the most tender and heart wrenching moment in the entire Stoppard canon when Jackson mentions to Housman that Rose, his girlfriend, suspects Housman to be sweet on Jackson. Housman, however, finally cannot lie to his friend, although at first he responds in the typically obscure fashion of the classics scholar:

> HOUSMAN: Theseus and Pirithous. They were kings.... They loved each other, as men loved each other in the heroic age, in virtue, paired together in legend and poetry as the pattern of comradeship, as the chivalric ideal of virtue in the ancient world. [...] well, not anymore, eh, Mo? [79].

Housman's pure reference to such "vice" will not suffice, necessitating that he become blunter:

> HOUSMAN: Will you mind if I go to live somewhere but close by?
> JACKSON: Why? Oh ...
> HOUSMAN: We'll still be friends, won't we?
> JACKSON: Oh!
> HOUSMAN: Of course Rose knew!—of course she'd know!
> JACKSON: Oh! [79].

And so, despite the fact that Jackson insists that they will still be friends, they more or less go their separate ways. Housman's poem in response to his loss speaks to the long-suffering purity of his love, and to the fact that this love found its complement in his other life (i.e., in the purity of his poetic and critical pursuits).

> He would not stay for me, and who can wonder?
> He would not stay for me to stand and gaze.
> I shook his hand, and tore my heart in sunder,
> And went with half my life about my ways [81].

Just as with his pursuit of classical scholarship, love for its own sake meant that it may be unrequited—and practiced from a distance. However, unlike his successful pursuit of classical scholarship, there would be no triumphant return to Cambridge when it came to Mo Jackson, who would marry, move to Canada, and fall out of touch.

The Un-political Unconscious

What does it mean, then, that love, criticism, and aesthetics are each recognized in *Invention* as enterprises which have an ideal form, except that Stoppard is engaged in defending grand narratives about the integrity and purity of each. Indeed, there is no attempt by Stoppard to employ any of his metanarrative playfulness in order to draw out the political unconscious of these grand narrative traditions. Rather, when Stoppard intends for his work to be political, it is most typically found to be overtly so, as in *Night and Day* and also in such shorts as *Every Good Boy Deserves Favour* and *Squaring the Circle*.

Perhaps *The Real Inspector Hound* stands as the single, early, exception to this rule. For in this case, Moon's affairs with various characters/actresses in the play — together with his shamelessness in promoting these actresses in his reviews — can be read as Stoppard using the metatheatrical form of his work to provide an ideological critique of the way in which theater reproduces the means of its production via the willful attempt by theater critics to seduce and/or be seduced by members of the cast such that they provide favorable reviews. According to this reading, the fact that Moon is drawn onto the stage and placed in the role of the philandering Simon is meant to draw overt attention to the way in which such behavior by critics affects the very content of the stage, making us question the theatrical ideological apparatus which both legitimates and is legitimated by the very theatrical content it is involved in producing. However, *Hound* is also unique in that it is one of only three plays (along with the even earlier *R & G* and *The Real Thing*) which is overtly concerned with the theater, meaning that even if this particular ideological reading really does stand up under scrutiny it would, at most, be one of only three plays which exhibits the sort of morphological features which lend themselves to the sort of postmodern politics described by Hutcheon (as we have seen, in *Night and Day* Stoppard actively rejects such an ideological view of the press).

That said, there is one metatheatrical feature of *Invention* which is ripe for this sort of ideological reading — the doubling of the actors in the

6. Metahistorical Detectives

play, itself a common technique of the Brechtian epic theater used to great effect by Caryl Churchill. For while there is a familiarity to many of the ontologically disruptive moments — such as AEH discussing love, poetry, and classical literature with his younger self— that it shares this familiar structure with *Travesties* means that these ontological disruptions can ultimately be accommodated in the minds of the audience as naturalist in scope in the same way that the ontological disruptions in *Travesties* are normalized (i.e., AEH is an unreliable narrator). More difficult to account for is the doubling of actors that the play calls for, and the way in which this doubling would overtly break the naturalist illusion for the audience, potentially drawing attention to the constructed nature of the play in a way which is unique in the Stoppard canon: "The two groups of characters appearing only in Act One or Act Two, respectively, may be played by the same group of actors" (unnumbered page, under "Characters").

Of course, there is a long tradition of productions making efficient use of the actors that are available through the doubling of roles. And as Stoppard explains it, this is intended to represent a theatrical possibility, not an essential requirement. That said, the initial production at the Royal National Theater included some very compelling casting choices; notably, the three actors who play Pater, Jowett, and Ruskin in Act One play Labouchere, Soans and Stead in Act Two, a fact that would hardly have gone unnoticed by the audience. Hersh Zeifman explains the importance of this feature of the play:

> When he was a youth the great minds who taught him at Oxford simultaneously revered the classics and condemned (or, worse, erased) all classical instances of "beastliness." ... And when Housman was an adult, equally powerful men — a trio of politicians and journalists played, in the original National Theater production, by the same actors — were instrumental in criminalizing homosexual acts ["Eros," 194].

While Zeifman doesn't take the point any further, its Brechtian influence would naturally encourage the audience into reflecting about the meaning of these particular choices. In Caryl Churchill such doubling is one more alienation technique among many meant to make the audience engage the socio-political conditions which give rise to the very subject matter of the play. In *Cloud Nine*, for instance, the role-doubling simultaneously emphasizes the constructed nature of the characters in Act One, while also emphasizing the reconstructed power dynamics of contemporary society. Unlike

Stoppard, however, in *Cloud Nine* Churchill specifically suggests, for instance, that the actor who plays Clive in the first act be played by Cathy in the second. This doubling, coupled with the fact that Clive fails to even appear on stage in the second act, points clearly to the development of a new power structure, which, simply, continues to construct identities, albeit according to new directives. Ironically, while Cathy becomes the most assertive character in Act Two, Clive has been so thoroughly reconstructed that he fails to even appear on stage.

It is hard not to draw similar conclusions about the implications of the casting choices of that first performance of *Invention* at the Royal National Theater. For instance, the heteronormative prudishness of Ruskin and the repressed sexuality of Pater very well may have played a significant role in the continued heteronormative prudishness of a generation of newspapermen and members of Parliament; a generation who ultimately fought for the Criminal Law Amendment Act of 1885, under which Oscar Wilde was eventually prosecuted and sent to prison for "gross indecency." Most notably, John Carlisle played both Benjamin Jowett, the master of Balliol College who dismissed Walter Pater for exchanging love notes with a student charmingly referred to by Jowett as "the Balliol Bugger," and W. T. Stead, editor of *The Pall Mall Gazetteer*, a newspaper instrumental in the passing of the 1885 amendment. One event is meant to mirror the other, as Walter Pater's dismissal is intended to prefigure Wilde's eventual prosecution and conviction. In turn, the heteronormative principles of one generation are explicitly seen as the product of the heteronormative classical scholarship of the previous generation. What are we to think except that Stoppard is arguing that the very means of production of homophobia are reproduced within the hallowed halls of academia. Foucault's conception of how power/knowledge reproduces itself comes to full fruition in the fact that the same three individuals are also identified as having "invented Oscar" only to see his fame grow so big that he got "away from us." How can this aspect of the play help but make us ever more suspicious of the role that various sorts of social media (including both newspapers and theater) play in defining our tastes (both aesthetically and morally). Even the Greek classics that Housman loves so much are characterized as having played a role in the apparatus: "Tibullus in my College library, the he loved by the poet is turned into a she: and then when you come to the bit where this 'she' goes

6. Metahistorical Detectives

off with somebody's wife, the translator is equal to the crisis — he leaves it out" (41).

Read this way, *The Invention of Love* comes across as something of an anomaly within Stoppard's career, not so much because of the overt politics of the work (for as we have seen, he does embrace political issues *in Night and Day*, among others), but, rather, because such a historically materialist perspective would typically be anathema to Stoppard (as it is in *Night and Day*). Equally problematic for my understanding of Stoppard's evolving aesthetic oeuvre is that this particular reading situates the play well within that body of work which Hutcheon suggests uses its postmodern features to ideological effect, since the play's consciousness about how texts — and the critics who champion them — serve the means of production of the status quo necessarily puts us in the position of asking the same thing of Stoppard, and of *The Invention of Love*; that is, is this a play which is conscious of its own role in reproducing heteronormativity? And, moreover, what does it mean that its postmodern formal conceits can so easily be accommodated to an ideologically progressive attitude on how heteronormativity is reinscribed within literary scholarship itself? And all this, from Stoppard, of all people.[6]

I find this political aside to present a compelling — if flawed — understanding of the play's attitude towards homosexuality. Compelling, because for whatever reason (for my money, because of the theatrical expediency of role-doubling), its metanarrative features in this case do lend themselves to a reading of the play which suddenly situates Stoppard as sharing something with so many politically progressive playwrights of his generation. And flawed, well, because situating himself within that camp quite simply insists on another interpretation which is so radically out of character with the arc of his career. That is why I stick to my earlier thesis. That the play is most centrally concerned with championing purity in aesthetics, criticism, and love. And that while telling Housman's story without casting occasional aspersions on a repressive system which forced him to avoid romance wasn't possible, at the end of the day Stoppard appears to have been most impressed by the purity and depth of feeling of that love, as evidenced in Housman's final tribute to Jackson, in which he provides a near quote of a poem from Theocrates, referred to by Andrew Sydenham Farrar Gow as the first romantic poem. Wilde then follows up with a bit of self-conscious wit appropriate to the occasion of his own death:

"Wickedness is a myth invented by good people to account for the curious attractiveness of others. One should always be a little improbable. Nothing that actually occurs is of the smallest importance" (105). This is a restatement of a claim attributed to him earlier in the play, made apparently in response to a question of whether he had really carried a lily down Picadilly, "It's not whether I did it or not that's important, but whether people believed I did it." Wilde's improbable action becomes one more tribute to aestheticism, leaving one with the distinct impression that if Wilde had not existed, Stoppard would have had to invent him. And just as Wilde has, fittingly, the final word on beauty, AEH gets the final word on literary criticism, where — among the various opposing traditions which made up the unique experience of "Oxford in the Golden Age" — we are left with "the study of classics for advancement in the fair of the world versus the study of classics for the advancement of classical studies" (105). In Housman, Stoppard finds his methodology (science) and his end game (for the advancement of classical studies). Each is grand enough to indicate a notable modernism in his metanarrative scope.

7

The Narrative Turn: Re-innovating the Traditional in *The Coast of Utopia*

> History has no purpose! History knocks at a thousand gates at every moment, and the gatekeeper is chance. It takes wit and courage to make our way while our way is making us, with no consolation to count on but art and the summer lightning of personal happiness.
> —(*The Coast of Utopia* 346)

The passage in the epilogue is quickly becoming one of the more oft-quoted passages from Stoppard's *The Coast of Utopia* (*Coast*), appearing in reviews in *The New York Times*, *The Houston Chronicle*, *The Wall Street Journal*, and *The Financial Times*, as well as in more academic discussions of the play, such as Robert Leo King's *The Ethos of Drama: Rhetorical Theory and Dramatic Worth*. That this quote has particular resonance should come as no surprise, since it is an idea that Stoppard has been working up to at least since *Arcadia*, and speaks in important ways to Stoppard's own likely realization that there are many doors other than Alexander Herzen's (the central character in the trilogy) that he may have opened. The rarely quoted continuation of this passage, however, is perhaps even more important: "Nothing, nothing.... The idea will not perish. What we let fall will be picked up by those behind. I can hear their childish voices on the hill" (346). The importance of the passage is made particularly evident by the fact that very similar passages appear in both *Arcadia* and *The Invention of Love*.[1]

That the quote comes so very late in the final scene of the third play in the trilogy—and has proven to be so quotable—suggests that it is a promising starting place for unpacking what precisely Stoppard is after in the trilogy, which has been described by many critics as a capstone to a brilliant career. Perhaps while denigrating the role of the historiographic critic in *Arcadia* and *Indian Ink* (who prove to be so hopeless in picking up what gets left behind) while privileging the more serious studiousness of Housman in *The Invention of Love* (who does so much to help pick up what has been left behind), maybe we are meant to consider what Stoppard himself has accomplished in this regard; that is, whether or not he has been successful at picking up what others have left behind in his historical treatment of key figures from the Russian intelligentsia.

According to this way of thinking Herzen, of course, is just one of those things that have been left behind by the unforgiving and random twists of history: At least partly obscured by the more flamboyantly radical Michael Bakunin, ignored by a Russian revolutionary movement that took a different path, and forgotten by intellectuals in the West as Russian social and political history became more and more remote as a consequence of cold war territorialism. Perhaps a literary treatment of Herzen — and the way in which he championed his ideals in the face of ideological pressure from all sides to conform to one tradition or another would do what history books — such as Carr's *The Romantic Exiles*, from which Stoppard borrows so freely — could not. As we will see, Stoppard makes use of Carr as both a resource and a model, in that Carr is at least as intent on telling a good story about Herzen as he is on providing an accurate representation of him.

Until his most recent plays (*The Coast of Utopia* and *Rock 'n' Roll*) Tom Stoppard was perhaps most well known as a theatrical innovator, devoted to exploring the way in which the unique features of theater might be used to query various philosophical issues, most especially the distinction between the real and the artificial, a fact which remains no less true even as he moves from rejecting realist ontologies to embracing them. For Stoppard, boundaries were meant to be transcended, whether that is the boundary between one play and another (*Rosencrantz and Guildenstern Are Dead*), a play and its audience (*The Real Inspector Hound*), the ontological distinctions between oil painting as art and theater as art (*After Magritte*) or even the various aesthetic boundaries which distinguish the work of a seemingly random assortment of notable modernists (*Travesties*). And while Stoppard has occasionally been diverted from this theatricalism (*Dirty Linen and New-Found-Land*, *Night and Day*), all of his most notable work has, in one way or another, been engaged with using theatrical boundaries

7. The Narrative Turn

to query epistemological and ontological issues (also *Jumpers*, *Arcadia*, *Hapgood*).

The Coast of Utopia and *Rock and Roll*, however, are each much more straightforwardly socio-realist history plays, which do not take their thematic meaning from formalist experimentation with the morphological features of theater (indeed, the first play of the trilogy, *Voyage*, has been linked with Chekhov for its traditional realism). Christopher Innes describes the realism of the play as follows[2]:

> [T]he characters throughout the trilogy are historical, and their actions are accurately represented, even if the speeches are only occasionally direct quotations from their writings. [...] In addition to this Realism, the structure of the trilogy is (for Stoppard, very unusually) chronological: it proceeds sequentially from play to play, with its high point in the middle of the central play — 1848, the Year of Revolution ["Post-millennial" 445].

I might add, moreover, that while Stoppard is well known for his playfulness, these works are deeply serious in their attitude towards their subject matter, striking a notable contrast from the Stoppard of *Jumpers*, and *Travesties*, where serious ideas are given decidedly unserious treatment.

However, to also suggest, as Innes does, that the works are part of some new "post-millennial mainstream" where Stoppard, together with David Hare and Max Stafford-Clark, "all have contributed in different ways to a radically rejuvenated factual and topical form of drama that has done much to define the contemporary scene," is to overstate the case. In fact, Innes' claim that the structure of the play is chronological is quite simply false, as the first play in the trilogy, *Voyage*, after tracking the various social, political, and intellectual engagements of the Bakunin's from 1833 to 1841 in Act One, returns in Act Two to 1834 and retraces its steps from a slightly different perspective, ending in this case in 1843.[3] One particularly notable feature of this chronological disruption is that while all of the scenes of Act One are set at "the Bakunin estate, a hundred and fifty miles north-west of Moscow" (7), every scene of Act Two except the last one (which brings a return to the Bakunin estate) is set in various locations in Moscow.

Indeed, while noting that the trilogy in many respects is an important step in Stoppard's evolving aesthetic, this chapter will also argue that there remains a significant link between these later works and the rest of Stoppard's work, not only because of the metatheatrical playfulness of the trilogy (muted as this is in the second two plays) but also because of the fact that underneath his playfulness Stoppard has always maintained a residual seriousness towards various philosophical issues. So while the balance between the playful and the serious may well have changed, something of Stoppard's central oeuvre yet remains. To this end it is essential to begin by remembering that even in his earliest and most theatrically innovative works, there is much more going on in Stoppard than mere theatricalism (as if that weren't enough). To be sure, the very refrain of this volume — that Stoppard has an ongoing commitment, as Vanden Heuvel put it, "to arraign [the postmodern] with deadpan irony or wit" — is suggestive of this serious side.

As such, one way of rephrasing the thesis of this book is by simply saying that this serious side has grown progressively more pronounced throughout his career, thus making his socio-realist works of the 20th century a logical outgrowth of his earlier work. In this respect, a play such as *Jumpers* is a natural — if more slapstick — counterpart to what we see in *Coast* given the play's more serious arraignment of philosophical issues.

An Ideal Voyage

The first play in the trilogy, *Voyage*, is dominated on the one hand by Michael Bakunin's tendency to chase each new philosophical fad in transcendental idealism — a running joke in the piece shows him continually attempting to explain some new concept to his father — and on the other by his not entirely unrelated (at least to his way of thinking) meddling in the romantic lives of his four sisters, beginning with his idealistically motivated protest against Liubov's arranged marriage to Baron Renne:

> MICHAEL: This marriage must not take place. We must save Liobuv. To give oneself without love is a sin against the inner life which is our only real life. The life of our bodily existence is mere illusion. I'll explain it to father later [14].

Of course, this being a Stoppard play, irony tracks Bakunin at every turn, such as when — just on the heels of this very speech — he shouts out "God, I'm starving" before pausing to "stuff his mouth with food from the table" (14). Consequently, just as with George in *Jumpers*, Michael's ideals are grounded at every turn. Loaded with unconscious irony, Michael fairly

7. The Narrative Turn

bristles at having to rely on his father to, as he explains it: "settle a few debts here and there in the world of appearances (24)." It eventually takes an outsider to his sheltered existence, the unlanded Belinsky, to really force him to ground:

> BELINSKY: I don't want to remember you for your overbearing vanity, your selfishness, your lack of scruple ... your bullying, your cadging, your conceit as a teacher and guide to your distracted sisters whose only philosophy is "Michael says" ...
> MICHAEL: Well!
> BELINSKY: ... and above all your permanent flight into abstraction and fantasy which allows you not to notice that the life of the philosopher is an aristocratic affair made possible by the sweat of Premukhino's five hundred souls who somehow haven't managed to attain oneness with the absolute [107].

This thread culminates near the end of the scene of August 1836, when Michael is seemingly abandoned by all his sisters at once (Varenka to write to her husband, Alexandra to assist with the baby, Liubov to a relationship with Stankevich and, most disturbing to Michael, Tatiana to an infatuation with Belinsky). In perhaps his only moment of self-irony vis-à-vis his rampant idealism in the entire trilogy (despite the way that irony surrounds his every action) he finally shouts "(*Ironically*) Illusion!— it's only illusion" when Belinsky informs him that he is also to be abandoned by their shared literary project, *The Telescope*, which "has been banned" (47).

As concerns the philosophical perspective of the trilogy (the play's most serious side), it is notable that German idealism and its romantic progenitors are nearly as skeptical of established truths as is postmodernism. In *Russian Thinkers*, (one of the two books Stoppard acknowledges as source material for the trilogy), Isaiah Berlin describes the German romanticism and idealism which influenced and was espoused by Stankevich and (of course) his best student, Bakunin, in all too familiar terms:

> If you wanted to know what it was that made a work of art; [...] then no general hypothesis of the kind adopted in physics, no general description or classification or subsumption under scientific laws or the behavior of sound, or of patches of paint, or of black marks on paper, or the utterances of human beings, would begin to suffice to answer these questions [157].

This is familiar both because similar formulations find their way into the mouth of Bakunin in *Voyage*—as Berlin explains, Stankevich and his followers were very skeptical about "the world of appearances," a phrase spoken by Bakunin in the play (and quoted above)—but also because it so closely resembles the sort of claims made by postmodern theorists; that, to reference Lyotard, we are of an era that has become increasingly skeptical of the sorts of grand narratives which "would begin to answer these questions."

In *Arcadia*, Stoppard himself made connections between romantic ideals and various skeptically charged contemporary perspectives about truth and reality,[4] and, to repeat, explained in an interview with Nigel Hawkes that in

> the period around the year 1800 ... you find that Blake and Wordsworth and Coleridge as young men are resisting the thinking of that time that science was rapidly finding out all the answers, and would solve all the mysteries. The sense, or illusion, that science is doing exactly that seems to accompany every age, and creates an opposing force [268].

Evidently, in early 19th century Russia Michael Bakunin was a part of that opposing force, albeit with an important caveat. For the Russian romantics did have their own grand narratives which they committed to even as they rejected Enlightenment narratives of truth and knowledge:

> You were told that if you simply listened to isolated notes of a given musical instrument you might find them ugly and meaningless and without purpose; but if you understood the entire work, if you listened to the orchestra as a whole, you would see that these apparently arbitrary sounds conspired with other sounds to form a harmonious whole which satisfies your craving for truth and beauty [Isaiah Berlin 163].

Oddly enough, this particular feature of Michael's romantic idealism never really surfaces in Stoppard's play, meaning that as Stoppard satirizes Michael, it is always and only the more epistemologically radical beliefs which he targets.

Stoppard being Stoppard, irony is hardly his only recourse against Bakunin's vapid idealism. Indeed, the play's very structure functions as a means of arraigning the philosophical idealism of several of the central characters as well. Consider Belinsky, in a long lecture to Michael's family about the poor state of Russian literature:

> [T]he answer is not out there like America waiting for Columbus, the same answer for everybody forever. The universal idea speaks through humanity itself, and differently through each nation in each stage of history [45].

And while the very structure of the play itself provides two sides to history—a structural indication if ever there was one of the concept that

7. The Narrative Turn

truth "is not out there like America" but is different for each person based on the perspective from which one views it — there is another reading of the odd chronology that Stoppard uses in the play, which is that it works to normalize various events which might otherwise prove to be ontologically discomfiting, just as the odd collages of *After Magritte* are normalized via a broadening theatrical perspective.[5] To this end, consider the following exchange in which a penknife Belinsky had apparently lost in Moscow appears in a carp at Premukhino:

> ALEXANDRA: He caught a carp — and it had a penknife inside it!
> VARENKA: A penknife?
> BELINSKY: It's my penknife which I lost last year in Moscow!
> ALEXANDRA: He says anything
> TATIANA: It's like a fairy tale [38].

This is apace with how the Bakunin women respond to much of what Michael brings with him to Premukhino from Moscow. For just as Michael is prone to spouting some disjointed and disconnected words of wisdom from German idealism, Belinsky, apparently, is also likely to "say anything." And like Michael, he is adored all the more for it (which of course — and ironically — only serves to get Michael's goat, much as he loves his sister's attention and strives to keep it to himself).

And soon enough, while debating German idealism with Alexander Bakunin, Belinsky says all too much once again:

> ALEXANDER (*losing patience*): God is all those things. That's the point!
> *Michael bows to patriarchal authority. Belinsky misses the warning.*
> BELINSKY: No, the point is, the question "how to make a clock" has the same answer for everybody.
> *The contradicting of Alexander disturbs everybody in different ways. Belinsky remains unaware* [42].

Why it is that Michael finally chooses this moment to bow to patriarchal authority is all too clear. For even as Michael bitterly complains at how Tatiana "runs after Belinsky like a puppy" (46) it is hard not to remember how he wielded romantic idealist notions to rail against Liubov's arranged marriage with Baron Renne. It is all cutting a little too close to the bone, what with Belinsky's poverty making Belinsky a very poor match for Tatiana in Alexander's eyes. Suddenly out of favor with Michael, who finds himself abandoned by all his sisters, Belinsky is encouraged to leave Premukhino upon hearing that the Telescope has been banned.

This is the last we hear of Belinsky in Act One. And soon enough in Act Two — now that he is no longer the romantic idealist threat to Tatyana's affections for Michael — we are also primed to find out how it was that he was able to conjure his lost knife out of a carp at Premukhino. The train of events leading to the surprise begins at Mrs. Beyer's open house, in Moscow, where we see Belinsky drop the knife in question. Before he can recover it Liubov has claimed it, believing that Stankevich has dropped it instead:

> *As she turns to leave, she sees the penknife on the floor. She gives a little cry of joy, and picks it up.*
> BELINSKY: Oh ... I think that is my penknife ...
> *Liubov presses the penknife to her lips and puts it in her neckline. She sees Belinsky.* [79].

Belinsky, however, is too embarrassed to ask for the knife more directly, his awkwardness in social situations being his signature trait. And now that the mystery of how the knife got as far as Premukhino has been resolved (i.e., it would have accompanied Liubov on her return), we only have yet to normalize the issue of how it got into the fish, which speaks to what is quickly becoming an all too familiar culprit. For in the face of Belinsky's idealistic ecstasy at the event, Liubov explains that: "Somebody threw it in the fishpond and the carp saw it and just gobbled it up." Very likely, Liubov herself, who had the object to hand some months earlier when Michael, in the midst of his most recent bout of fury with his father's unreasonable rejection to fund yet another philosophical enterprise, whisks Stankevsky away to Moscow just as he and Liubov are breaking through their shyness:

> LIUBOV: I found this. I think it's your penknife.
> STANKEVICH: Mine? No, it's not mine.
> LIUBOV: Oh. Didn't you lose one?
> STANKEVICH: No. (*pause*) Perhaps I should have one.
> LIUBOV: Yes. Well, you can —
> *Michael bursts in with bulging satchel over each shoulder.*
> MICHAEL: We're leaving! [27].

At least to some degree, Stoppard's use of realism turns out to provide just what he has been striving towards his whole career. Sure, it is a realism dosed with a fair bit of theatricality, so that he can continue to "arraign [radical concepts] with deadpan irony or wit," but there is a privileging

7. The Narrative Turn

of the real all the same, most notably in how the dual narratives, in what by now has become a familiar technique of Stoppard's, serve to normalize what on first viewing appears to be a decidedly extraordinary turn of events in the play. Soon enough, the furniture is no longer piled against the door as a man in waders changes a lightbulb. Soon enough, the mystery surrounding the penknife in the carp is explained.

Meanwhile, Michael's idealistic illusions follow a similar pattern as the "normalization" of the penknife. For while Liubov's illness and death remain something of a mystery in Act One, in Act Two it becomes increasingly evident that she died for love. For by the time the opening words of Act Two are voiced — in which Mrs. Beyer expresses her concern to Liubov that she will "Die an old maid [...] Baron Renne was a catch"— we already know that her words will prove prophetic, although it takes working through the bonfire procession of 1838 for a second time (the second time being necessary, presumably, because Michael had dominated the event with yet another argument with his father) to come to this realization. The procession is presented in dream sequence, as Tatiana reflects back on the occasion: "I always think of Liubov at this time of day in the garden.... Once, not long before she died, Michael made a bonfire, just over there" (56). But what we don't know until late in Act Two is that Liubov dies while awaiting an opportunity to join Stankevich at the spas in Germany, which Stankevich is visiting for his health. All we get is the following vague exchange with Varenka:

> LIUBOV: He has to go, he's ill, he has to go to the spas.
> VARENKA: Why can't he marry you and take you with him? You need to go to the spas as much as he does.
> LIUBOV: What do you mean?
> VARENKA: You know you do [50].

In turn, Michael's meddling in his sister's affairs for the sake of romantic idealism becomes all the more tragic, and all the more telling. How sorry are we supposed to feel for Michael when, after finally borrowing enough money to travel to Germany, he arrives only to hear that "Nicholas (Stankevich) had died a month before in Italy" (55). How indeed when, at least in part as a result of his romantically idealist meddling, Liubov has died at home, alone.

More to the point, Alexander Bakunin gets in the final word about objective reality when, despite his blindness (it is 1844, 11 years after the first scene) and apparent mental confusion about what year it is (Varya has to remind him that "Vasilly's been dead for years" [117]) he remains quite certain that he has witnessed the sun going down at the end of the play[6]:

> TATIANA: Yes. It's strange ... Michael never cared about politics at Premukhino, We were above all that. High above.
> ALEXANDER: Has it set?
> TATIANA: Yes. I said yes.
> ALEXANDER: I saw it go down [119].

Of course, while Michael and his cohort may have been high above politics with their heads in the clouds of German idealism, it is hard not to see how the blind Alexander's witnessing of a physical event that would have come under so much scrutiny by Bakunin's band of German idealists in "the world of illusion" is meant to bring them back to earth again. To be sure, this moment serves as quite a contrast with the philosophical idealism of Michael's erstwhile mentor Stankevich, who had earlier professed that:

> The world outside of me has no meaning independent of my thinking it. (*pausing to look*) I look out of the window. A garden. Trees. Grass. A young woman in a chair reading a book. [...] Perhaps the only thing that's real is my sensory experience, which has the *form* of a woman reading — in a universe which is in fact empty [24].

Now, Stankevich is dead. And Michael, apparently, has lowered himself to engaging in politics, having quit the military and "refused an official summons to return home" (119). The warmth of the setting sun is perhaps cold comfort for the continued intransigencies of the prodigal son. For while Alexander may not have seen his son go down, at least in his eyes Michael's "banishment to Siberia for an indefinite period with hard labour" has been a long time coming.

Shipwrecked *Ideals*

The next play in the trilogy, *Shipwreck*, changes the focus from Bakunin to Alexander Herzen, who made only fleeting appearances in *Voyage*. After opening on Herzen surrounded by his entourage (Ogarev, Turgenev, Ketscher, Granovsky) in Moscow, Herzen soon receives word that he has been approved to travel to Europe with his wife, Natalie, and family.

7. The Narrative Turn

Act One follows him to various European cities (Salzbrunn, Paris, Nice), where Herzen continues to be surrounded by various intellectuals and revolutionaries. In Paris he witnesses the 1848 revolution, only to be quickly disabused of its potential for real change, an event which challenges his romantic ideals. Act Two focuses on his and Natalie's relationship with George and Emma Herwegh. Natalie starts an affair with George, which, when finally discovered, further tests Herzen's romantic ideals.

As he is considered by many to be the father of pragmatic philosophy — a field of thought specifically devoted to rejecting the sort of radical epistemological and ontological idealism which Bakunin was so committed to by appealing to a common-sense approach to accepting material reality — we may well expect *Shipwreck* to serve as a pragmatic response to the more whimsical elements of *Voyage*, and we would be half right. For while the flighty Bakunin comes off as something of a buffoon in *Voyage*— for all his grounding in the reality of the moment — Herzen comes across as a bit of a bully in *Shipwreck*, this perhaps being Stoppard's way of trying to give opposing arguments equal weight, which, as we have seen, is a familiar Stoppardian trope going back at least as far as *Travesties*. Stoppard's professed love for Michael notwithstanding, much of this play continues to devote itself to the buffoonish Michael giving "shallow arguments" so that the bully Herzen can knock them down. And, all other things being equal, it becomes fairly clear by the end of the play that we are meant to side with the intelligent bully in this case. Indeed, with some reservations Stoppard basically admitted as much himself:

> About Michael Bakunin's virtues there is no dispute. He was courageous, inspiring, big-hearted and tireless. But his way of jumping from one enthusiasm to another, his erratic pursuit of mutually contradictory goals and his staggering metamorphoses between intellectual analyst and romantic idealist, and back again, are a challenge to those who admire him [xiii].

To the extent that Stoppard does continue to target Bakunin, it is this characteristic which becomes his focus, perhaps largely because while Bakunin's philosophical principles continue to be radical, they become, rather, the radical principles of the revolutionary anarchist, for which the "achieved inner peace" (Berlin 161) which characterized his allegiance to Stankevich would be something of an anathema. To be sure, he is a far cry from the apolitical philosopher for whom Tatiana expresses nostalgia at the end of *Voyage*.

Shipwreck is well titled after the optimism of *Voyage*. And Herzen is well chosen as its central figure, as all the grand political idealism about revolution in Europe is gradually recognized by Herzen as a situation in which one problematic power has simply been replaced by another:

> Virtue by decree. They're building prisons out of the stones of the Bastille. There's no country in the world that has shed more blood for liberty and understands it less. I'm going to Italy [157].

To this end, the very realism of *Shipwreck* speaks to the common-sense pragmatism of Herzen — which arises in part from the unfulfilled political revolutions in France. His is not a popular position, such that the running gag of Bakunin jumping from one strained philosophical position to another in *Voyage* is replaced in *Shipwreck* by Herzen's brutal pragmatism, which places strains on relationships on all sides. As a result, Herzen is continually apologizing for one slight or another (except, as Stoppard mentions, to the ever affable Bakunin).

Freedom and Representation

Herzen's disenchantment with revolution in France stops just short of nostalgia for Russia; it turns out, moreover, that Belinsky is of the same frame of mind, if for very different reasons, as earlier in the same conversation he argued that the situation of the writer is preferable in Russia in part *because* of the censorship practiced there:

> At home the public looks to writers as their real leaders. The title of poet or novelist really counts with us. My articles get cut by the Censor, but a week before the *Contemporary* comes out students hang around Smirdin's bookshop asking if it's arrived yet ... and then they discuss it half the night and pass copies around.... Writers here, they think they're enjoying success. They don't know what success is. You have to be a writer in Russia [155].

It is hard not to be reminded of Andy Warhol's insistence that "in the future, everyone will be world-famous for 15 minutes," a claim often interpreted as suggesting that the attention span of the new media is such that while it offers many more people the opportunity to have their moment in the spotlight, that moment is typically only fleeting at best. Unsurprisingly, Baudrillard was much taken by this quote,[7] which would appear to be one step towards Baudrillard's own position that too much information doesn't simply obscure the real, but actually replaces it: "Everywhere one

7. The Narrative Turn

seeks to produce meaning, to make the world signify, to render it visible. We are not, however, in danger of lacking meaning; quite the contrary, we are gorged with meaning and it is killing us" (Ecstasy 63). And so we find one more way in which Stoppard travels the postmodern terrain, if, perhaps, unwittingly, as the Russian intelligentsia in Paris begins to see how the multitude of voices kills their own.

As to how best to read Stoppard's transit of this particular parcel of the postmodern terrain, it is hard to say. For there is no explicit rejection of Belinsky's way of thinking. Rather, his listeners are sympathetic: "*He is met with silence. Then Bakunin embraces him, and Herzen, mopping his eyes, does likewise*" (155). Our best bet for unpacking this lies elsewhere in Stoppard's work — an argument in *Night and Day* between Ruth and Hannah over whether or not the corporate press inhibits free speech. Belisnky would seem to share the concerns of Wagner, who responds to Ruth's argument that the freedom of the press is evident in how the country is "littered with papers pushing every political line from Mao to Mosley and back again" by arguing, "It's absurd to equate the freedom of the big battalions to the freedom of the pamphleteer to challenge them." Like Belinsky, it appears that Wagner is concerned for the individual ability to have one's voice heard, while Ruth is concerned about publishing freedom more generally, replying, "A state of affairs where only a particular, approved, licensed and supervised non-millionaire can have a newspaper is called, for example, Russia" (83). There is very little one-to-one correspondence here. For it is nothing but coincidence that Ruth proffers Russia as an example that might convince Wagner (we are talking of two very different Russias, separated by some 150 years). But that Stoppard clearly favors Ruth's opinion certainly suggests a general lack of concern with the idea that even with a free press there are ways in which truth is obscured. And as we will see, there are many other ways that *Shipwreck* commits itself to knowable truths and representable realities.

For just as Stoppard ups the ante in *Voyage* regarding how common sense about overwrought philosophical issues might come from surprising places — with the blind Alexander confident that he is a credible witness to the setting sun — in *Shipwreck* Stoppard uses Herzen's deaf son Kolya to similar effect. To his mother Natalie's query about whether or not Kolya "can have thoughts if he has no names to go with them," Turgenev appropriates a poetic mode in response:

TURGENEV: He's thinking muddiness ... flowerness, yellowness, nice-smellingness, not-very-nice-tastingness.... The names for things do not come first, words stagger after, hopelessly trying to catch up [133].

Natalie is surprised, responding: "How can you say that, you a poet." To which Ogarev replies "That's how we know." Turgenev is, in return, deeply affected by Ogarev's reply: "I thank you. As a poet. I mean, you as a poet. I myself have started writing stories" (133).

Despite the pretension of Turgenev's original response, it is a sweet moment, which says something of Stoppard's preference for literary treatments (both Turgenev's and Stoppard's) of philosophical subjects as compared with philosophical ones. But soon enough this response is trumped by more mundane issues. Surrounded on all sides by philosophical speculation concerning the nature of reality, Kolya boldly (and silently) makes his own way through the play, from place to place. The world is his to be discovered, with or without his hearing. And, of course, the adults that surround him prove — despite their philosophical protestations to the contrary — to be so immersed in the real world that they continue to call out to him when he goes missing, despite the fact that he can't hear — and despite the fact that they continue to remind themselves of this very fact: "NATALIE: I call to him as if he can hear me. I still think one day I'll say 'Kolya!' and he'll turn his face to me" (133).

Still later, as they all gather in Paris to discuss the ongoing revolutionary struggles, Kolya (as always, his father's son) is identified by Stoppard as somehow more cognizant than the rest about approaching trouble:

Kolya is left alone.
There is the distant sound of thunder, which Kolya doesn't hear. Then there is a roll of thunder nearer. Kolya looks around, aware of something [164].

In one of the few breaks with realism in the play, the scene leading up to this episode is repeated at the end of Act One (September 1847 Reprisal). The reprisal occurs just on the heels of Herzen having learned that Belinsky has died (June 1848). And while during the first time through, the scene had been witness to a multitude of conversations, all speaking over one another (it is Belinsky's going-away party), during the reprisal all of the conversations except Belinsky's are muted. Belinsky is expounding on the pleasures of literature for its own sake (after previously having been drawn away from that belief by the idea that literature should be political). He has witnessed the shipwreck of ideology and, upon his return to Moscow, dies. Herzen comes to pieces. And his pragmatic politics becomes even more deeply engrained.

And then Kolya — this second time through and against all odds — suddenly speaks his own name. To himself. This is the inverse of the skeptical philosophical idealism which had, in part, led to the rise of revolutionary movements against the Crown. Does a deaf-mute speak his name in an empty room when nobody is there to hear it? And against the backdrop of thunderstorms and revolutions? Does a blind man see the sun go down? What does this mean except that the common sense of deaf children has trumped the skeptical idealism of Bakunin. And then — only a couple of years later — Kolya dies in a real shipwreck. There is no mistaking the pain this causes his family with anything other than real physical trauma.

This is Stoppard at his most touching, along with the deeply felt pain of Housman as he "went with half his life about his ways," and the pain of Septimus as Thomasina burns to death in the fire. It is much noted that Stoppard only successfully wrote love late in his career. Pain — and what it owes to love — only came later as well. And is as indicative of anything else in his works of a move towards embodying reality on stage.

THE LUNCHEON ON THE GRASS

In the other significant break with realism in *Shipwreck*, the scene of June 1849 in Act Two presents an opening tableau which is meant to anticipate Manet's *Dejeuner sur l'herbe* (The Luncheon on the Grass). Stoppard gives a lengthy explanation of the intended effect, which is suggestive of the way in which the tableau will eventually be normalized for the audience:

> There is a tableau which anticipates — by fourteen years — the painting by Manet. Natalie is the undressed woman sitting on the grass in the company of two fully clothed men, George and Herzen. Emma, stooping to pick a flower, is the woman in the background. The broader composition includes Turgenev, who is at first glance sketching Natalie but is in fact sketching Emma. The Tableau, however, is an overlapping of two locations, Natalie and George being in one, while Herzen, Emma, and Tergenev are together elsewhere [196].

Not being privy to the stage directions, the audience only gradually catches on to what is happening. As it eventually becomes clear to the audience that it is in fact witnessing two separate scenes, the effect is a familiar one from the Stoppard canon, reminiscent, once again, of *After Magritte*, where the opening tableau of that play mirrors the ontologically confounding imagery of a Magritte painting.

In this case it is, rather, the *social-culturally* confounding image of Manet's famous painting which stands in need of the Stoppardian normalizing treatment, what with its seemingly unselfconscious juxtaposition of female nakedness with men in dinner dress. Paul Tucker captures the surprise of the painting:

> What attracted avant-garde artists to the picture and what made it so controversial when it was first exhibited are not necessarily what viewers today generally find so startling—namely, the boldness of the female figure who sits without a stitch of clothing on in front of us and her male companions and who has the audacity to stare at us in such a self-conscious, unflinching manner. She knows that we know she is naked. She also is fully aware that we are staring at her with the same directness that she foists upon us. This curious exchange makes most people feel slightly uneasy or at least a bit perplexed, particularly because Manet offers no clues as to what is occurring in the picture or what our relationship is supposed to be to the scene as a whole. Have we stumbled upon some kind of intimate sexual encounter? Are we implicated in some way? Why does the woman look at us so unabashedly, and why are the men beside her so disengaged [from] her and each other? [7–8].

The image is quite ontologically disconcerting. But just as he does in *After Magritte*, Stoppard quickly normalizes the scene. Natalie isn't naked among a group of people dressed in their Sunday best, but is naked only for George, with whom she has been carrying on an extended affair.

And while given the thesis of the book as a whole I might hope for some compelling distinction between the two episodes (one in *Magritte* and the other here) to point towards Stoppard's continued transition away from postmodernism, the fact that it is here at all—within a play that is largely realist in its dramatic form—is a bit confounding. Yes, it does unfold in a way that normalizes that which might otherwise come across as rejecting traditional ontologies. But why even include the scene at all? If my larger thesis is correct, then it would seem that *After Magritte* is of such a different era that putting such a scene in a nominally realist text is beside the point. Is Stoppard suddenly trying to tell us that his is but one perspective of these events? And that other perspectives (i.e., other "little narratives") are perhaps equally valid? That the subjectivism of the scene is ultimately normalized does nothing to explain why it is there in the first

7. The Narrative Turn

place, except, perhaps, as an overture to the fact that Stoppard has lived so long amongst the ideas of the postmodernists that, seeing an opportunity, he just can't help himself.

One thing we should remember, however, is that the Herzen circle did actively challenge social-cultural sensibilities (and, moreover, that in the given context this marginally different target is potentially significant). To this end it is worth noting that in the immediately preceding scene Natalie had met with Maria (Ogarev's estranged wife), who described for Natalie how she often sat as a nude model for her current lover, and encouraged Natalie to do the same. Driven out of her comfort zone, Natalie lashes back in unfamiliar fashion for one so committed to romantic ideals: "Your portrait, by the way, doesn't look much like you. But that in itself is neither here nor there; technique by itself means nothing — in art or in love." Unable to help herself, she concludes by insulting Maria as well: "I know what it is. He's got your tits too high and your arse too small" (193).

And yet that Maria has awakened romantic sensibilities in Natalie is evidenced by how Natalie is driven to strip naked for George. So the scene is not simply normalized according to the way in which the image plays itself out — it is also further "normalized" for how it fits the historical narrative of their lives. On this score it is notable that the founder of realism himself, Emile Zola, famously saw fit to defend the painting against those who would have censored it:

> The crowd has kept itself moreover from judging *The Luncheon on the Grass* like a veritable work of art should be judged; they see in it only some people who are having a picnic, finishing bathing, and they believed that the artist had placed an obscene intent in the disposition of the subject, while the artist had simply sought to obtain vibrant oppositions and a straightforward audience. Painters, especially Édouard Manet, who is an analytic painter, do not have this preoccupation with the subject which torments the crowd above all; the subject, for them, is merely a pretext to paint, while for the crowd, the subject alone exists [*The Imagist*].

According to Zola, the painting never needed normalization in the first place, which is something coming from a committed realist such as Zola. By contrast with Zola, Stoppard's experiment in the form is an expansive realism, grounded in its socio-cultural narrative subject matter, and yet willing to include bits and pieces of other narrative tropes as he sees fit and as it suits his purposes.

The final scene provides one last break with realism, as we find ourselves in "Sokolovo, as before: a continuation of the first scene. Distant thunder. Ogarev and Sasha." Again, it is 1846. Sasha, Herzen's eldest, who to this point has done no more than run across the stage in the opening scene, finally makes a substantial appearance in a quiet moment with Ogarev. Sasha speaks here for the first time in the play, as if he will stand in as a replacement for his younger brother. Ogarev explains to Sasha his connection to the family, that he (Ogarev) is Herzen's best friend. "Sasha: No you aren't. I don't know you" (227). The scene is a stark reminder of all that will be lost in the shipwreck that follows. Unfaithful spouses. Friendships strained and lost. Revolutions turned bad. Family members lost to shipwrecks and grief. To close on Herzen's excitement at having been granted leave to travel to Europe — and excitedly sharing the news with Ogarev (whose faithless wife will refuse to divorce him so that he can remarry) — only compounds the tragedy.

Salvaged *Truths*

In the final play, *Salvage*, the realist disruptions are scarcer still. Most notably, Bakunin makes several ghost-like appearances to Herzen during which they argue through various sociopolitical issues regarding the means and ends of revolutionary endeavors. Each scene, however, is easily recognized as Herzen simply arguing with himself. More surprising is a scene which closes with Stanislaw Worcell, a Polish nationalist, falling asleep in an armchair in one scene where he then "remains to awake in the next scene." Moreover, this next scene is a little more than a year later, and when Worcell wakes up Herzen teases him about the "experience":

Worcell's congested chest wakes him.
WORCELL: What?
HERZEN: *(pauses to think)* I said "Why don't you have a nap" [273].

The scene's playfulness resonates in several different ways. Certainly it at least partly refers to Worcell's homelessness, and to the amount of time he spends with the Herzen's as a consequence. In fact, only a few lines later Herzen offers to let him stay on permanently in two of his rooms. This resonance would be even more pronounced, however, except for the fact that Herzen follows up his little joke on Worcell by letting us in on the idea that Worcell had really only fallen asleep some little time earlier, even while teasing Worcell that it had been some time:

7. *The Narrative Turn*

WORCELL: You've changed the furniture.
HERZEN: Yes, we moved house while you were asleep, we're in Finchley [273].

Soon enough, Worcell remembers the truth, ("Of course, I remember." [273]) just as one might when slowly awakening to familiar if impersonal surroundings. What this means is that even while Stoppard begins by using the stage directions to create a disruption in the realism in a way which would have quickly normalized itself as the play progressed, he then follows up by having Herzen himself push the meme a bit further, before, finally, allowing Worcell to remember the truth. It is a clever gambit, which nicely captures the open house atmosphere of the Herzen home described by Carr:

> The traditional hospitality of the Russian *grand seigneur* asserted itself even in foggy *bourgeois* London. Herzen kept open house, and any exile could come, any evening, to drink his wine, to smoke his tobacco, and to talk, gaily or gravely as the mood served, till any hour of the night [*Romantic Exiles* 123].

It seems fitting to reflect for a moment on how far we have come. From the metatheatrical playfulness of *R & G*— meant to draw attention to the artificial environment which seemingly traps its characters for time immemorial within the confines of text and stage — to a variety of theatricalism meant, rather, to capture a bit of history, and doing it in a way that supersedes the possibilities provided by dramatic realism proper.

CONSTRUCTING HISTORY

Innes' discussion of *Coast's* constructivist attitude towards history provides a useful means to conclude this discussion, given that it diverges so widely from my own:

> History (as Walter Benjamin has argued) is written by the victors, who expunge the opposing versions of events espoused by the vanquished and even erase their images (as Stalin did to Trotsky). Still more to the point, because of the links between history and art, there is, as Hayden White asserts, no such thing as a stable and unified historical record but only competing, pluralistic "histories." White points out that these "histories'" are literally "stories," using rhetorical tropes and constructed on fictional lines in order to offer specific moral explanations for events ["Allegories from the Past" 229].

In addition to making this case about *Coast*, Innes finds similar evidence which he suggests implies that constructivist attitudes towards history pervade both *Travesties* and *Arcadia*. In another essay Innes writes:

"Arguably, *Travesties* could be seen as being about historical revisionism" ("Towards a Post-millennial Mainstream?" 444). And then in both essays, Innes focuses on an image of Lenin which appears in the play, and which is famous for having been retouched by Stalin to "expunge Kamenev and Trotsky who featured prominently in the original" (*Travesties* 84). In the earlier essay Innes explains how it is that in Stoppard "The way reality is distorted by subjective perception is a central theme" ("Allegories from the Past" 228). In the latter essay he writes of *Travesties*, "The endlessly revised version Stoppard presents is history as myth" ("Towards a Post-millennial Mainstream?" 444).

As covered in Chapter 3, however, it would seem that *Travesties* provides an all too obvious response to anyone who would see it as espousing either perspectivism or historical revisionism, given that all of the historical constructions that we witness in the play represent the confused memories of a man on his deathbed. To assume that the overtly artificial collage which results from these delusions is somehow meant to suggest that Stoppard has a constructivist attitude towards history would be to assume that historians are no better at recovering the past than is a man suffering the sort of delusions so common to the elderly who are so mortally afflicted. Inne's additional implication that Stoppard might have been directly influenced by Hayden White's *Metahistory: The Historical Imagination in Nineteenth-Century Europe*, which came out the same year, is quite a fanciful leap, especially considering how comfortable Stoppard is with referencing his influences rather directly in his prefaces and interviews. Indeed, there is, simply, no specific indication that *Travesties* is meant to be read this way.

As we have seen in Chapter 5, Stoppard's rejection of historical constructionism becomes ever clearer in *Arcadia*. Innes, however, sees things differently, and writes:

> Stoppard's formulation ... corresponds to the views of White, since Stoppard too denies the significance of historical "fact" and calls on the power of imagination. In doing so he implies that artistic vision trumps historical records ["Allegories from the Past" 234].

Now, while Stoppard may well believe that artistic vision trumps historical records (I return to argue something similar below), he certainly does not go so far as to "den[y] the significance of historical fact." For even while Bernard makes very foolish assumptions in tracking Byron's actions at the

7. The Narrative Turn

estate, as we have seen the play ultimately privileges the epistemologically conservative method of conjecture and refutation as a means of ferreting out truth in historiography. So, too, in my discussion of *Indian Ink* Pike's version of history is shown to be refuted by the same method. And in *The Invention of Love*, Housman is seen as very much in favor of the scientific method of conjecture and refutation which moves beyond construction to truth. It would seem, then, that what Innes fails to recognize is that for every Stalin who, as Stoppard himself explains, has a photo "retouched so as to expunge Kamenev and Trotsky who figured prominently in the original" (quoted in Innes 444), there is always someone such as Housman or Stoppard (or even Innes) who will inevitably come along and correct the historical record just as Hanna does in *Arcadia*, and Houseman does in *The Invention of Love*.

A much better example of Stoppard presenting history as a constructed phenomenon — and doing so in a way which accords with Hayden White's theory of history — can be found in his earlier television play, *Squaring the Circle* (1984). In *Unnatural Voices*, Brian Richardson explains how the play's narrator continually disrupts the storyline to point out how unknown bits of historical information are invented according to the needs of the story:

> It pushes the generative narrator to new extremes by applying the technique to historical events that were largely unknowable at the time of its filming. It has a narrator, whose role at first seems to be merely that of the conventional pseudo-objective voice-over. Soon, however, the voice contradicts the enacted events. After introducing Brezhnev and Gierek talking together on a beach at a resort on the Black Sea, the narrator goes on to state "this isn't them, of course." In close-up we then see the (suddenly) bodied narrator who, looking directly into the camera, continues speaking, "and this isn't the Black Sea. Everything is true except the words and pictures. If there was a beach, Brezhnev and Gierek probably didn't talk on it" (21–22). The deceptively omniscient documentary voice is here demystified and revealed to be a single, situated speaker with his own positionality and limited knowledge [110].

According to this perspective, there is no objective position from which history can be written. However, it is hardly surprising that a short play from relatively early in his career might address such themes. A more compelling reading of *Coast* is that, after a period of satirizing the way in which historiographers create their subject in *Arcadia* and *Indian Ink*, in *Coast* Stoppard is much more given over to simply obscuring the way in which historical gaps are filled for the sake of coherent story-telling rather than reflecting on them in a way that is meant to remind us of White.

That said, I do think that at the end of the day Stoppard does favor artistic treatments of historical events over purely historiographic ones. For even when marginally anti-realist elements — such as Worcell remaining on stage between scenes — are explored, in addition to being normalized in fairly standard Stoppardian fashion, they also function as a means of representing a historical fact: Herzen was a benefactor for many impoverished Poles, and that Worcell often stayed with the Herzens. So, too, the scene based on Manet's *Dejeuner sur l'herbe*, where the way in which the play represents the simple fact of the Herzen, Natalie, George love triangle trumps the idea that it is somehow representative of an inherent subjectivity in historiography.

Moreover, after two plays in which he denigrated historiographic research (*Arcadia* and *Indian Ink*) and another in which he found his hero in Houseman, it is hard to believe — were he really as committed as Innes suggests to pointing "out that these 'histories' are literally 'stories,' using rhetorical tropes and constructed on fictional lines in order to offer specific moral explanations for events" — that he would have created such a faithful treatment of the rise and exile of the Russian intelligentsia without in some much more explicitly self-conscious way exposing his own naive part in what he had constructed. Instead, when Marx himself finally enters as a character in *Salvage*, and suggests to Natalie and George that an unknown political unconscious may be at play in their lives, he is explicitly derided as attempting to perpetuate a paranoid ideology in his peers:

> NATALIE: Every time you want to argue back, Marx just says "Well, you would think that, because as a product of your class you can't think anything else."
> GEORGE: I agree. But then I would, wouldn't I, because et cetera.
> NATALIE: You say, "Karl, I don't agree morality is defined entirely by economic relations," and Marc replies–
> GEORGE: "Well, you would thing that because you're not a member of the proletariat!" [*Shipwreck* 183].

Even as the play refuses to commit to the sort of ideologically driven understanding of how representation is always and already a function of power, Stoppard proves once again how distant Hassan's theorization of postmodern Immanence is from his own field of vision.

7. The Narrative Turn

STOPPARD'S SOURCES

One of the odder features of the trilogy is that it treats E. H. Carr's *The Romantic Exiles* so uncritically, a feature which is particularly odd given how dismissive Stoppard had been of historiography in the near past. Aside from the few differences of perspective mentioned above (and the more obvious fact that not everything from the book could possibly fit even into a pair of plays, *Shipwreck* and *Salvage*)[8] the plays remain quite faithful to the book. In fact, a fair bit of the dialogue from the trilogy comes directly from Carr's work (not that there is anything wrong with that, as Stoppard is quite generous in his attribution to Carr). For instance, in Stoppard we find the following exchange between Herzen and his wife regarding a painting of herself that she commissioned which is meant to be a present to her lover, George Herwegh:

> NATALIE: Do you like it?
> HERZEN: Very much. If Herwegh will permit it, I'll order a copy made for myself.
> NATALIE: You're angry.
> HERZEN: What would I have to be angry about?
> NATALIE: Take it for yourself, then.
> GEORGE: Nothing would induce me [210].

In Carr we find:

> "Do you like it?" asked Natalie.
> "So much," said Herzen with icy sarcasm, "that if Herwegh permits, I will have a copy made for myself."
> "Take it yourself," said Natalie with tears in her eyes.
> "On no account. Are you jesting?" [87].

What is particularly odd about this, however, is that the dialogue does not appear to have come from any of the surviving letters that Carr had at his disposal, nor does it appear in Herzen's *My Past and Thoughts*,[9] meaning that it must have been written with fair bit of creative license on the historian's part (how does Carr know, for instance, that Herwegh replied with "icy sarcasm").

Moreover, in Appendix D of Carr's volume, Carr includes a short play of eight scenes titled *Bedlam, or, A Day of Our Life*, also, apparently, composed by Carr from what he has culled from the letters, as Carr does not attribute the short play to anyone else. The scene in this instance is London, several years after the affair between Herzen's wife and Herwegh. His friend Ogarev is visiting, and Herzen has begun an affair with Ogarev's wife, also named Natalie. Stoppard also lifts lines from this short play which he puts to use in *Salvage*:

> HERZEN: (*pause*) So, how are you today? Still cross? No — just say. Are you cross or not? Oh, I can see you are.
> NATASHA: Why, what am I doing?
> HERZEN: You're just cross, don't deny it. It's because of what I said yesterday about that sign at the zoo [*Shipwreck* 300].

In Carr we find:

> HERZEN (*to* NATALIE): Well, how are you today? Still cross? (NATALIE *frowns*.) No, just say! Are you cross or not? Oh, I can see that you are cross.
> NATALIE: Why, what am I doing?
> HERZEN: I can see! It is all because of what I said yesterday. (330)

What this means is that Carr was much more willing to take expositional liberties than is generally expected of a historian, turning expository biographical narrative and family letters into dialogue. And yet, in his own introduction Carr talks down the amount of creative license he took: "I have refrained where possible from judgments of my own; but I have not been able to avoid giving from time to time my own interpretations of the situations and events described" (10).

That Stoppard, so often critical of academics, thought so highly of his sources in this case is also indicated in the preface to the trilogy, where Stoppard writes, "Berlin is one of the two authors without whom I could not have written these plays, the other being E. H. Carr, whose *The Romantic Exiles* is in print again after nearly seventy years, and whose biography of Bakunin deserves to be" (ix). All of which begs the question of why it is acceptable for Carr to construct so much of his own material from whole cloth without so much as a peep of self-reflection from Stoppard, while Bernard and Pike were treated as buffoons for doing much the same thing.

While perhaps a full investigation of the provenance of the passages Stoppard culls from Carr is in order, there is room for at least some conjecture about what Stoppard's use of Carr means to our larger question of Stoppard's preference regarding the appropriate means of historiography (and, of his own play's participation in historiography). To this end, *The Romantic Exiles* is quite notable for how much attention it gives to simply telling a good story — to engaging its readers — rather than with producing

7. The Narrative Turn

the facts as fully and objectively as possible (or, rather, to simply fulfilling the needs of an academic career such as we find with Bernard and Pike). Its generous use of dialogue is just one example of how it sacrifices objectivity for aesthetics; and, as we have seen, while Stoppard is surprisingly committed to reproducing the sources he has on hand (at least by comparison with what we see in *Travesties*) he, too, yet sacrifices objectivity for aesthetics, as he occasionally strays from Carr's narrative (Stoppard, for instance, situates the conversation Natalie is so cross about as having taken place at the zoo; for Stoppard, quite naturally enough, if there was a conversation, it must have had a location).

Even more surprisingly — given Stoppard's faith in Carr — there are occasional moments when Carr makes historiographic assumptions that are all too reminiscent of the sort made by Bernard and Pike, given how unfounded and salacious they are. In telling how Herwegh had obsessively stalked Herzen via the post in order to take revenge on him for reclaiming Natalie, Carr discusses a letter Herwegh sent to Herzen challenging him to a duel. According to how Herzen describes the letter in his biography, the letter ended with the inflammatory suggestion to Herzen that:

> Fate has decided between you and me, by drowning your progeny and your family in the sea. You wished to end the affair in blood when I still thought a humane ending possible. Now I am ready and I demand satisfaction [Carr 96].

Carr goes on to explain that while the original letter was lost, a draft of the letter exists in the archives, which "sufficiently corresponds with Herzen's account to justify the conviction that it has not materially altered in form" (96). After reproducing the draft in full, Carr follows up:

> The draft breaks off here. The reference to fate and the drowning of Herzen's mother and son does not occur in it, and must — for Herzen can scarcely have invented it — have been a brilliant afterthought [97].

The similarity to Bernard making historiographical leaps of causal logic is clear. For while Bernard's mistake was trusting too much in Byron's mythic persona, Carr, similarly, puts a lot of faith in Herwegh to play the ultimate cad, and in Herzen to be too decent to have slandered him out of spite so many years later. While Stoppard omits this salacious bit from his own play, our ever evolving theory of Stoppard holds, that even while Stoppard has embraced historical subjects, his attitude towards historiographic indiscretions may have changed. To be sure this is quite a compelling tidbit, made all the more compelling for Carr's telling of it. By contrast, Bernard does not seem so much interested in spinning a great yarn for its own sake in his research into Byron, but, rather, with playing a trump card against his fellow Byron critics.

Carr is also prone to disarming passages of psychological introspection which go well beyond what would appear to come through in the letters and journals:

> This correspondence filled Natalie with dull despair. She felt more and more that she was living in a world of mean and ignoble slanderers, incapable of comprehending the breadth and purity of her own ideal [98].

And, of course, Carr also has a keen eye for cribbing the best material from his sources, such as this wonderful bit from Herzen's biography concerning the fact that even while leaving town, Emma took time to make purchases against Herzen's accounts:

> Caesar [Herzen sardonically concludes his chapter] could read, write and dictate at the same time; such was the richness of his genius. But to think about children's stockings and the purchase of cloth on economical terms at a moment when families are being shattered to pieces, and men feel at their throats the cold steel of Saturn's blade! The Germans are a great race [82].

Finally, Carr's narrative often refuses the straightforward chronological form so common to traditional history texts, by leaping a bit ahead in his storytelling so as to build suspense (and as we have seen, Stoppard is even more playful with chronology than Carr). What does this mean, then, except that in Carr Stoppard has found a historian he can admire—and perhaps even emulate—in writing what remains his most factually accurate and (until *Rock 'n' Roll*) his most formally realist play (albeit one which occasionally strains against both facts and realism).

And, of course, Stoppard goes on to take his own liberties with the material, as he does in his representation of Herzen and Herwegh's relationship in the immediate aftermath of Herwegh's failed campaign to lead a revolution in Germany (but before Herwegh and Natalie's affair). Carr describes the time as follows:

> Herzen encouraged these visits. He had found few acquaintances, and no intimates, among the French; and his Russian friends, with the single exception of Turgenev, had fled from Paris since the revolution. Herzen was still young enough to feel the need of constant society. He thirsted for companionship; and, like many others, he fell in love at first sight with the vivid intelligence

7. The Narrative Turn

and social charm of the German poet. Political affinities sealed the friendship. Herwegh was not merely a democrat, but a martyr in the cause of revolution. Herzen was far at this time from accepting the stories of Herwegh's cowardice at Dossenbach which he afterwards retails with so much gusto in My Past and Thoughts [49].

In *Shipwreck*, however, Stoppard portrays Herzen as skeptical of Herwegh from the very beginning (a characterization which suggests to the audience that perhaps he is suspicious of an affair between Natalie and Herwegh much earlier on than would be the case if he represented the episodes the way Carr explains them. In Stoppard we find Herzen making fun of George immediately upon his return from his campaign in Germany, teasing him for having shaved his beard: "My dear fellow! Mon Brave!" Natalie defends him: "There was a price on his head" (173). Notably, this is an issue that Carr admits is left ambiguous by the historical record. That Stoppard differs from Carr, however, simply means that like Carr he has once again let his choice be determined by what makes for a more compelling narrative.

Moderated Politics

Carr explains the political differences which eventually drove Herzen and Bakunin apart as follows (I quote at length because this difference between the two consumes Stoppard's representation of the pair in the trilogy):

> [W]hen he [Bakunin] came to England at the end of 1861 and found his former friend deeply committed to the cause of Russian democracy, the ways of the two men parted forever. Bakunin stood far nearer than Herzen to his own countrymen; and he shared to the full the instinctive Russian distrust of democracy. He saw no logical reason, on the romantic hypothesis, to prefer the chains of democracy to the chains of autocracy. If human nature merely requires the enjoyment of its native freedom to achieve perfection, it follows that the constraint imposed by states and governments is in itself noxious, irrespective of the form of the state or the composition of the government. The true believer could only advocate a return to nature, and the destruction of all governmental units or institutions resting on force; and anarchism, which was the ultimate goal of Bakunin's political thought, was merely the logical outcome — or the logical reduction ad absurdum — of the romantic doctrine [197–198].

Given Stoppard's moderate politics, it is hardly surprising that he would find Herzen so compelling, and, moreover, that he would be so discomfited by Bakunin's anarchist aspirations. Even more important to Stoppard, however, would be the way in which *The Romantic Exiles* serves as something of a *reductio ad absurdum* of the entire romantic movement. And while Carr does not explicitly spell out this implication, on reflection it is clear that many of the tragedy's which the Herzen family faced over the years (the three longest of Carr's 17 chapters use the word "tragedy" in the title, while several other titles point towards other difficulties) are characterized as having arisen from the difficulties of putting romantic ideals into practice — most notably, the way in which the various love triangles (first Herzen, Natalie and Herwegh and later Ogarev, the Second Natalie and Herzen) failed so miserably in practice.

No novice himself when it comes to employing the *reductio ad absurdum* to its full theatrical effect (employed so successfully in *Jumpers* against George) Stoppard picks up on this thread of *The Romantic Exiles* and plays it to its fullest, both in how the love triangles — and their human costs — are so central to the second two plays in the trilogy, and in his continual belittling of Bakunin's tendency to espouse romantic ideals even while failing to live according to them (which, as we have seen, is put into full effect in the first play, but crops up in the later plays as well).

Perhaps equally interesting to Stoppard would have been Carr's characterization of how Bakunin, having chosen his causes, threw himself into them with the full force of his overwhelming personality. Carr poignantly quotes the following passage from Herzen's biographies about a conversation between Herzen and Bakunin soon after Bakunin had arrived in London:

> "Only in Poland there are some demonstrations," said Herzen; "but perhaps the Poles will come to their senses and understand that a rising is out of the question when the Tsar has just freed the serfs. Clouds are gathering, but we must hope that they will disperse."
> "And in Italy?"
> "All quiet."
> "And in Austria?"
> "All quiet."
> "And in Turkey?"
> "All quiet everywhere, and nothing in prospect."
> "Then what are we to do?" said Bakunin in amazement. "Must we go to Persia or India to stir things up? It's enough to drive one mad; I cannot sit and do nothing" [193].

This is the political charlatan whom Stoppard picks up on and develops so carefully in the trilogy. In fact, Stoppard was so given over to characterizing various of Bakunin's absurdist properties that he finally couldn't help collecting himself and having second thoughts about him, worrying that he had done Bakunin an injustice:

> This was my picture of Bakunin. Then, in New York, I began to question my treatment of him. I saw that I had adopted Alexander Herzen's perspective of his old comrade. Herzen regarded Bakunin as an oversized, irresponsible child, endearing, infuriating, fickle and occasionally admirable. And Herzen was my hero, after all. But as the long process of rehearsal and performances continued, I had the sense that I had let Bakunin down. I had short-changed him, undervalued him. He always came off worse in the exchanges with Herzen. He'd get egg on his face and carry on without resentment or deviation. I began to love him [*Coast* xiv].

The thing that Stoppard began to love is well described by Carr: "From a practical standpoint, Herzen was perfectly right. [...] But human sympathy is on the side of 'big Liza'" (196).[10] It seems, then, that Bakunin's overwhelming personality finally had the strength to charm even the skeptical Stoppard, all these years later. That said, Stoppard was hardly ready to give up his (long held) dual concern with how political agitators have such difficulty marrying their theoretical positions with practical concerns and, moreover, with the idea that all too often political agendas are more akin to a kind of moral exhibitionism than they are the sincere concerns of those espousing them — which also become the dual themes of Stoppard's next play, *Rock 'n' Roll*. The realism of *Coast* shadows the pragmatism of Herzen, never overwhelming Stoppard's powerful metatheatrical instincts. In *Rock 'n' Roll*, however, it finally does.

Encore: *Rock 'n' Roll*

Referring to *Rock 'n' Roll* as the encore performance in Stoppard's long and distinguished playwriting career will hopefully prove to be premature. At seventy-four, Stoppard is still quite active, and is as of this writing working on a screenplay of Tolstoy's *Anna Karenina*. In an interview in 2010 with Mark Lawson he left the impression that he was not currently writing a play:

> What he craves is a new play. By his age (72), Beckett and Pinter were content with one-acts and fragments; Stoppard is still aiming for two acts and three hours, interval drinks and last-train tickets. Inspiration, though, is intermittent and mercurial.

And so while Stoppard very well may yet return for an additional encore performance, *Rock 'n' Roll* will have to stand in as the final set of the night for this volume; as concerns my own needs, it fulfills this role quite nicely.

Rock 'n' Roll is unique in that unlike *Utopia*, with its occasional theatrical flourishes, for the first time Stoppard has written an entirely realist play, with none of the metatheatrical disruptions he became famous for. Of course, this in and of itself should prove sufficient to complete my argument that he has moved away from postmodern representational modes towards more traditional representational modes. Add to this the fact that while in *Coast* he continued to traverse the postmodern terrain by critiquing postmodern ideas (most notably, in his critique of German idealism and what it shares with the postmodern), in *Rock 'n' Roll* he refuses even that, leaving very little to write about without, finally, turning to how the play's politics refuse the postmodern (a tricky task, to say the least).

Rock 'n' Roll divides its time between Prague and Cambridge, covering the years from 1968 to 1990. Both dates are important ones in recent Czechoslovakian history; in 1968 the Prague Spring witnessed a brief period of liberalization, before Soviet tanks rolled in the following August, while in 1989 what became known as the Velvet Revolution finally saw a restoration of democracy. What this means is that in many respects this is a history play, albeit one populated with fictional characters. Christopher Innes takes proper notice of this characteristic of the work:

> As with *The Coast of Utopia*, all the public events are factual and well documented. [...] The true life figures are not politicians (as in *The Coast of Utopia* [...]) but rock and roll musicians: in particular, Syd Barrett, whose drug fueled break-up with Pink Floyd is chronicled in the play, as well as a Czech band rejoicing in the unlikely name of the Plastic People of the Universe ["Post-Millennial" 446].

Innes is equally convincing in his explanation of how Max and Jan each have real-world counterparts (Max is "modeled on Eric Hobsbawm" and Jan on "Jan Patocka" 447). All the same, I am more sympathetic to Carol Rocamora's view, as she argues that Jan is best understood as Stoppard's alter ego, especially given that Stoppard, like Jan, was born in Czechoslovakia before becoming something of an exile in the face of advancing German forces:

> So in *Rock 'n' Roll*, Stoppard does some time-traveling — just as his characters did in *Arcadia* — only this time it is he himself who takes the journey, going back in time and rewriting his own personal history. Through his character Jan, he imagines the life he might have lived and the choices he might have faced: to return to Prague or not after the Russian invasion, to remain passive or become a dissident, and so on [126].

In any case, it is clear that "Stoppard overlaps his main characters with recognizable people" (Innes 447), and that it contains notable elements of a history play even as it "establish[es] new standards of authenticity and realism" (Innes 448–449).

Despite their differences, the play resurrects *Coast's* concern with the tension between theory and practice, a theme most strongly embodied in Max, a philosophy professor and Communist party member. Jan, a Czech exile and Cambridge student, is Max's protégé, and equally important in this regard. The play follows Jan's return to Czechoslovakia, where he is eventually imprisoned at least as much for his fixation on rock music as for any overtly dissident activity. Meanwhile, back in Cambridge Max's Marxism is becoming increasingly out of date, in part because of the evolving plight of Marxism in capitalist Britain, and in part because of inconsistencies which naturally crop up as Max attempts to negotiate his politics with being a British citizen, husband, and college professor. The challenge finds Max admitting early on that he is:

> [D]own to one belief, that between theory and practice there's a decent fit — not a perfect fit but decent: ideology and a sensible fair society, it's my double helix and I won't be talked out of it or shamed out of it. We just have to do better [8].

Of course Max's rhetoric — that he is willing to give up all other beliefs to salvage this one — only points to how increasingly tenuous the position of the Communist Party member really is, especially as various countries in the Soviet bloc fight for and win increasing levels of sovereignty from Soviet control — a fact which further serves to belabor Max's beliefs. Eventually Max finds himself so isolated in his commitment to the party that — like George in *Jumpers* — his obsessive commitment to his belief system forces him to ignore various problems on the home front, where he is hardly more than a part-time support system for his wife as she battles cancer:

> MAX: The struggle was for socialism through organized labour, and that was that. What remains of those bright days of certainty? Where do I belong? The Party is losing its confidence in its creed. [...] Why do people go on as if there's a danger we might forget Communism's crimes, when the danger is we'll forget its achievements? I've stayed in because they meant so much to me. Now that they seem to mean so little to anyone else, I sometimes think ... Nell, what do you think? Should I ...? [50].

But in the face of what increasingly appears to be an inevitable death from cancer, Nell is hardly interested: "I don't care! I don't care about it! Stay in — get out — I don't care, Max!" For she recognizes that communism — just like the disease which is taking her life — doesn't care for her as an individual: "My body is telling me I'm nothing without it, and you're telling me the same" (50).

As such, even while there are very few of the sort of stylistic flourishes that make up the bulk of Stoppard's canon — not even a tendency to engage and arraign postmodern ideas in a more naturalist fashion, such as in *Coast* — this tendency to focus on the gap between theory and practice remains prototypically Stoppard. Eventually the tension becomes so great that Max must eventually leave the party — or, rather, see it leave him, a fact which becomes all too evident in a conversation with his daughter's boyfriend, Stephen. Indeed, Stephen espouses such a self-satisfied view about the rise of communism that it quite simply evades Max's more nuts-and-bolts attitude, a difference made manifest in Max's reaction to how communism has accommodated itself to commerce:

MAX: Now, now. Come upstairs and tell me what the comrades are doing now that history has ended,
STEPHEN: Can't, I have to lay the table. Why don't you read the journal, then you'd know.
MAX: *Marxism Today?* It's not so much the Eurocommunism. In the end it was the mail order gifts thing. I couldn't take the socks with the little hammers and sickles on them.
STEPHEN: Well, read the *Morning Star* and keep up with the tankies.
MAX: The tankies ... How the years roll by. Dubcek is back. Russia agrees to withdraw its garrisons. Czechoslovakia takes her knickers off to welcome capitalism. And all that remains of August '68 is a derisive nickname for the only real communists left in the Communist Party. I'm exactly as old as the October Revolution [80].

Apparently, the party has refused to commit to Max's core beliefs about accommodating practice to theory. To Max's way of thinking, communism has sold out.

It can hardly be a coincidence that the play comes just two years after *The Motorcycle Diaries* (2004), a film which coincided with a veritable revolution in the commercialization of the Marxist revolutionary Che Guevera, whose face came to be seen on T-shirts marketed and sold around the globe:

> Today, his image is so ubiquitous it has become fodder for couture. Even Paris Hilton could be forgiven for thinking Ernesto "Che" Guevara was the greatest accessory designer since Jimmy Choo. Model Gisele Bündchen strutted down the catwalk in a Che bikini, and Elizabeth Hurley club-hopped across London with a $4,500 Che-embroidered Louis Vuitton handbag. Even teen star Lindsay Lohan dons a tight-fitting Che shirt in "Confessions of a Teenage Drama Queen" [Armstrong].

Stoppard, of course, would have been all too quick to pick up on the irony in Che Guevara's image becoming ubiquitous in and around London (especially among the leftists of the arts and theater scene). And similar as this cultural turn of events is to the situation Max faces as Marxism becomes a fad, it is not much of a leap to conclude that it is this very cultural environment which at least in part inspired *Rock 'n' Roll*.

Meanwhile, Jan faces increasing pressure to join the Czechoslovakian dissidents. When Jan refuses to sign an anti-government document Ferdinand is circulating, Ferdinand "walks out without a word" (19). In still another argument with Ferdinand, Stoppard finally identifies the importance of rock-and-roll music to Czechoslovakian social-political liberty.

As Jan explains it, a country that allows for the proliferation of the sort of apathy which is part and parcel of the rock-and-roll environment actually does more to prove itself to be a more open society than one that simply allows for occasional voices of dissent:

> Jirous doesn't cut his hair. It makes the policeman angry, [...] What difference does long hair make? The policeman is angry about his fear. [...] He's frightened by his indifference. [...] The policeman isn't frightened by dissidents! Why should he be? Policemen love dissidents, like the inquisition loved heretics. Heretics give meaning to the defenders of the faith. Nobody cares more than a heretic [36].

Should *Rock 'n' Roll* ultimately turn out to be Stoppard's swan song, the way in which the play champions the importance of rock music in fighting for and maintaining liberal democracy and free expression would prove fitting. By contrast, in *The Real Thing* Henry admits to embarrassment about some of the music that he listens to: "I'm going to look like a complete idiot, aren't I, announcing that while I was telling Jean-Paul Sartre and the post-war French existentialists where they had it wrong, I was spending the whole time listening to the Crystals singing 'Da Doo Ron Ron'" (17). *Rock 'n' Roll*, however, contains a full-throated admission on Stoppard's part as to rock music's importance to both his literary career and beyond.

After having described *Coast* as postmodern it is with some comfort that I find that Christopher Innes has determined that *Rock 'n' Roll* is largely realist, as it means that we are at least in agreement that there has been a transition of sorts towards the real with this latest play — although with Innes it doesn't seem so much to be a gradual and inevitable transition, as a full scale aesthetic revolution. For Innes goes even further, claiming that Stoppard (as well as both David Hare's *Stuff Happens* and Max Stafford Clark/Robin Stoan's *Talking to Terrorists*) "deals in a hard-nosed, factual way with very recent history and the events of the day, establishing new standards of authenticity and realism (449)." And while I am not so sure I would go so far as Innes in suggesting that it appropriates a documentary style (albeit what it shares with the other plays that he discusses on that score seems to me to be rather slim indeed), it is hard to argue with a position that fits so well with my own conclusions about the trajectory of Stoppard's career.

That said, it is well worth acknowledging how Stoppard's realism differs from the realism of his late nineteenth-century precursors. On this score, I think that gradual transition away from the postmodern which brought him to this point is decidedly important to understanding *Rock 'n' Roll*—just as the pre-realist career which led to Ibsen's naturalism is quite important to understanding his unique variety of realism.[1] With this in mind, that the play refuses theatricalism is perhaps even less relevant than that it contains so little material which might be seen as arraigning the postmodern; at least, that is, unless we once again turn to Linda Hutcheon's theorization of the postmodern, taking particular note of her thinking about how self-reflexive formal techniques — such as those which are so common in the rest of Stoppard's work — are so easily read as drawing attention to the way in which postmodern inscriptions so often employ their self-conscious constructivity to ideological effect by implying that their construction always and already serves power:

> What is foregrounded in postmodern theory and practice is the self-conscious inscription within history of the existing, but usually concealed attitude of historians towards their material. Provisionality and undecidability, partisanship and even overt politics — these are what replace the pose of objectivity and disinterestedness that denies the interpretive and implicitly evaluative nature of historical representation [71].

By contrast, just as throughout the bulk of his career Stoppard can be seen as arraigning various ontological and epistemological attitudes common in postmodernity, so to can he be seen as arraigning this particular "ideological" feature of the postmodern (such as it is) in *Rock 'n' Roll*. For even while he is all too keen to foreground the historiographic partisanship of the Bernards and Pikes of the world in *Arcadia* and *Indian Ink*, he does very little to indicate the "evaluative nature of [his own] historical representations" in his increasingly realist history plays. Apparently, there is a right way of completing and representing history and which needs no ironic apologies when done correctly.

One possible reading of such an omission — especially given the trajectory of his career from the postmodern to the real — is indicative of a growing understanding on Stoppard's part that a blending of history, politics, and theatricalism is a recipe for political radicalism of one sort or another, and one that he would just as soon avoid.[2] As indicated in the Introduction, it is this very foregrounding of the collusion between critic and actress in *The Real Inspector Hound*— made all the more noteworthy because of the way in which the fourth wall is bridged by the critic —

which means that the play is all too easily accommodated to a politically postmodern reading, such that the critic's "pose of objectivity and disinterestedness" is always and already seen to be just that, a pose. And to be sure, one who is inclined to read a social-political agenda into *R & G* could make much of the way in which ROS and GUIL — trapped as they are by the very structure of the text and environment of the theater — embody humanity's powerlessness in the face of the various social institutions which control our lives and shape our destinies (according to this reading, the playwright, director, and actor might be conflated with the politician, the business owner and the policeman). Neil Sammells, for instance, suggests something along this line when he argues that "The choices faced by the two courtiers, and the pressures that envelop them, are clearly political pressures: the pressure of individuals trying to assert themselves against collectivism" (111).

While Sammells at least has the good sense to read the "political pressures" in a way which is consistent with Stoppard's oft professed political antipathy for socialism, other critics haven't been as careful. In *Gesher: Russian Theater in Israel: A Study of Cultural Colonization*, Olga Gershenson provides a clear instance of such a reading. Gershenson provides an account of a performance of *R & G* at the Gesher Theater in Israel, and describes the effect of metatheatricalism in the production as having created a Brechtian style alienation technique which had the effect of "distancing the audience from the characters of the show, and making the audience aware of the stage nature of the production" (40). Gershenson goes on to explain how in some of its more carnivalesque moments the play "destroys the boundaries between genres ... and ultimately shatters hierarchies of power" (41). Now, it is not clear from the description whether or not this particular production of *R & G* went out of its way to encourage an ideological reading — or whether Gershenson reads ideology into it herself (although I strongly suspect the latter, since there is no admission that the play itself is in any way metatheatrical). But in either case, it proves my point. A slight shift of one's perspective means that the work can suddenly be appropriated as chock-full of ideological intent. And, to be sure, there would very likely be many more such readings of Stoppard were he not so vocal about his moderate conservatism. (Among my colleagues who have seen or read a Stoppard play, they are universally surprised to find out that he is a moderate conservative).

Encore: Rock 'n' Roll

By contrast, Alan Sinfield explains how it is that one might read the play as driven by ideological concerns, before dismissing such a reading:

> Formally, *Rosencrantz and Guildenstern Are Dead* may seem to offer the radical undermining of ideology that we associate with a Brechtian alienation-effect. In that effect, no discourse is allowed to become established as simply dominant, as the natural and self-evident way to think about the action. The audience is denied the secure relationship with the text that characterizes the process through which ideology normally normalizes itself; the activity of language and ideology, in making the world rather than reflecting it, comes into view [130].

This nicely sums up much of what I have been saying about how the play's form can be read to ideological ends; that is, that when constructivism presents itself as an epistemological or ontological norm, it is, perhaps, quite natural to consider the place of "language and ideology" in those constructions. Holderness, however, goes on to dismiss this reading of *R & G*, ultimately arguing that a much more conservative reading of the text is in order:

> However, *Rosencrantz and Guildenstern Are Dead* is actually a very conservative play. As the discourses of the text are reduced to the one set of notions (illusion, allusion, contrivance, acting, joke, logical play), a new meta-discourse emerges behind them, controlling them and reassuring the audience. It is the metadiscourse of metadiscourse. The disturbance of Hamlet, and of all other discourses in the play, become what the play is about; we have not a surface and a rupture, but a theme, almost a statement [131].

In other words, when the play is about the artificial environment of the stage—and the way in which it traps ROS and GUIL into reliving their deaths over and over again—it is about that for its own sake. The point is not that the artificiality is the product of some ideologically sinister situation. Rather, the artificiality is itself the point. When Stoppard traverses and investigates the artificial terrain of the postmodern, he does so because he finds it fascinating in itself, not because he wants to get to the center of who might have created it, and why.

Neil Sammells finally decides that *R & G* itself serves as something of a corrective to the ideological plight of Rosencrantz and Guildenstern, suggesting that:

> Stoppard succeeds where Rosencrantz and Guildenstern fail: he manages to act upon Shakespeare's original, restyling it with Beckett's help. In effect, an act of criticism—that is both interpretive and transformational—becomes, in

a way that is simultaneously Wildean and characteristically postmodern, an act of creation [112].

Sammells comes very close here to conflating the postmodern with the political. Indeed, in an age when Shakespeare is so often decried as being too central to the canon — as exerting too much control over the Rosencrantzes and Guildensterns of academia — it is not surprising to find someone reading Stoppard in just this fashion. But I would counter that even while it is true that one needs a less-than-rigid attitude about the sacrosanctity of Shakespeare in order to appreciate what Stoppard has accomplished, Stoppard yet means to honor Shakespeare, not to bury him. What Joyce in *Travesties* says of the effect his version of *Ulysses* will have on Homer's similarly applies here, that Stoppard with his version of Hamlet "will double that immortality, yes, by God there's a corpse that will dance for some time yet and leave the world precisely as it finds it." Well, Stoppard is far more modest than Joyce, but you get the idea.

According to this perspective, until *Rock 'n' Roll* only *Night and Day* would have been entirely immune to this type of misreading, given how explicitly it rejects the idea that corporate power yields too much influence vis-à-vis the production and distribution of knowledge. In that case, given how straightforwardly the case is made for a media unfettered by union control, it is impossible to read any irony into the play's argument. *Rock 'n' Roll*, moreover, can be seen as making much the same point: that organized labor in all its manifestations — from the closed shop to the closed country — is the only significant means by which power threatens freedom of expression. With Max muted by a changing socio-political culture — and with the Soviet Union overturned — Jan and Esme (Max's granddaughter) are finally able to relax into themselves for a tender moment in a pub; so much so that Esme — apparently assuming that the Czech waiter would not understand her English — decides that she is free enough from social constraints to tell Jan that she would like to be "shagged senseless." So, too, the bartender is free to learn English, which means just as there is no longer a secret language which might keep him from pursuing various other sorts of freedom, he is also free to indicate to Jan and Esme that he has overheard their private communiqué. And all of them are free to run off to see the Rolling Stones play their famous Prague concert. According to Stoppard's way of thinking, this is what liberal democracy allows. There is nothing to his realist picture about the conditions under which liberal democracy allows it; and no complex theatrical structure which might — albeit inadvertently — give such generous license to a politicized rethinking of the play's intent. Despite everything — theaters, players, critics, surrealists, philosophers, dadaists, news reporters, unions, actors, chaos, academics, quantum mechanics, thermodynamics, love, anarchists, capitalism, communism, and disingenuous authors — the world remains both a known and knowable locale.

Chapter Notes

Chapter 1

1. Simard's work is typical not only of how Stoppard is too quickly lumped into the postmodern, but of how much of the early work in postmodern drama uses it as little more than a convenient label with which to explain various forms of experimentation in contemporary theater. Marvin Carlson's *Deathtraps: The Postmodern Comedy Thriller* (1993) is notable for how it implements the description of the postmodern outlined by Linda Hutcheon in order to recognize that a postmodern element exists in contemporary dramatic murder mysteries. Here again, however, the focus is decidedly narrow; by contrast, I hope to use the term in a way that is more widely applicable (although Carlson is put to fair use below in my discussion of *The Real Inspector Hound*). And as we will see in my discussion of *The Coast of Utopia* in the concluding chapter, Innes simply gets Stoppard wrong.

2. William W. Demastes expresses a similar attitude towards Stoppard in a recent essay on Arcadia: "Challenging our powers of observation and data reconstruction, and offering multiple possible resolutions at the same time are all part of Stoppard's agenda" (231). For a fuller treatment of Demastes' essay, see Chapter 5, note 12.

3. While never explicitly addressing this issue, Hutcheon is always careful to distinguish between postmodern forms and their use by political movements, as she does in her Epilogue to *The Politics of Postmodernism*: "What these various forms of identity politics share with the postmodern is a focus on difference and ex-centricity, an interest in the hybrid, the heterogeneous, and the local, and an interrogative and deconstructing mode of analysis. Each of these however has had its own specific artistic and social history" (166).

4. Tim Brassell, in *Tom Stoppard: An Assessment* (New York: St. Martin's Press, 1985), for instance, explains that while there is a whole range of work that Stoppard invites comparison to, "Chief among these is Pirandello's self-conscious exploration of inescapably defined roles in *Six Characters in Search of an Author*" (47). Neil Sammels unwittingly presents one possibility for how this influence might have happened in his suggestion that Stoppard may very well have read Lionel Abel's *Metatheatre* (1965). Sammels finds the fact that Abel explains how "the self-referentiality of Hamlet expresses itself not just in the explicit commentary on actors and acting, but in the way the play is constructed as a continuing conflict between different dramatists" ("The Early Stage Plays," *The Cambridge Companion to Tom Stoppard*. Ed. Katherine E. Kelly. Cambridge University Press: Cambridge, 2001. 110). Had Stoppard read Abel, he would have been introduced to Pirandello's work there, as well as to a treatment of it which may well have proved very suggestive to him.

5. It should be said that Hunter's way of putting this serves as a nice explanation

Chapter Notes

for how *R & G* paves the way for *Jumpers*, which pursues similar philosophical questions, albeit more directly.

6. McHale recognizes an ontological disparity in how the law of the excluded middle is broken, as two different characters, Malone and Molloy, appear to be one.

Chapter 2

1. That this has resonance with Magritte's work is directly commented upon in the text itself as Harris explains the presence of a tuba to Inspector Foot by explaining that his mother is an admirer of Magritte (22).

2. Zekiyi Er does a nice job of putting together the various quotes from Stoppard explaining the impetus behind these particular scenes, quoting Stoppard on *Jumpers* as follows:

> There are tiny bits of that in *Jumpers*: a man carrying a tortoise in one hand and a bow and arrow in the other, his face is covered in shaving foam. A trick I enjoy very much is when, bit by bit, you build up something ludicrous — and then someone walks in [Gussow 8].

But Er is wrong to see anything remotely new historicist in Stoppard's attitude towards how witnesses react to these oddities. Indeed, Er suggests, "What new historicists tend to do is not much different from Stoppard's intention here: that is, to show the reasons behind seeing a man with a peacock in his hand, his face covered with shaving foam, running into the street" (232). This is such a general claim about the interpretive process that it could describe just about any interpretive mode. Moreover, Stoppard doesn't ever just show the "reasons" behind his anomalous scenes; in each case, rather, there is a specific sequence of events which lead to the scene in question, and which the audience is well aware of. Er's mistake seems to be confusing Stoppard's having traveled this postmodern terrain (which he does), with committing to it (which he does not). Oddly enough, while Er quotes the same Vanden Heuvel essay from which I take this very terminology, he continues to write as if Stoppard is a thoroughgoing postmodernist in his new historicist approach to literary history.

3. Perret correctly notes that "the confrontation between Dotty and Bones occasions a fine theatrical joke" with very similar "appearance-reality" implications; as in the previous scene, given the way in which the meeting is accompanied first by "Mozartian trumpets" and then "a loud animal bray" and, finally, the dropping of a vase: "A noise such as would have been made had he dropped it down a long flight of stone stairs." Perret notes that this "mystery is resolved by the subsequent action."

4. See Introduction. Jonathan Bennet also sees philosophical interest in *R & G*. See below.

5. Ironic because his namesake at Cambridge, G. E. Moore, was a logical positivist (although, admittedly, his ethical philosophy was not the mainstream logical positivism variety).

6. As Jill Oliphant, Jon Mayled, "Emotivism [the ethical theory most commonly linked to logical positivism] is sometimes known as the Boo/Hurrah theory, as in saying 'murder is wrong' we are saying 'boo to murder,' and in saying 'giving to charity is good' we are saying 'hurrah for giving to charity'" (15).

7. John Fleming quotes Stoppard's own take on George's neglect of home and family: "While George has the right ideas, he is also a culpable person; while he is defending his ideas and attacking the opposition, he is neglecting everyone around him and shutting out his wife who is in need, not to mention shooting his hare and stepping on his tortoise" (quoted in Fleming 95).

8. One of the "bizarre" things that only

Chapter Notes

philosophers could convince themselves of, no doubt, would be the Foucauldian idea that the human sciences are an institution of oppression.

9. This, perhaps, is what Stoppard gets from Wittgenstein, who took it on himself to cure philosophers of the desire to philosophize. Wittgenstein was extremely critical of the sorts of questions philosophers asked.

10. Fleming explains that in an early version of the play the dream is attributed to George. Stoppard wrote, "It may as well be stated now that a rational explanation of this coda, if such an explanation is required, is that it is George's dream" (274).

11. See Fleming (99).

12. This is a joke that is later recycled in *Arcadia*, when Bernard proclaims, "I've proved Byron was here and as far as I'm concerned he wrote those lines as sure as he shot that hare" (*Arcadia* 89). However, in that case the punch line (that Byron had shot neither the Hare nor Chater) is much more central to the text, indicting Bernard as complicit in creating knowledge rather than discovering — with the corollary more determinist implication that if he had not been so eager to publish he would have determined the truth — which eventually does become clear (see Chapter 5). In this case, of course, the truth outs itself as well, but not so much in a way that implicates George's behavior as an academic, but, rather, his behavior as a husband. As such, the episode's connection to the play's larger concern with whether or not it is reasonable to treat moral and aesthetic principles as contingent social norms is tenuous at best — with the result that the play remains much more engaged with teasing out these issues rather than simply indicting the critics that are engaged in them (as is the case in *Arcadia*).

Chapter 3

1. See Stephen Sicari's essay "Rereading Ulysses: 'Ithaca' and Modernist Allegory."

2. For a lively and informative treatment of this connection — which would appear to suggest a much more complex relationship than I (or perhaps even Stoppard) give to this relationship — see Ira Nadel's essay on the play in the *James Joyce Quarterly*.

3. In Stoppard we find: "JOYCE: ... what, reduced to their simplest reciprocal form, were Tzara's thoughts about Ball's thoughts about Tzara, and Tzara's thoughts about Ball's thoughts about Tzara's thoughts about Ball. TZARA: He thought that he knew that he would ride the tiger, whereas he knew that he thought that he knew that he would not" (*Travesties* 60). Compare this to Joyce: "What reduced to their simplest reciprocal form, were Bloom's thoughts about Stephen's thoughts about Bloom and about Stephen's thoughts about Bloom's thoughts about Stephen. He thought that he thought that he was a jew whereas he knew that he knew that he knew that he was not" (558).

4. For Brian Richardson, "Carr is a clear specimen of what I have elsewhere termed the 'fraudulent narrator,' whose averred narrative stance is so clearly preposterous that it is not intended to be believed" (684).

5. In arguing that the play is indicative of Stoppard's new historicist credentials (see Chapter 2, note 2) Zekiye Er misunderstands the epistemological function of Carr when he writes, "The end of the play is another opportunity for Stoppard to show that reality is no more than a mere fiction created in the mind of a man (here Old Carr), and that what the audience has been watching so far is just his illusionary, misleading reminiscence" (235). There is, however, very little that is ultimately misleading about an old man confused about his youth, especially when he admits to the confusion himself (and in so doing "normalizes" the anomalies).

6. Zeifman quotes from a Tom Stoppard interview with Roger Hudson, Catherine Itzin, and Simon Trussler (6).

7. Toby Zinman sees this as one more way in which the title of the play resonates with the content, explaining how Henry's "dreadful hackwork ... is writing for alimony money, and not the real thing at all" (133).

8. See Mark Lawson's interview with Tom Stoppard, "Tom Stoppard: I'm the Crank in the Bus Queue."

9. Of course, for many feminist critics this would be quite beside the point, as proof of Stoppard's misogyny would be found in the positivism itself.

Chapter 4

1. In *Tom Stoppard and the Craft of Comedy* (153) Katherine Kelly claims that Stoppard followed this debate closely, and that he would have been versed in the commission's report (Ann Arbor: University of Michigan Press, 1991).

2. For a more thorough discussion of the way in which *Serious Money* is conscious of its own role in the power/knowledge hierarchy, see my essay "Serious Money Becomes 'Business by Other Means': Caryl Churchill's Metatheatrical Subject," *Comparative Drama* 38:2,3 (2004): 1–29.

3. In "Science in *Hapgood* and *Arcadia*" (in Kelly, ed., *The Cambridge Companion to Tom Stoppard* Cambridge, UK: Cambridge University Press, 2001), Paul Edwards tracks the different reception that the two plays received, *Hapgood* negative and *Arcadia* positive. That my discussion diverges significantly from Edwards' is made explicit in the fact that after limited discussion of *Hapgood*, Edwards explains, "There is not room here to explore the remaining intricacies.... What must be said, however, is that working these intricacies out does not — as it ideally should — take us deeper into them" (175). In *Arcadia*, as well, Edwards focuses more on the way in which chaos theory serves as an analogy to the complexity that arises out of human emotions than on the epistemological and ontological implications of the play.

Chapter 5

1. To revel in a work's "anti-epistemological implications" would mean reveling in the fact that knowability is an impossibility.

2. It is important to note that they focus on its epistemological implications, rather than its ontological features.

3. See the discussion in Plotnitsky, 179–180.

4. For an example of how conspiracy derives from complexity in such a way as to create postmodern effect, see my essay "Theatrical Collusion with Multinational Capitalism in Caryl Churchill's Serious Money." Text and Presentation 21 (2000): 117–134.

5. Coincidentally, in *After Magritte* a white umbrella glimpsed in passing becomes first an ivory cane and then a blind man's walking stick. The play is shot through with examples of how perspective skews perception, except that in Stoppard's case the situation is finally decidable when the two who are in disagreement about the identity of the object find out that the object was most certainly an umbrella.

6. I also don't mean to suggest that had Stoppard only been more postmodern, the play would have been a greater success. Paul Edwards nicely articulates a likely reason for why it is the least successful of Stoppard's plays to date, both commercially and critically, arguing that "science should, through the sideways slant of its analogies, illuminate the human world" and that "if the balance is wrongly weighted, or the production wrongly calculated, emotion and meaning are not just unspoken but lost altogether" (172–173). According to Edwards, Stoppard gets this wrong in *Hapgood*, where "the remoteness of its action is [too far removed] from everyday life," but gets it right in *Arcadia*, which "turns such remoteness to its advantage" (176).

7. Vees-Gulani is convinced that Stoppard's work implies similar sentiments:

Chapter Notes

"Intuition, then, is a useful tool for understanding when it is based on the evidence available. Stoppard, however, never fails to make clear that prediction, no matter which technique is applied, will always be fragmentary and cannot be guaranteed to be flawless" (422). As we will see, however, Stoppard is anything but a strict intuitionist, nor does he have much in common with other anti-epistemological trends in hermeneutics. For Stoppard does believe firmly in the scientific method of conjecture and refutation — a process that identifies, on seemingly arbitrary criteria, some data as "less flawless" than other data. How, for instance, are we to believe that the information which "refutes" Bernard's theory hasn't itself been corrupted by time and chaos?

8. W. K. Wimsatt, Jr., and Monroe C. Beardsley, "The Intentional Fallacy." 1946. In Wimsatt, *The Verbal Icon*. Lexington: University of Kentucky Press, 1954. 3–18.

9. See, for example, the essay "What Is an Author?" in *Michel Foucault, Language, Counter-Memory, Practice*. Trans. Donald F. Bouchard and Sherry Simon. Ithaca: Cornell University Press, 1977. 113–138.

10. This is the scientific method of conjecture and refutation as Karl Popper explains it: "The method of science is the method of bold conjectures and ingenious and severe attempts to refute them." Bernard gets the bold part right but fails miserably when it comes to offering up refutations. Popper continues: "We can never make absolutely certain that our theory is not lost. All we can do is to search for the falsity content of our best theory" (81). For Popper, every theory remains, at best, a hypothesis, always and already subject to the method of conjecture and refutation. This is Valentine's point when he claims that "it can only not prove to be false yet" (Arcadia 74). Popper continues: "And if we fail to refute a new theory, especially in the fields in which its predecessor has been refuted, then we can claim this as one of the objective reasons for the conjecture that the new theory is a better approximation to the truth than the old theory" (Popper 81). Everyone is convinced, moreover, that Bernard's theory about Byron has been rejected by Hannah in favor of one that "is a better approximation of the truth than the old theory." Finally, Popper's requirement that theories be "bold" means that these theories must be refutable when considered according to empirical evidence. Vague theories that can stand come what may are, simply, unscientific; consider, for instance, how Bernard's thoughts about Byron made Byron capable of anything — even that he might have "borrowed the book, written the review, posted it, seduced Mrs. Chater, fought a duel and departed, all in the space of three days" (59). Of course Stoppard's invocation of Popper is a mini-lesson in Stoppard's ultimate rejection of constructivist theories of truth in general; consider, by contrast, Thomas Kuhn, who believes that scientific knowledge doesn't accumulate in the way that Popper describes, but rather that science goes through a series of revolutions and that each new scientific perspective is neither more nor less true than the previous one.

11. In a recent essay William W. Demastes presents a theory of Stoppard's career that complicates my own view that Stoppard's primary mode involves serving up odd and ontologically anomalous versions of reality, before normalizing them in one way or another (according to this perspective, Stoppard's invocation of Popper's scientific method comes in as his latest tool for accomplishing this end). Demastes also sees a similar connection between Stoppard and Popper (although he fails to quote my own earlier *Comparative Drama* essay on *Arcadia* which also makes this same connection, largely repeated herein):

> Philosopher of science Karl Popper famously framed the matter by ask-

ing, "Under what conditions would I admit that my theory is untenable?" Popper clarifies: "In other words what conceivable facts would I accept as refutations, or falsifications, of my theory" (41). Stretching limits of credibility and observing what ensues, challenging our powers of observation and data reconstruction, and offering multiple possible resolutions while at the same time are all part of Stoppard's agenda [231].

This sounds quite close to my own position — especially that through the falsification method Stoppard is committed to "rejecting subjectivity and randomness." Demastes, however, goes on to complicate the picture unnecessarily:

> It's to begin with an assumption of communal habituation against which Stoppard will push in order for us to reconsider our smug, generally upper-middle-class, self-congratulatory (and generally Newtonian) perspectives on existence [233].

Put this way, of course, he provides only half the picture — for as we will see, Stoppard also proves himself quite capable at pushing us "to reconsider our smug, generally upper-middle-class, self congratulatory (and generally [Einsteinian]) perspectives on existence." (Put this way, Demastes sounds more than half wrong, as I have actually met many more people among the upper class who are prone to defending relativist positions, than I have among the working class). While Demastes finally determines, "Between the improbable and impossible is where Stoppard's theater thrives" (233), I argue, by contrast, that even while in one sense this may well be true of Stoppard, it is also true that Stoppard strives for ever greater determinability as his career progresses.

12. Gleick, Chaos, 6; quoted by Prapassaree and Kramer, "Stoppard's Arcadia," 4.

13. Paul Edwards describes one scene which very nearly approximates what I am talking about: "A coffee mug set down in a 'modern' scene at the beginning of the play should remain on the table in a nineteenth-century scene that occurs later in the play (and vice versa for the props placed there in the nineteenth century). At the end of the play, the table has accumulated a variety of objects that, if one saw them without having seen the play, would seem completely random and disordered" (181). However, despite the fact that there is an overture on Stoppard's part to the postmodern potential of this particular invocation of the chaos metaphor, Edwards describes the final effect as in fact normalizing the anomaly: "Entropy is high. But if one has seen the play, one has full information about the objects and the hidden 'order' of the arrangement, brought about by the performance itself. Entropy is low; this can be proved by reflecting that tomorrow night's performance of the play will finish with the table in a virtually identical 'disorder'— which therefore cannot really be disorder at all" (181). I might have written this last bit myself, for how it corresponds with my explanations of how similar scenes in *After Magritte* and *Jumpers* normalize themselves.

14. As we have seen in Chapters 1 and 3, Stoppard has written about both Shakespeare and Joyce, and from a standpoint which is largely dismissive of critical excess; but he does not suggest that extreme uninterpretability is the result.

15. Ironically, Gleick's own narrative about the history of chaos theory is fairly traditional epistemologically. Ultimately he reconstructs a grand historical narrative about his subject and makes his own opinion — that chaos is the next great scientific achievement — all too apparent; moreover, like all success stories Gleick's has its heroes (Feigenbaum and Mandelbrot, who in the face of much skepticism, yet prevail) and its villains (those who stood

in Feigenbaum's and Mandelbrot's way). And yet we might wonder, "Aren't the historical circumstances from which chaos theory sprang themselves chaotic?" If so, what inspires Gleick's confidence in his particular narrative construction? Doesn't a tenuous epistemology require a new narrative form?

Chapter 6

1. Clearly, I would strongly disagree with such readings of Stoppard as that of Zekiye Er, who argues that Stoppard essentially uses drama to defend new historicist attitudes about interpretation as construction and the unavailability of history:

> New historicist critics are less fact- and event-oriented than historical critics used to be, perhaps because they have come to wonder whether the truth about what really happened can ever be purely and objectively known. *Arcadia* and *Travesties* are based on this very assumption of the impossibility of a "real" reality. New historicists (like Stoppard) are less likely to see history as linear and progressive, as a movement developing toward the present or the future (teleological), and they are also less likely to think of it in terms of specific eras, each with a definite, persistent and consistent Zeitgeist.

By contrast, I argue that Stoppard believes both that there are facts and that they can be recovered by those who carefully pursue the very linear method of conjecture and refutation.

2. In a sustained Orientalist critique of the play, Bhatia notes an unintentional irony in Stoppard simultaneously criticizing the excesses of academic criticism, while writing a play so invested in academic style research as well:

> If, indeed, Stoppard's intention is to reveal the unknowability of history and the impossibility of reconstructing history through academic analyses, then it is all the more ironic that his play is extremely academic and keeps providing footnotes to his own construction of the empire and its aftermath. These include references to the British Library, the University of Texas Library, and the University of Maryland English Department, and to the letters of Emily Eden, Macaulay and the politics of English, the Theosophical Society, Bloomsbury, Gertrude Stein, Virginia Woolf, Bernard Shaw, Rudyard Kipling, "Gunga Din," and *A Passage to India* [233].

It is hard to dismiss Bhatia's point of concern here; Bhatia is right to notice that one way of reading the implications of Stoppard's "attack on Pike" is that it "serves to foil academic reassessment of imperial history and of the play itself" (233), potentially silencing Bhatia's very critique of Stoppard.

3. The Lee quote is from page 17 of *Indian Ink*.

4. See 103–104, where Houseman questions whether he remembers the boating incident properly.

5. Or, at least according to one accounting of why Housman would fail his exams, although this is not the one which dominates the play (i.e., that Housman deliberately failed to stay near Jackson). Fleming lists others, including that "Housman spent idle time with Jackson when he should have been reading and studying" and that "over confidence bred of contempt for the Oxford establishment" and "his father's serious illness" (299).

6. With the current penchant for Queer deconstructions of texts, I must admit to being a bit surprised by the fact that this play is yet to be targeted for reinforcing heteronormativity — for championing a gay figure who embraces such a austere and celibate lifestyle. Aside from

the fact that such a reading would presuppose that Wilde is meant to be viewed negatively by comparison (which as we have seen, is hardly an open and shut case), more fundamentally I think this would be a very odd conclusion to make about a playwright who has written a play which unselfconsciously demonstrates the passion and tenderness of feeling that one man might have for another. As such, I read this as a play which — to the extent that it engages such debate (which it does very minimally) hopes to put the debate behind us. Or, at least, simply finds a debate about homosexuality's legitimacy irrelevant to the deeper issue of attempting to understand what love is. According to this reading, while the play is not postmodern in any of the self-conscious ideologically driven ways which Hutcheon describes, it is post gay — "The notion that homosexuals should be able to define their identities by something other than sexual preference (Urbandictionary.com)" — all the same. Housman loves Jackson, but ultimately seeks to define himself by the academic work that he does and the poetry that he writes more than by whom he loves.

Chapter 7

1. Discussed in Chapters 5 and 6. Roberta Barker notes this similarity as well:

> Herzen, meanwhile, balances his final dismissal of imaginary Utopias with a plea to those who will take up his lifelong revolutionary struggle. "The idea will not perish," he declares in words strongly reminiscent of Septimus' speech in Arcadia. "What we let fall will be picked up by those behind." He bids these inheritors "[t]o go on, and to know there is no landfall on the paradisal shore, and still to go on" (Salvage Promptbook 118). The possibility of a final resting-place may be gone, but the drive for progress continues [718].

Barker goes on to convincingly show — while querying the feminist implications of Stoppard's different uses of circular and linear time — how in various forms it extends back to the beginning of Stoppard's career.

2. Although oddly enough, in an earlier essay Innes is less convinced by the play's realism — see below.

3. And while Innes may simply have been expressing surprise at the fact that one play picks up where another leaves off, the fact that he would ignore this non-chronological feature when discussing this particular issue — that is, his expressed concern with the plays' realism — is an odd bit of scholarship all the same

4. See Chapter 5.

5. See Chapter 2.

6. As I discuss in the introduction, Rosencrantz and Guildenstern fixate on whether the sun has risen, and do so in a way that draws attention to the medium of theater. In this case, that medium is obscured and the illusion of realism restored.

7. See "Mass Media Culture," *The Jean Baudrillard Reader*, ed. Steve Redhead. Edinburgh: Edinburgh University Press, 2008. 14.

8. There is very little from Carr's book in *Voyage*.

9. Most of the available letters are ones written from Natalie to Herwegh, who saved them. Natalie burned all of Herwegh's letters to her. All indications are that most of the dialogue is composed by Carr. It is not set apart in block quotes as other quotes are, and a review of Herzen's biography doesn't turn up the relevant quotes. Moreover, when the dialogue does come from the letters, Carr is explicit on this fact, prefacing one bit of dialogue by writing, "The conversation with Natalie is recorded by Emma herself."

Chapter Notes

10. "Big Liza" being the name they used for him in London, after their youngest, Little Liza, who was so enamored of him.

Encore

1. This perspective would to some extent account for seeming inconsistencies, given that in a 1979 interview with Kenneth Tynan Stoppard said of naturalism (realism), "I think that sort of truth-telling writing is as big a lie as the deliberate fantasies I construct. It's based on the fallacy of naturalism. There's a direct line of descent which leads you down to the dregs of bad theater, bad thinking, and bad feeling" (64). (Thanks to Neil Sammells for drawing my attention to this quote.)

2. *Night and Day* is perhaps Stoppard's second most political play — and, perhaps, his second least metatheatrical one, a fact which I occasionally use to make a similar point in Chapter 4.

Bibliography

Allen, Paul. "Third Ear" (Interview). In Delaney, *Tom Stoppard in Conversation*. 239–247.

Armstrong, Elizabeth. *Che Chic. The Christian Science Monitor*, March 5, 2004. Accessed September 15, 2011. http://www.csmonitor.com/2004/0305/p13s02-algn.html.

Arndt, Susanne. "'We're All Free to Do as We're Told': Gender and Ideology in Tom Stoppard's *The Real Thing*." *Modern Drama* 40:4 (Winter 1997): 489–501.

Baudrillard, Jean. *Cool Memories: 1980–1985*. Trans. Chris Turner. London: Verso, 2003.

———. *The Jean Beaudrillard Reader*. Ed. Steve Redhead. Edinburgh: Edinburgh University Press, 2008.

———. *Simulacra and Simulation*. Ann Arbor: University of Michigan Press, 1994.

———. "The Superficial Abyss." *The Ecstasy of Communication*. New York: Semiotext(e), 1988.

Bennett, Jonathan. "Philosophy and Mr. Stoppard." *Philosophy* 50:191 (January 1975): 5–18.

Berlin, Isaiah. *Russian Thinkers*. 2nd ed. New York: Penguin, 2008.

Bhatia, Nandi. "Reinventing India through 'A Quite Witty Pastiche': Reading Tom Stoppard's *Indian Ink*." *Modern Drama* 52:2 (Summer 2009): 220–237.

Bragg, Melvyn. "The South Bank Show." London Weekend Television. November 26, 1978. reprinted in Delaney, *Tom Stoppard in Conversation*.

Brassell, Tim. *Tom Stoppard: An Assessment*. New York: St. Martin's Press, 1985.

Bull, John. *Stage Right: Crisis and Recovery in British Contemporary Mainstream Theatre*. New York: St. Martin's Press, 1994.

———. "Tom Stoppard and Politics." In Katherine E. Kelly, ed. *The Cambridge Companion to Tom Stoppard*. Cambridge, UK: Cambridge University Press, 2001. 136–153.

Carr, E. H. *The Romantic Exiles: A Nineteenth-Century Portrait Gallery*. London: Serif, 2007.

Churchill, Caryl. *Cloud Nine*. London: Theatre Communications Group, 1995.

———. *Serious Money*. London: Methuen, 1987.

Corballis, Richard. "Wilde ... Joyce ... O'Brien ... Stoppard: Modernism and Postmodernism in 'Travesties.'" In Patrick Gillespie, ed. *Joycean Occasions*. Newark: University of Delaware Press, 1991. 157–170.

Corso, Gregory. *The Happy Birthday of Death*. New York: New Directions, 1960.

Delaney, Paul, ed. *Tom Stoppard in Conversation*. Ann Arbor: University of Michigan Press, 2001.

———. *Tom Stoppard: The Moral Vision of the Major Plays*. New York: St. Martin's Press, 1990.

Demastes, William W. "Portrait of an Artist as Proto-Chaotician: Tom Stoppard Working His Way to Arcadia." *Narrative*, 19:2 (May 2011): 229–240.

Bibliography

Eagleton, Terry. "Awakening from Modernity." *Times Literary Supplement*, February 20, 1987.

Edgar, David. *The Second Time as Farce: Reflection on the Drama of Mean Times*. London: Lawrence & Wishart, 1988.

Edwards, Paul. "Science in *Hapgood* and *Arcadia*." In Katherine E. Kelly, ed., *The Cambridge Companion to Tom Stoppard*. Cambridge, UK: Cambridge University Press, 2001. 171–184.

Er, Zekiye. "Tom Stoppard, New Historicism, and Estrangement in *Travesties*." *New Theatre Quarterly* 21:3 (August 2005): 230–240.

Feynman, Richard. *The Character of Physical Law*. 1965. Cambridge, MA: MIT Press, 1967.

Fish, Stanley. *Is There a Text in This Class?* Cambridge, MA: Harvard University Press, 1980.

Fleming, John. *Stoppard's Theatre: Finding Order amid Chaos*. Austin: University of Texas Press, 2001.

Foucault, Michel. *This Is Not a Pipe*. Trans. James Harkness. Berkeley: University of California, 1983.

Frayn, Michael. *Copenhagen*. London: Methuen, 1998.

Gershenson, Olga. *Gesher: Russian Theatre in Israel: A Study of Cultural Colonization*. New York: Peter Lang Publishing, 2005.

Gleick, James. *Chaos: Making a New Science*. New York: Penguin, 1987.

Gollob, David, and David Raper. "Trad Tom Pops In" (Interview). In Delaney, *Tom Stoppard in Conversation*, 150–166.

Gow, Andrew Sydenham Farrar. *The Greek Bucolic Poets*. Cambridge, MA: Harvard University Press, 1996.

Gussow, Mel. "*Jumpers* Author Is Verbal Gymnast" (Interview). In Delaney, *Tom Stoppard in Conversation*, 73–76.

Hassan, Ihab. "From Postmodernism to Postmodernity: The Local/Global Context." *Philosophy and Literature* 25.1 (2001): 1–13.

_____. *The Postmodern Turn: Essays in Postmodern Theory and Culture*. Bowling Green: Ohio State University Press, 1987.

Hawkes, Nigel. "Plotting the Course of a Playwright" (Interview). In Delaney, *Tom Stoppard in Conversation*, 2001.

Hewett, Ivan. "Ineffable or Just Indefinable." *Prospect Magazine* 41. May 1999. Accessed August 14, 2010. http://www.prospectmagazine.co.uk/article_details.php?id=3932/.

Hinden, Michael. "*Jumpers*: Stoppard and the Theatre of Exhaustion." *Twentieth Century Literature* 27. 1 (Spring 1981): 1–15.

Hofstadter, Douglas R. *Gödel, Escher, Bach: An Eternal Golden Braid*. New York: Basic Books, 1979.

Hudson, Roger, Catherine Itzin, and Simon Trussler. "Ambushes for the Audience: Towards a High Comedy of Ideas." (Interview.) *Theatre Quarterly* 4 (May–July 1974): 3–17.

Hunter, Jim. *Tom Stoppard*. London: Faber and Faber, 2000.

_____. *Tom Stoppard's Plays*. New York: Grove, 1982.

_____. *About Stoppard: The Playwright and the Work*. London: Faber and Faber, 2005.

Hutcheon, Linda. *The Politics of Postmodernism*. New York: Routledge, 1989.

Innes, C. D. "Towards a Post-millennial Mainstream? Documents of the Times." *Modern Drama* 50:3 (Fall 2007): 435–452.

_____. "Allegories from the Past: Stoppard's Uses of History." *Modern Drama* 49.2 (Summer 2006): 223–237.

Jameson, Fredric. "Postmodernism and Consumer Society." In Hal Foster, *The Anti-Aesthetic: Essays on Postmodern Culture*. Seattle, WA: Bay Press, 1983. 111–125.

_____. *Postmodernism, or, The Cultural Logic of Late Capitalism*. Durham, NC: Duke University Press, 1991.

_____. *The Geopolitical Aesthetic: Cinema and Space in the New World System*.

Bloomington: Indiana University Press, 1992.

Jenkins, Anthony. *The Theatre of Tom Stoppard*. Cambridge, UK: Cambridge University Press, 1990.

Jensen, Henning. "Jonathan Bennett and Mr. Stoppard." *Philosophy* 52:200 (1977): 214–217.

Jernigan, Daniel. "Tom Stoppard and 'Postmodern Science': Normalizing Radical Epistemologies in *Hapgood* and *Arcadia*." *Comparative Drama* 37 (Spring 2003): 3–35.

Kaplan, Laurie. "*In the Native State/Indian Ink*: Footnoting the Footnotes on Empire." *Modern Drama* 41:3 (Fall 1998): 337–346.

Kelly, Katherine E., ed. *The Cambridge Companion to Tom Stoppard*. Cambridge, UK: Cambridge University Press, 2001.

Kerensky, Oleg. "Tom Stoppard" (Interview). In Delaney, *Tom Stoppard in Conversation*, 85–88.

Kershaw, Baz. "Discouraging Democracy: British Theatres and Economics, 1979–1999." *Theatre Journal* 51:3 (1999): 267–283.

Kramer, Prapassaree and Jeffrey Kramer. "Stoppard's *Arcadia*: Research, Time, Loss." *Modern Drama* 40 (1997): 1–10.

Kreps, Barbara. "How Do We Know That We Know What We Know in Tom Stoppard's *Jumpers*?" *Twentieth Century Literature* 32:2 (Summer 1986): 187–208.

Lawson, Mark. "Tom Stoppard: I'm the Crank in the Bus Queue" (Interview). *The Guardian*. April 2010. Accessed September 15, 2011. http://www.guardian.co.uk/stage/2010/apr/14/tom-stoppard-the-real-thing.

Lavender, Andy. "Theatre in Crisis: Conference Report, December 1988." *New Theatre Quarterly* 5 (1989): 211–213.

Lee, Josephine. "*In the Native State* and *Indian Ink*." In Katherine E. Kelly, ed. *The Cambridge Companion to Tom Stoppard*. Cambridge, UK: Cambridge University Press, 2001. 38–52.

Lyotard, Jean-François. *The Postmodern Condition*. Minneapolis: University of Minnesota Press, 1984.

McHale, Brian. *Constructing Postmodernism*. London: Routledge, 1992.

———. *Postmodernist Fiction*. London: Routledge, 1987.

McGregor, O. R. *Royal Commission on the Press: Final Report*. London: Her Majesty's Stationery Office, 1977.

Mendelsohn, Daniel. "The Tale of Two Housmans." *The New York Review of Books*. August 10, 2000. Accessed October 15, 2011. http://www.nybooks.com/articles/archives/2000/aug/10/the-tale-of-two-housmans.

Murphy, Neil. "Flann O'Brien." *Review of Contemporary Fiction* 25:3 (Fall 2005): 7–41.

Nadel, Ira. *Double Act: A Life of Tom Stoppard*. London: Methuen, 2002.

———. "*Travesties*: Tom Stoppard's Joyce and Other Dadaist Fantasies, Or History in a Hat," *James Joyce Quarterly* 45:3–4 (Spring–Summer 2008): 481–492.

O'Brien, Flann. *At Swim-Two-Birds*. New York: Walker, 1966.

Oliphant, Jill, and Jon Mayled. *Religious Ethics for AS and A2*. London: Routledge, 2007.

Perret, Roy W. "Philosophy as Farce, or Farce as Philosophy." *Philosophy* 59:229 (July 1984): 373–381.

Pirandello, Luigi. *Naked Masks*. New York: Dutton, 1952.

Plotnitsky, Arkady. *Complementarity: Anti-Epistemology after Bohr and Derrida*. Durham, NC: Duke University Press, 1994.

Pynchon, Thomas. *The Crying of Lot 49*. Philadelphia: Lippincott, 1966.

Reckford, Kenneth. "Stoppard's Housman." *ARION*. 9:2 (Fall 2001): 108–149.

Richardson, Brian. "Voice and Narration

in Postmodern Drama." *New Literary History* 32:3 (Summer 2001): 681–694.

———. *Unnatural Voices*. Columbus: Ohio State University Press, 2006.

Rocamora, Carol. "The Parallel Worlds of '*Rock 'n' Roll*': Tom Stoppard Imagines a Life He Might Have Lived in the Country of His Birth" (Theater review). *American Theatre* 23:8 (2006): 122–127.

Sammells, Neil. "The Early Stage Plays." In Katherine E. Kelly, ed. *The Cambridge Companion to Tom Stoppard*. Cambridge, UK: Cambridge University Press, 2001. 104–119.

Schmidt, Kerstin. *The Theatre of Transformation: Postmodernism in American Drama*. New York: Rodopi, 2005.

Shaw, George Bernard. *Our Theatre in the Nineties*, Standard Edition, Vol. 1, London: Constable, 1932, 42–43.

Sinfield, Allen. "Making Space: Appropriation and Confrontation in Recent British Plays." In Holderness Graham, ed. *The Shakespeare Myth*. Manchester, UK: Manchester University Press, 1988. 128–144.

Sicari, Stephen. "Rereading Ulysses: 'Ithaca' and Modernist Allegory." *Twentieth Century Literature* 43 (Fall 1997): 264–290.

Stoppard, Tom, and Mel Gussow, *Conversations with Stoppard*. London: Nick Hern Books. 1995.

Stoppard, Tom. *After Magritte*. New York: Samuel French, 1994.

———. *Arcadia*, London: Faber and Faber, 1993.

———. *The Coast of Utopia*. New York: Grove Press, 2002.

———. *Hapgood*, London: Faber and Faber, 1988.

———. *Indian Ink*. London: Faber and Faber, 1995.

———. *The Invention of Love*. London: Faber and Faber, 1997.

———. *Jumpers*. New York: Grove Press, 1972.

———. *Night and Day*. New York: Grove Press, 1979.

———. *Night and Day*. London: Faber and Faber, 1978.

———. *The Real Inspector Hound*. In *Tom Stoppard: Plays One*. London: Faber and Faber, 1993.

———. *The Real Thing*. Winchester, MA: Faber and Faber, 1984.

———. *Rock 'n' Roll*. New York: Grove Press, 2007.

———. *Rosencrantz and Guildenstern Are Dead*. New York: Grove Press, 1967.

———. *Travesties*. New York: Grove Press, 1975.

Stoppard, Tom. Reply by Daniel Mendelsohn. "'The Invention of Love': An Exchange." *The New York Review of Books*. September 21, 2000. Accessed October 15, 2011. http://www.nybooks.com/articles/archives/2000/sep/21/the-invention-of-love-an-exchange.

Tucker, Paul. *Manet's le dejeuner sur l' herbe*. Cambridge, UK: Cambridge University Press, 1998.

Tynan, Kenneth. *Show People: Profiles in Entertainment*. New York: Simon and Schuster, 1979.

Vanden Heuvel, Michael. "'Is Postmodernism?': Stoppard Among/Against the Postmodern." In Katherine E. Kelly, ed. *The Cambridge Companion to Tom Stoppard*. Cambridge, UK: Cambridge University Press, 2001. 213–228.

Vees-Gulani, Susanne. "Hidden Order in the 'Stoppard Set': Chaos Theory in the Content and Structure of Tom Stoppard's *Arcadia*." *Modern Drama* 42 (1999): 411.

Watts, Stephen. *Postmodern/Drama: Reading the Contemporary Stage*. Ann Arbor: University of Michigan Press, 1998.

Wetzsteon, Ross. "Tom Stoppard Eats Steak Tartare with Chocolate Sauce." *The Village Voice*, November 10, 1975.

Whitaker, Thomas. *Tom Stoppard*. New York: Grove, 1983.

Wilde, Oscar. *The Importance of Being Earnest and Other Plays*. New York: Penguin, 1985.

Wimsatt, W. K., Jr., and Monroe C.

Beardsley. "The Intentional Fallacy." 1946. In Wimsatt, *The Verbal Icon*. Lexington: University of Kentucky Press, 1954.

Zeifman, Hersh. "Comedy of Ambush: Tom Stoppard's *The Real Thing*." *Modern Drama* 26.2 (1983): 139–149.

———. "The Comedy of Eros: Stoppard in Love." In Katherine E. Kelly, ed. *The Cambridge Companion to Tom Stoppard*. Cambridge, UK: Cambridge University Press, 2001. 185–200.

Zinman, Toby. "*Travesties, Night and Day*, and *The Real Thing*." In Katherine E. Kelly, ed. *The Cambridge Companion to Tom Stoppard*. Cambridge, UK: Cambridge University Press, 2001. 120–135.

Zola, Emile. "Le Déjeuner sur l'herbe: Edouard Manet: 1863." *The Imagist*. Accessed September 27, 2011. http://theimagist.com/node/4391.

Index

aesthetics 2, 5–7, 9, 11, 25, 28, 30, 51, 58, 60–64, 66, 71, 77, 80, 84, 93, 107–108, 116, 119, 123, 127, 130, 143, 146–147, 150, 152, 154–156, 158–159, 181, 190
After Magritte 2, 6, 30, 31, 32, 35, 36, 38, 40–44, 49, 158, 163, 172
Analytic philosophy 42, 48, 50–52
Arcadia 6, 9, 12, 14, 32–34, 42, 53, 57, 83, 97–98, 111–117, 119–121, 123–124, 127, 129–132, 135–136, 143–144, 146–149, 157–159, 162, 175–178, 187, 191
L'Assassin menacé 36–37, 39

Bakunin, Mikhail 158–163, 166–169, 171, 174, 180, 183–185
Barker, Clive 92
Bataille, Georges 103
Baudrillard, Jean 10–13, 90, 168, 204; *Cool Memories* 11–12; *Simulacra and Simulation* 11
Beardsley, Monroe C. 115
Beckett, Samuel 15, 31, 54, 186, 193; *Malone Dies* 31; *Molloy* 31; *The Unnamable* 31; *Waiting for Godot* 54
Bennett, Jonathan 50–51
Berlin, Isaiah 161–162, 167, 180
Bohm, David 104–105
Bohr, Niels 9, 103, 108, 110
Brassell, Tim 46–48
Brecht, Bertolt 15, 153, 192–193
Bull, John 6–7, 30, 105

Carlson, Marvin 7
Carr, E.H. 158, 175, 179–185
Carr, Henry 65, 67, 68, 69, 70, 71, 144, 198
chaos theory 9, 12, 33, 98, 111, 112, 114–115, 118–121, 124–125, 133, 148
Chekhov, Anton 34, 159
Chinese box worlds 16, 72–76
Churchill, Caryl 92, 94–95, 97, 123, 153–154

Coast of Utopia 1, 6, 34, 84, 157–159, 187
Communism 188, 189
constructivism 119, 131, 142, 193
Cool Memories 11–12
Coover, Robert 64–65
Corballis, Richard 7, 58, 59, 61
Corso, Gregory 20
The Crying of Lot 49 110, 131–132

Dadism 66, 195
deconstruction 109
Delaney, Paul 25
Derrida, Jacques 103–104, 108–109
Dirty Linen and New-Found-Land 158

Eagleton, Terry 61
Edgar, David 90, 92
Edwards, Paul 117
Einstein, Albert 9, 104–105, 108
Enlightenment 116, 119–121, 125, 162
entropy 117, 134, 202
epistemology 1–3, 5, 8–9, 11–14, 27–33, 36–40, 42, 47–48, 50, 53, 67–68, 80–84, 97, 102–104, 107–112, 115–127, 132, 136, 138, 144, 149, 159, 162, 167, 177, 191, 193
Euler, Leonhard 101, 104
Every Good Boy Deserves Favour 91, 152

Feigenbaum, Mitchell 119–120
Feynman, Richard 102–103
Finnegans Wake 80
Fleming, John 6, 25, 43, 46–47, 56, 73, 77, 79, 82, 91, 96, 135, 139, 145–146
Ford, John 75–76
Foucault, Michel 37–39, 52, 84, 115, 154; *The Order of Things* 38–39; *This Is Not a Pipe* 37–38
Frayn, Michael 110
"From Postmodernism to Postmodernity" 10, 29, 53
Fuentes, Carlos 64–65, 70

211

Index

Genet, Jean 15, 32
The Geopolitical Aesthetic 107, 115–116
German idealism 161, 163, 166, 168
Gleick, James 114, 119–124
Gödel, Kurt 9, 10, 109
Goethe, Johann Wolfgang von 119
Grass, Günter 64

Hall, Peter 93–94
Hamlet 17–20, 22, 24, 193–194, 197
Hapgood 3, 9, 32, 33, 83, 97–102, 104–107, 109–112, 115, 125, 138, 159
Hare, David 159, 190
Harkness, John 38
Hassan, Ihab 9–11, 29, 40, 178; "From Postmodernism to Postmodernity" 10, 29, 53; *The Postmodern Turn* 10
Heisenberg, Werner 9, 104, 110; uncertainty principle 104
heterotopia 38–43
historiography 33, 70–71, 177–180
Hofstadter, Douglas 38–39
Holderness, Graham 193
Housman, A.E. 127, 129, 143–151, 153–156, 158, 171, 177
Hume, David 53
Hunter, Jim 7, 8, 11, 19, 44, 60, 64–65
Hutcheon, Linda 8–9, 12–13, 29, 59, 68–70, 83, 125, 142, 152, 155, 191

immanence 10–11, 29, 178
In the Native State 127, 140–141
indeterminacy 9–12, 18, 29, 40, 109
Indian Ink 6, 33, 34, 42, 53, 57, 126–130, 132–140, 143–144, 146, 158, 177–178, 191
Industrial Relations Act 86
Innes, Christopher 7, 159, 175–178, 187, 190
intertextuality 58–59, 61, 63, 66–67, 70, 75, 136
The Invention of Love 33, 126–127, 129, 132, 143, 147, 155, 157–158, 177

Jameson, Fredric 7–13, 28, 52, 59, 63, 101–102, 106–107, 115–116, 121, 123; *The Geopolitical Aesthetic* 107, 115–116; *Postmodernism* 11, 28, 63, 101, 123; "Postmodernism and Consumer Society" 52
Jenkins, Anthony 36, 47–48, 72
Joyce, James 32, 54, 58–69, 71, 108; *Finnegans Wake* 80; *Ulysses* 52, 59–61, 64, 67, 69, 194
Jumpers 2, 31, 32, 35, 42–57, 127, 145, 147, 159, 160, 184, 188

Kelly, Katherine 7
Kendal, Felicity 79, 128

Lenin, Vladimir 32, 58, 60–61, 63–68, 84, 127, 138, 147, 176
London 81, 85, 92, 94, 128, 133, 144, 175, 179, 184, 189
Lord Byron 112–115, 117–118, 124, 130–131, 135, 137, 144, 147, 149, 176, 181–182
Lyotard, Jean-François 3, 7–9, 10, 12, 41–42, 46, 98, 103, 107–108, 115–116, 120–121, 162; *The Postmodern Condition: A Report on Knowledge* 9, 98, 107–108

Magritte, René 36–42, 53, 172; *L'Assassin menacé* 36–37, 39; *The Treachery of Images* 37–39
Malone Dies 31
Mandelbrot, Benoît 120
Manet, Edouard 171–173, 178
McHale, Brian 1–3, 8–11, 13–18, 20, 25, 27, 30–31, 38, 59, 64–67, 70, 72–73, 75–76, 81, 130, 136; postmodernist fiction 2, 14–16, 20–21, 26, 30, 64–67, 72–73, 75
Mendelsohn, Daniel 144–145, 147
metanarrative 9, 15, 20, 40–41, 45, 63, 98, 103, 107, 115, 122–124, 152, 155–156
metatheater 7, 11, 13, 17, 21, 27, 29, 34, 51, 57, 72, 75, 107, 152, 159, 175, 185, 186, 192
Molloy 31
Moore, G.E. 198
Mulligan Stew 16–18
Munch, Edvard 123

Nabokov, Vladimir 15
Nadel, Ira 65, 128–129, 147
National Union of Journalists 85, 87
Nietzsche, Friedrich 103–104, 109
Night and Day 12, 29, 33, 83, 84–87, 89–93, 95–97, 128, 138–139, 147, 152, 155, 158, 169, 194

O'Brien, Flann 122
ontology 1–3, 5, 9, 11, 13–21, 23, 25–33, 36–42, 44, 48, 57, 64–67, 70, 72–73, 76–77, 80–81, 84, 96–97, 99, 102–104, 122–125, 130–132, 144, 153, 158–159, 163, 167, 172, 191, 193
The Order of Things 38–39

Palin, Sarah 13
parody 6, 16, 28, 51–53, 56, 59, 63, 66–67, 74, 89, 91, 115, 116

Index

pastiche 28, 59–61, 63, 65–67, 69, 116
Pater, Walter 145, 148, 150, 153–154
Pinter, Harold 92, 186
Pirandello, Luigi 15–18, 27, 29, 32
Plotnitsky, Arkady 3, 103, 105, 108, 109
Popper, Karl 132
Positivism 45–47, 57, 82
The Postmodern Condition: A Report on Knowledge 9, 98, 107–108
Postmodern/Drama: Reading the Contemporary Stage 8
The Postmodern Turn 10
Postmodernism 11, 28, 63, 101, 123
"Postmodernism and Consumer Society" 52
Postmodernism in American Drama 8
Professional Foul 48, 91
Pynchon, Thomas 61, 64, 110, 131–132; *The Crying of Lot 49* 110, 131–132

quantum mechanics 3, 9, 33, 98–99, 101–112, 120–121, 125, 195

The Real Inspector Hound 2, 12, 17, 25–29, 32–33, 36, 45, 72–73, 98, 107, 124, 130, 147, 152, 158, 191
The Real Thing 1, 6, 14, 32, 71–72, 74, 76–79, 81–82, 84, 124, 128, 130, 152, 190
Realism 1, 34, 84, 97, 159, 164, 168, 170–171, 173, 175, 182, 185, 187, 190–191; dramatic 1, 34, 97, 175; neo-realism 1
Reed, Ishmael 64
Richardson, Brian 177
Rock 'n' Roll 12, 29, 33, 34, 84, 158, 182, 185, 186–195
Romanticism 116, 118–120, 161
Rosencrantz and Guildenstern Are Dead 1–2, 6–7, 14, 17–22, 24–25, 28, 32, 36, 44–45, 51, 57–58, 61, 64, 96, 98, 145, 152, 158, 175, 192–194
Royal Commission on the Press 86
Royal Shakespeare Company 94
Rushdie, Salman 64
Ruskin, John 145, 148, 154

Salvage 174, 178–180
Sartre, Jean-Paul 80, 190
Schmidt, Kerstin 8; *Postmodernism in American Drama* 8
Self-reflexivity 63, 191
Shadow Arts Council 93–94
Shakespeare, William 17–20, 25, 124, 193–194; *Hamlet* 17–20, 22, 24, 193–194, 197; Royal Shakespeare Company 94

Shipwreck 166–174, 178–180, 183
Simard, Rodney 7
Simulacra and Simulation 11
Socialism 188, 192
Sophocles 24, 121, 148, 149
Sorrentino, Gilbert 16–19; *Mulligan Stew* 16–18
Squaring the Circle 152, 177
Stafford-Clark, Max 159, 190; *Talking to Terrorists* 190
Stankevich, Nikolai 161, 164–167
Stoppard, Miriam 79, 128
Stoppard, Tom 1–25, 27–36, 40; *After Magritte* 2, 6, 30, 31, 32, 35, 36, 38, 40–44, 49, 158, 163, 172; *Arcadia* 6, 9, 12, 14, 32–34, 42, 53, 57, 83, 97–98, 111–117, 119–121, 123–124, 127, 129–132, 135–136, 143–144, 146–149, 157–159, 162, 175–178, 187, 191; *Coast of Utopia* 1, 6, 34, 84, 157–159, 187; *Dirty Linen and New-Found-Land* 158; *Every Good Boy Deserves Favour* 91, 152; *Hapgood* 3, 9, 32, 33, 83, 97–102, 104–107, 109–112, 115, 125, 138, 159; *In the Native State* 127, 140–141; *Indian Ink* 6, 33, 34, 42, 53, 57, 126–130, 132–140, 143–144, 146, 158, 177–178, 191; *The Invention of Love* 33, 126–127, 129, 132, 143, 147, 155, 157–158, 177; *Jumpers* 2, 31, 32, 35, 42–57, 127, 145, 147, 159, 160, 184, 188; *Night and Day* 12, 29, 33, 83, 84–87, 89–93, 95–97, 128, 138–139, 147, 152, 155, 158, 169, 194; *Professional Foul* 48, 91; *The Real Inspector Hound* 2, 12, 17, 25–29, 32–33, 36, 45, 72–73, 98, 107, 124, 130, 147, 152, 158, 191; *The Real Thing* 1, 6, 14, 32, 71–72, 74, 76–79, 81–82, 84, 124, 128, 130, 152, 190; *Rock 'n' Roll* 12, 29, 33, 34, 84, 158, 182, 185, 186–195; *Rosencrantz and Guildenstern Are Dead* 1–2, 6–7, 14, 17–22, 24–25, 28, 32, 36, 44–45, 51, 57–58, 61, 64, 96, 98, 145, 152, 158, 175, 192–194; *Salvage* 174, 178–180; *Shipwreck* 166–174, 178–180, 183; *Squaring the Circle* 152, 177; *Travesties* 2, 11, 14, 31, 32, 58, 59, 61–71, 77, 81, 84, 124, 127, 138, 143–144, 147, 153, 158–159, 167, 175–176, 181, 194; *Voyage* 159–161, 166–169
Swift, Jonathan 6

Talking to Terrorists 190
Theater in Crisis 92–96
thermodynamics 118, 121, 195

INDEX

This Is Not a Pipe 37–38
Travesties 2, 11, 14, 31, 32, 58, 59, 61–71, 77, 81, 84, 124, 127, 138, 143–144, 147, 153, 158–159, 167, 175–176, 181, 194
The Treachery of Images 37–39
Tzara, Tristan 32, 58, 60–64, 66–67, 127, 138, 147

Ulysses 52, 59–61, 64, 67, 69, 194
uncertainty principle 104
University of Texas 3, 128, 134, 203
The Unnamable 31

Vanden Heuvel, Michael 5–8, 11, 13, 160
Voyage 159–161, 166–169

Waiting for Godot 54
Wallace, David Foster 61
Warhol, Andy 168
Watt, Stephen 8; *Postmodern/Drama: Reading the Contemporary Stage* 8
Whitaker, Thomas 48
White, Hayden 175–178
Wilde, Oscar 58, 60, 62, 65–67, 77, 146–148, 150, 154–156, 194
Wittgenstein, Ludwig 35, 42, 49, 51
Wood, John 145–146
Woolf, Virginia 2, 14

Zeifman, Hersh 74, 77, 153
Zeno's paradox 49, 55–56

www.ingramcontent.com/pod-product-compliance
Lightning Source LLC
Chambersburg PA
CBHW032054300426
44116CB00007B/741